# Fixing Women

The Birth of Obstetrics
and Gynecology in
Britain and America

**Perspectives in Medical Humanities**

Perspectives in Medical Humanities publishes peer reviewed scholarship produced or reviewed under the auspices of the University of California Medical Humanities Consortium, a multi-campus collaborative of faculty, students, and trainees in the humanities, medicine, and health sciences. Our series invites scholars from the humanities and health care professions to share narratives and analysis on health, healing, and the contexts of our beliefs and practices that impact biomedical inquiry.

**General Editor**

Brian Dolan, PhD, Professor, Department of Humanities and Social Sciences, University of California, San Francisco (UCSF)

**Other Titles in this Series**

*Heart Murmurs: What Patients Teach Their Doctors*
Edited by Sharon Dobie, MD (2014)

*Humanitas: Readings in the Development of the Medical Humanities*
Edited by Brian Dolan (2015)

*Follow the Money: Funding Research in a Large Academic Health Center*
Henry R. Bourne and Eric B. Vermillion (2016)

*Soul Stories: Voices from the Margins*
Josephine Ensign (2018)

*Memory Lives On: Documenting the HIV/AIDS Epidemic*
Edited by Polina Ilieva (2020)

**www.UCMedicalHumanitiesPress.com**

This series is made possible by the generous support of the Dean of the School of Medicine at UCSF, the UCSF Library, and a Multicampus Research Program Grant from the University of California Office of the President. Grant ID MR-15-328363.

mh

# *Fixing Women*

## The Birth of Obstetrics and Gynecology in Britain and America

Marcia D. Nichols

University of California
Medical Humanities Consortium
Department of Humanities and Social Sciences
UCSF (Box 0850)
490 Illinois Street, Floor 7
San Francisco, CA 94143-0850

Cover Art from Fabian Gautier d'Agoty, *Anatomie generale des viscères* (1752).
Courtesy of the National Library of Medicine.
Designed by Virtuoso Press

---

Library of Congress Control Number: 2020951919

ISBN: 978-1-7355423-0-0

Printed in USA

# Contents

# Acknowledgments

The long gestation of this project, from an idea, to dissertation, to different ideas, and now to book would not have been possible without the aid and support of innumerable mentors, colleagues, librarians, friends, and family. If books are the products of a gravid mind, then this one was a malpresentation and tedious labor that has required their timely interventions and skillful aid. I am grateful to my mentors, without whose encouragement and advice, I would have given up long ago. Recognition is owed to all of the colleagues throughout the years who have listened to parts of this project or who have read drafts, without whose critiques and encouragement this "ill-formed offspring of my brain" would be even more blemished. The project would not have been possible if librarians at the College of Physicians of Philadelphia, the Library Company of Philadelphia, Bard College, and many other libraries had not been willing to share their secrets and insights. Finally, I would be amiss to forget the family and friends who have never ceased expecting the presentation of my monographical first born. Thank you all.

Special acknowledgment is owed to the McNeil Center for Early American Studies, the Library Company of Philadelphia, and the University of Minnesota for the generous funding to do the archival research to write this book and to the Wellcome Collection, the National Library of Medicine, the Library of the College of Physicians of Philadelphia, the Library Company of Philadelphia, and the Wangensteen Historical Library of Biology and Medicine at the University of Minnesota for their gracious permission to use images of items in their collections.

# Introduction

Iremember sitting in an undergraduate British literature class when the professor casually dropped what was for me a bombshell: in the Renaissance, people believed that women had to orgasm in order to conceive. My mind was blown. This was the 1990s, and American culture was still rebelling against "Victorian" prudery. The existence of female orgasm, the "G-spot," and the function of the clitoris were all still being hotly debated. Authors like Barbara Keesling were promising to teach women how to have super orgasms,[1] John Gray was assuring us that men and women were from different planets,[2] and *Cosmo* and other women's magazines were providing us a heady mix of sexual self-objectification and empowerment. What then was I to make of the fact, that, four hundred years earlier, people would have been confused as to *why* we were having this debate—of course women were highly sexed beings— and that was why they needed to be subordinated to men? How, I wondered, had we gotten from the belief that women needed to orgasm to conceive in 1598, to orgasm as being pathological (or at most a hysterical paroxysm) in 1898, to 1998, when women were still struggling to reclaim the orgasm against a biomedical and social milieu that resisted seeing them as desiring beings, while at the same time constantly hypersexualized and reduced them to sexed bodies? Indeed, how, twenty years later, are we still debating if the female orgasm has—or needs—a function, what the actual anatomical shape of the clitoris is, and whether there's such a thing as a "vaginal orgasm" or if all orgasms are clitoral in origin?[3] How did Anglo-American culture forget that women could orgasm?

Throughout the rest of my undergraduate and graduate studies, that question never entirely left me. It has remained an undercurrent in this project, which examines medical writings by men about the female body in the long eighteenth century. Despite the ongoing cultural attempts to separate coitus from maternity, pregnancy and labor are sexual acts in themselves, and ones that always, at least until the 1970s, occurred because of an act of coitus. Dismissing the female orgasm as fictional or unimportant was a byproduct of male midwifery writers' quest for professional and social respectability. This project will examine the work of three important midwifery authors—

William Smellie, Thomas Denman, and Samuel Bard—to argue that each help popularize the discursive persona of the "hero-accoucheur." In effect, these authors made themselves the heroes not only of their own stories but, in a larger sense, of a professionalizing medical story that allowed them to claim authority over female bodies. In doing so, they constructed women as "damsels-in-distress," in need of rescuing from their faulty, sexed bodies.

Medicine as a whole was revolutionizing during the long eighteenth century. Traditionally, in Britain, there were three branches of medicine: physicians, who possessed a medical degree from a university and who concerned themselves with medical theory and diagnosis; barber-surgeons, who had served apprenticeships and who undertook any physical examinations or treatments a patient might require; and apothecaries, who also had served an apprenticeship and who concerned themselves with the making and dispensing of drugs. Midwives were a sort of fourth branch, as many of them had also served apprenticeships and were technically supposed to have an ecclesiastical license (this, however, was only haphazardly enforced). The reality of the medical marketplace was much messier. In addition to these three (or four) categories of supposedly formally-trained practitioners, were an abundance of quacks and lay practitioners such as oculists, bonesetters, and tooth-pullers. Moreover, there was much blurring between the three medical branches. Many apothecaries also practiced surgery; some surgeons went on to obtain an M.D. from one of the Scottish or Continental schools that only required a thesis and letters of recommendations; and many physicians were not above hawking "specifics"—drugs they claimed could cure whatever might ail you. And, by the late seventeenth century, some surgeons were billing themselves as men-midwives.

Medicine began professionalizing as the members of the formally-trained branches began the process of trying to distinguish themselves from the legions of lay practitioners. Since no one—neither those formally trained nor the quacks—could claim superior therapeutics, greater importance was laid on educational experience and formal membership. Hence, the College of Surgeons broke away from the Barbers in 1745 in order to increase the professional éclat of surgeons. The University of Edinburgh and many French and German universities offered superior hands-on medical training that many British and colonial practitioners sought, and in London, private medical classes and the chance to walk the wards of the many charitable hospitals began being offered. Even as these efforts to improve training and professional standing were underway, however, the lines among the three branches—but especially physic and surgery—continued to blur. Man-midwifery was a major cause of this erosion.

Struggling against the professional and social mistrust that perceived them as quacks and sexual predators, men-midwives had to convince medical colleagues to take them seriously and to convince lay men and women to let them have access to women's bodies in a much broader scope than their traditional role. Before the eighteenth century, most men-midwives were only called for obstetric emergencies, during which they usually employed obstetrical instruments to destroy the fetus in a last-ditch effort to save the mother's life. To convince "the Faculty"—the medical establishment—that man-midwifery was a legitimate medical field, men-midwives had to establish their authority over obstetrics and gynecology, a task that was not fully accomplished until the late nineteenth century. While eighteenth-century men-midwives could and did cite historical precedence for their work—Hippocrates, Galen, and other medical greats all wrote about women's health—the new demand for empirical evidence based upon scientific inquiry meant that they also had to demonstrate their authority through experience and anatomical knowledge.

For this, men-midwives needed access to women's bodies during all stages of pregnancy and all types of labors. To gain it, they had to convince women themselves and their husbands to break long-standing taboos against letting medical men touch and observe married women. It was not enough to simply castigate midwives as ignorant, superstitious, and dangerous, though they did that as well. At first, most men-midwives did not seek to entirely replace midwives. Instead, men-midwives, much as American obstetricians and gynecologists continue to do today, had to create a need for their services by expanding the definition of emergency to include even the most remote of possibilities. Then they had to present themselves as the only viable option to circumvent the danger. Men-midwives first gained access to the labors of the poor and the elite. To get permission to attend the poor, they styled themselves as charitable and heroic gentlemen, willing to provide free medical care and to support poor women during their lying-ins. Many men-midwives did this privately; later in the century, after men-midwives had acquired some professional and social authority, they set up charitable lying-in hospitals with the support of wealthy backers. In the resulting case studies published in treatises and periodicals, men-midwives described situations in which poor women, betrayed by their own bodies, were unable to give birth without the timely intervention of masculine reason and strength.

Although access to the pregnancies and labors of poor women gave men-midwives some medico-scientific authority, it did not give them the professional and social éclat—not to mention income—that having patients from the elite or even the middling classes would bring to them. It was one thing to do experiments on subaltern women; it was another to ask for access to their social betters outside of an obstetric emergency. Men-midwives had to convince "respectable" people that there was a need, not only for male birth attendants, but also for male practitioners to superintend all aspects of women's health. Performance played a large part in the achievement of prestige and professional recognition. Public display and lectures convinced other men to invest authority over the body in medical men, while personal interaction at the bedside with patients and their families was an important means of reaching women. Display was only part of the story, however; the writings of men-midwives played just as important a role in their self-presentation.

In their written performances—in midwifery treatises and home health guides—men-midwives cast themselves in an archetypal hero story, in which they, as the hero, rescued the damsel-in-distress held hostage by her weak, inferior body. By drawing upon archetypal tropes, such a story has deep psychological and emotional appeal. Moreover, by using the tropes of hero and damsel-in-distress, men-midwives were able to convince "respectable" people of their good intentions. By casting themselves as heroes, they assured men and women that they were honorable men on an honorable quest and not dastardly lechers. By casting women as damsels-in-distress, they made that quest a necessity. The figure of damsel-in-distress was appealing to both men and women. While it reified masculine superiority by locating women's need of male protection within their bodies, it also bestowed upon all women traits of delicacy and weakness—traits normally applied only to elite women. This was appealing to middling women because it meant treating them with the deference and respect given to their social betters. The expansion of their practice enabled men-midwives to make claims about the nature of Woman— that all women were "naturally" weak, modest, submissive, and maternal— which in turn constructed a need for their profession and for their professional authority.

The investing of authority is reciprocal. When other men accepted men-midwives' authority over feminine nature, they could in turn use that authority for their own ends. In *Birthing the Nation*, Lisa Foreman Cody argues that the emergence of Georgian man-midwifery coincided with and reinforced emerging political and imperial identities. The body politic never escaped the body actual, especially the reproductive body. Men-midwives, natural historians, and other searchers into the mysteries of sex and birth claimed authority to know the secret processes of life, and their research "provided the bedrock for nineteenth-century evolutionary and embryological theories, but these various facts of life were also mobilized to make claims about ethnic, racial, national, and other forms of human identity."[4] Reproductive processes and reproductive bodies became metaphors with which Britons understood themselves and their relationships with others. Cody provides valuable insight on the ways in which the practices and social presence of men-midwives in part accounted for their newfound authority that proved impermeable to critics' assaults.

Similarly, in *Sensibility in the American Revolution,* which examines the rhetoric of sensibility in the revolutionary moment, Sarah Knott argues that British-trained early American doctors, such as William Shippen, presented themselves as men of feeling in order to construct a professional image and stance toward the female body that opened for them the bedrooms of elite American women. In turn, this stance affected how lay people viewed and understood feminine "nature."[5] I use Knott's analysis of sensibility to examine the use of sensibility and novelistic techniques in medical guides written by American and British physicians at the turn of the nineteenth century. This rhetoric cast women as delicate and weak and medical men as enlightened heroes protecting them from their own bodies. These texts made the image of the medical man of feeling available to literate women across the early republic who may not have actually had contact with university-trained physicians.

Dana D. Nelson's *National Manhood* argues that white manhood in the United States constituted itself by imagining itself as a fraternity of individuals bound together and separated from women and people of color. Mid-nineteenth century gynecology offered an arena for medical men to form one such fraternity, allowing them to "project" "worries about being a man" and professional competition onto the bodies of women.[6] Nelson's insights have influenced my understanding of the medical textbook as an imagined community or fraternity constituted upon the bodies of women.

I've attempted to avoid the pitfalls of victimology in examinations of historical gendered interactions. Too often we look at the past in stark contrasts of power and subjugation, but rarely can lines be so neatly drawn. It is true that in the Enlightenment era, women were legally and politically bereft of most rights, but to look at the past and paint them merely as victims of patriarchy does disservice to both men and women. Victimology caricatures men as merely self-serving misogynists and belittles even their best intentions. Moreover, victimology accomplishes what patriarchy, even at its most virulent, cannot fully manage—it takes away women's agency by refusing to recognize it. However limited women's agency might be or might have been, it always deserves acknowledgment.

Women's agency in the rise of man-midwifery has gained some visibility. Adrian Wilson's eminent history of eighteenth-century obstetrics, *The Making of Man-Midwifery*, argues that, in the end, the ascendancy of man-midwifery was due to women choosing to hire men as primary attendants rather than to male possession of obstetrical instruments. He suggests that they did so as a fashion statement because men's higher fees made them accessible to only the wealthy few.[7] I have taken Wilson's caution not to discount a woman's power to choose her attendants to heart and found it verified in obstetric case studies. These narratives reveal that women did choose their attendants—even poor women. They sometimes chose male attendants, chose to obey them and appear, at least to the man-midwife who recorded the case, to live up to the passive ideal. Others, however, chose to have female attendants. After all, midwives have never ceased to exist, to cease practicing their art, despite the best efforts of some nineteenth-century male practitioners to wish them away. Other women resisted or disobeyed the men-midwives who did attend them, refusing to be touched or examined, refusing to take medicine or lie still—in sum, refusing to be submissive and passive.

Wilson's account of man-midwifery, moreover, has provided a solid historical foundation and background upon which to build my rhetorical analysis of midwifery manuals. Wilson's history argues against the grain of traditional histories of obstetrics that traced the rise of the man-midwife from the forceps revolution in the early eighteenth century. In contrast, Wilson notes that men were entering the field in greater numbers before knowledge of the forceps was widespread. He argues that in the early eighteenth century there were two schools of man-midwifery: those who were anti-forceps tended to be Whigs, while forceps practitioners tended to be Tories. This divide was finally bridged by William Smellie, a moderate Whig and forceps practitioner. After Smellie, however, men-midwives began taking a non-interventionist stance, which they opposed to the meddling midwifery that they claimed was practiced by women. This is best demonstrated by the career of William Hunter, who rose from Scottish obscurity to professional prominence as the queen's obstetrician.

While Wilson, Cody, and Knott focused more upon the performative aspects of man-midwifery—that is, obstetric practice itself and professional lectures and demonstrations—and man-midwifery's influence upon larger social trends, Eve Keller, in *Generating Bodies and Gendered Selves*, turned to the rhetorical constructions of identity in seventeenth-century embryology and obstetrics. Keller locates the emergence of the masculinist "modern, liberal self" in seventeenth-century embryology that envisioned the male fetus as primary, often reducing the female body to cavernous uteri. In that process, early midwives of both genders constructed themselves as rational, cool-headed individuals. As Keller argues:

> the Enlightenment hero, who, having sought knowledge from books, values equally the knowledge of experience, who is endowed with a native liberty that only the ignorant would deny, and how, because of that knowledge and the exercise of that liberty, is able to be generous and compassionate toward those who suffer. This is of course a masculine model more than a generically human one, and the construction of this model in the texts of male practitioners who were making their way into a workplace that had previously been female suggests the importance of gender in the process of its construction. But the gender issue here is not simply tied to the sex of the competing practitioners, because the rhetorical effect of this model is to general medical authority even as it evokes a mode of masculine identity…. [M]edical authority gets established in the birthing room as the agents who practice there represent themselves, regardless of their sex, in accordance with emerging ideals of masculine subjectivity.[8]

I have quoted this passage at length because Keller's argument has greatly influenced the direction and goals of my project. I sought to build and expand upon her argument by analyzing the ways in which authors of eighteenth-century midwifery manuals styled themselves as masculinist heroes. Keller found that embryological writers identified with the fetus, granting it masculine individuality. This was perhaps best illustrated by seventeenth-century images of fetuses *in utero*: they depicted fetuses as little men, standing, jumping and kicking in the empty bottle-like space of disembodied uteri (see Figure 2.21). This changed in the eighteenth century. My research suggests that midwifery authors stopped identifying with the (male) fetus, instead constructing it as passively in need of the man-midwife's aid in much the same way as its mother. She, in turn, takes on greater importance, not as a subject, but as the primary object and field of the heroic man-midwife's efforts.

I also draw upon the scholarly debate about the construction of the sexed body. For example, the influential *Making Sex* by Thomas Lacqueur has been a useful starting point. Lacqueur argues that Early Modern European medicine was dominated by a one-sex theory of the body that was based on the writings of Galen. In this schema, male and female bodies were considered analogous, but, in the logic of humoral medicine, because women were believed to be colder and wetter, their genitalia were inside the body, whereas men produced enough body heat for theirs to protrude. According to Lacqueur, over the course of the eighteenth century, this theory was replaced by a two-sex model that, by the nineteenth century, viewed sex as a somatic phenomenon that resulted in two fundamentally incommensurable sexes.[9] Helen King, however, maintains that the two-sex model was always dominant. She argues that while Galenic medicine had its heyday in the early modern era, it was grafted onto Hippocratic-Aristotelian medicine, which had at its core a two-sex model of the body.[10] What I have found in my research is that both of these positions have merit. As Karen Harvey points out in her exploration of eighteenth-century erotica, *Reading Sex in the Eighteenth Century*, authors mingled one- and two-sex theories to serve a particular rhetorical need.[11] This strategy extends to medical authors who actively constructed the sexed female body yet sometimes could not escape the language of commensurability. Similarly, these writers often commingled conflicting accounts of female desire and chastity.

Other scholars have traced the entrenchment of the sexed body, in particular Ornella Moscucci and Londa Schiebinger. In *The Science of Woman*, Moscucci analyzes nineteenth-century obstetrics and gynecology for the ways in which those medical sciences constructed a definition of femininity that was limited by a woman's sexual functioning (her sexuality in a broader sense than merely her erotic desire, one that encompasses all the characteristics attributed to her biology. I follow Moscucci in this broader usage). Woman, ruled by her ovaries, became "the Sex."[12] Schiebinger, in *Nature's Body*, turns her attention to eighteenth-century natural history and comparative anatomy, exposing the ways in which male scientists located traits gendered feminine within the very bones and bodies of female animals and racial Others. Comparative anatomists and natural historians were thereby able to define femininity as bodily, while distinguishing and privileging white womanhood over racial Others.[13] Both of these authors make it clear that by the end of the eighteenth century, medical men had located sexual differences in the capacious female pelvis. Ludmilla Jordanova and Roberta McGrath have extended this line of thinking by analyzing anatomical atlases and other medico-scientific presentations of the female body that rendered it submissive and eroticized.[14]

*Fixing Women* builds upon these scholars' pioneering work by examining vagaries of the sexed body as it appears in midwifery manuals and anatomical atlases. The white female body was an uneasy signifier. On the one hand, according to the four-stage theory accepted by many of the writers discussed in this project, women were the civilizers, the keepers of the hearth who caused men to evolve from primitive hunter-gatherers to mighty men of state. On the other, their weak, faulty bodies made them closer to animals and to racial Others. The Anglo-American woman embodied a host of contradictions: civilized and therefore physically weak; a woman and therefore imperfect and closer to animals; emblem of erotic beauty, yet sexually chaste; domestic goddess, yet in need of mothering instruction from male physicians, who held up the primitive Other as their guide. Anglo-American women were borderlands, dividing civilization from primitiveness, whiteness from Otherness.

My work attempts to elucidate a nuanced history of the rhetorical constructions of masculinist selfhood and the sexed female body in midwifery manuals. My contribution is a comparative analysis of the material texts themselves that enriches the current scholarly understanding of obstetrics, gender, and sex. Much of my research has been to compare and contrast multiple editions and iterations of the same titles across the long eighteenth century. Such comparisons shed new light on the interactions of authors, publishers, and readers and expose the ways in which ideas about gender and sex were formed, transformed, and entrenched over time. The construction of women as "the Sex" emerged gradually, in correlation with the perceived authority of man-midwifery. The profession's authority derived in great measure from the successful deployment of the trope of what I call the "hero-accoucheur."

Chapter One examines the three-volume *Treatise on the Theory and Practice of Midwifery* (1752-1764) by William Smellie. Smellie's teachings and writings were widely influential. Not only was his *Treatise* read by thousands of medical practitioners who regarded him as the father of modern obstetrics, he reached a wider audience when his books were used as the primary source for the article on midwifery in the first edition of the *Encyclopedia Britannica* (1771). I argue that Smellie's *Treatise* borrows the rhetorical valences of the picaresque and romantic modes in order to redeem man-midwifery from its bad reputation. The *Treatise* constructed a collective, heroic identity that was borrowed by later authors. This identity was created by appropriating cases from many male practitioners and by using ambiguous pronouns in these cases and elsewhere. This story, in turn, allowed a corporate identity to emerge that the male reader could then project himself into, irrespective of nation. This strategy made available a pan-Euro-American male identity that empowered medical men on the British imperial periphery, namely the Scottish and American writers discussed in this project.

Additionally, the depiction of women was as influential as his construction of a collective masculine identity. In Smellie's *Treatise*, women were often depicted as ideally helpless and passive—traits that later writers would locate within the female body itself. In Smellie's works, however, the female body was depicted as a *terra incognita*, waiting for further explorations by future men-midwives. To illustrate his textbook, Smellie produced one of the most widely circulated anatomical atlases of the era. In Chapter Two, I analyze Smellie's *Set of Anatomical Tables* for what it can tell us about how masculine medicine viewed the female body. The descriptions of the female body in the textbook evinced a desire to fix and control what Smellie perceived as mutable and ultimately unknowable. The *Anatomical Tables* provided a sort of map to this feminine *terra incognita*. In keeping with the hyperrealism favored in anatomical drawings of the time, Smellie's *Tables* created an illusion of dissection captured *in media res* through the careful posing of female and infant cadavers. Moreover, by focusing on genitalia copiously adorned with hair, Smellie codified a view of women that defined them through their contradictory sexuality: they were idealized as chaste child-bearers yet depicted as erotic objects of masculine desire. I argue that, for the original audience, knowledge of the corpses' origin—they were the bodies of poor women—was a means of reconciling this contradiction by containing the erotic potential within a classed body. However, the images from Smellie's *Tables* were reprinted multiple times in small, cheap formats on their own and as illustrations for other books. They were also borrowed to illustrate many other books, including the *Encyclopedia Britannica*. This proliferation called for new strategies for erotic containment, such as censoring some images and depilating others. Because they stayed in print, in a wide array of contexts, much longer than the *Treatise* itself, the images reached an even wider audience. Combined, the textbook and the *Tables* worked to convince middling and elite men not only that men-midwives had mastered the female body but also of their good and honorable intentions toward their wives.

Chapter Three turns to the work of Thomas Denman, whose textbook, *An Introduction to the Practice of Midwifery* (1785), stayed in print for over fifty years. By Denman's time, man-midwifery was well established as a specialty; however, it still faced criticism for being a disreputable business. I argue that, in order to distance himself and man-midwifery from the sexual scandal caused by Smellie's blunt presentation of women's bodies and to increase the professional respectability of the man-midwife, Denman constructs the "Accoucheur of Feeling"—a heroic persona akin to those found in domestic fiction, whose refinement and sensibility would prevent any suspicions of sexual predation. Thus, Denman's textbook functioned as a conduct manual as much as a textbook, and, like the actual conduct manuals and novels I argue it borrows from, envisioned Woman as bourgeois, domestic(ated), and white.

Although Denman acknowledged women were susceptible to "the passions," he claimed that their primary passion was fear—and rightly so, as their weak bodies needed the superintendence of a well-trained man-midwife in order to survive pregnancy and childbirth.

The final chapter turns to the work of American Samuel Bard, whose textbook, *A Compendium of the Theory and Practice of Midwifery* (1808), transformed, over the course of a decade, from a patronizing guide for female midwives into a sophisticated textbook for male medical students that triangulated the work of Smellie and Denman. Tracing this evolution provides insight into how attitudes toward female midwives changed dramatically as increasing numbers of young men matriculated from the newly minted American medical schools in Philadelphia, New York, and elsewhere. Moreover, Bard's work created an obstetrical republic of letters that allowed the American hero-accoucheur to imagine himself a part of an international fraternity constituted through the exchange of textualized female bodies. By envisioning themselves as part of this international fraternity, American medical men could imagine themselves, not as provincial bunglers, but as cosmopolitan professionals on a footing with colleagues in Britain and Europe.

In what follows, I hope to provide a nuanced account of male-authored British and American texts on gynecology and obstetrics, primarily published between 1752 and 1819. My goal is to treat the ideas and personages of the past as complex entities. Although men-midwives idealized women as passive damsels-in-distress, on some level, they recognized that idea as a fiction of their own making in order to obfuscate that much of their professional, masculine authority derived from the approbation and complicity of the fair sex. Although the voices of actual women are, unfortunately, largely absent from this account, I hope to demonstrate that eighteenth-century medical attitudes towards them and depictions of them were not monolithic but variegated and often contradictory. My work does not seek to reconcile the contradictions found in medical writings about women's bodies and desires or the contradictions about the practices or beliefs of men-midwives themselves. Rather, I hope to allow these contradictions to surface so that we have a richer understanding of the variegated past. To paraphrase Walt Whitman, people and our histories are large and contain multitudes.

# Endnotes

1   Barbara Keesling, *Super Sexual Orgasm* (New York: HarpersCollins, 1997).

2   John Gray, *Men Are from Mars, Women Are from Venus* (New York: HarpersCollins, 1993).

3   See, for instance, Helen E. O'Connell, Kalavampa V. Sanjeevan, & John M. Hutson, "Anatomy of the Clitoris" *The Journal of Urology* 174 (2005): 1189-1195; Barry R. Komisaruk, Carlos Beyer-Flores, & Beverly Whipple, *The Science of Orgasm* (Baltimore: Johns Hopkins University Press, 2006); Stuart Brody & Rui Miguel Costa, "Vaginal Orgasm is Associated with Less Use of Immature Psychological Defense Mechanisms," *Journal of Sexual Medicine* 5 (2008): 1167-1176; Vincenzo Puppo & Guilia Puppo, " Anatomy of Sex: Revision of the New Anatomical Terms Used for the Clitoris and the Female Orgasm by Sexologists," *Clinical Anatomy* (2014): 293-304; Nicole Prause et al, "Clitorally Stimulated Orgasms Are Associated with Better Control of Sexual Desire, and Not Associated with Depression or Anxiety, Compared with Vaginally Stimulated Orgasms," *The Journal of Sexual Medicine* 13 (2016): 1676-1685; Roy J. Levin, "The Clitoral Activation Paradox—Claimed Outcomes from Different Methods of its Stimulation," *Clinical Anatomy* (2018): 650-660.

4   Lisa Forman Cody, *Birthing the Nation* (Oxford: Oxford University Press, 2005), 8.

5   Sarah Knott, *Sensibility and the American Revolution* (Chapel Hill: University of North Carolina Press, 2009).

6   Dana D. Nelson, *National Manhood* (Durham, NC: Duke University Press, 1998): 137.

7   Adrian Wilson, *The Making of Man-Midwifery* (Cambridge, MA: Harvard University Press, 1995).

8   Eve Keller, *Generating Bodies and Gendered Selves* (Seattle: University of Washington Press, 2007), 182.

9   Thomas Lacqueur, *Making Sex* (Cambridge, MA: Harvard University Press, 1990).

10   Helen King, *Midwifery, Obstetrics, and the Rise of Gynecology* (Burlington, VT: Ashgate, 2007).

11   Karen Harvey, *Reading Sex in the Eighteenth Century* (Cambridge: Cambridge University Press, 2004).

12   Ornella Moscucci, *The Science of Woman* (Cambridge: Cambridge University Press, 1990).

13   Londa Schiebinger, *Nature's Body* (New Brunswick, NJ: Rutgers University Press, 1993).

14   Ludamilla Jordanova, *Sexual Visions* (Madison: University of Wisconsin Press, 1989); Roberta McGrath, *Seeing Her Sex* (Manchester: Manchester UP, 2002).

# Chapter One

# Man-Midwife as Picaresque Hero: William Smellie's *Treatise on the Theory and Art of Midwifery*

William Smellie, who began his life as an obscure apothecary-surgeon practicing in rural Scotland, is now recognized as the most important obstetrical pioneer of the eighteenth century. His achievements were the result of a lifelong quest to perfect medical knowledge about pregnancy and childbirth, a quest that took him from Scotland to Paris and London and from one of the lowest rungs of the medical profession to that of a respected physician and pioneering specialist esteemed by much of the medical establishment. Along the way, he taught nearly a thousand male and an unknown number of female students everything he had learned about the theory and practice of midwifery. Impressive as these accomplishments are, as Adrian Wilson points out, Smellie's place as founder of modern obstetrics was not completely assured during his own day. It was not until the publication of his three-volume *A Treatise on the Theory and Practice of Midwifery* (1752-1764) and an accompanying volume of anatomical plates that he became "the biggest name in midwifery in England and possibly in Europe."[1] To these places, one should add America—the first scientific/medical plates engraved in the newborn United States were John Norman's 1786 version of Smellie's *Sett of Anatomical Tables* (originally printed in 1754). Samuel Bard, author of one of the first American midwifery textbooks, complained that Smellie's "works are in the hands of almost every practitioner in this country, and more generally read than any other," a fact to which he attributed what he saw as widespread and unnecessary forceps use.[2]

Smellie is most associated with teaching and promoting forceps delivery, a legacy that is perhaps undeserved. In *The Making of Man-Midwifery*, Wilson painstakingly recreates Smellie's ambiguous relationships with the forceps. Wilson argues that although Smellie had learned of the forceps and received training in their use in 1737-39, he largely eschewed them until 1746. Smellie began teaching midwifery in London in 1740, and, even after forceps became a regular tool in his primarily emergency practice, he emphasized in his lessons to young practitioners that most births were normal and did not need instrumental intervention.[3]

Obstetrical techniques were only a slice of his pedagogical goals. Culled from his lectures, the textbook was a substitute lecture hall for "young practitioners in general" to leaf through at their leisure, to perfect "the art or science" of midwifery.[4] Smellie believed his textbooks, written explicitly for the novice, would fill a need not met by the many other midwifery texts available. He educated on every aspect of midwifery including sartorial advice and bedside manner; interacting with other midwives, male and female; handling recalcitrant patients and their families; and, most importantly, the character and role of the man-midwife in society at large.

However, it was not the breadth of his goals that sets Smellie's work apart, but rather the style in which they were presented. The *Treatise* picked up on a heroic stance found in many earlier works on midwifery and embryology[5] and developed it into a collective male identity available to his readers. The conjunction of literariness and the formulation of the hero-accoucheur created a juggernaut that would influence generations of medical practitioners and authors. Applying a literary lens, in particular the related modes of the picaresque and the romantic, enables an analysis of the *Treatise*'s rhetorical constructions of the character-types that appear in his three volumes: the man-midwife as hero, the "good" midwife as squire, the faulty practitioner as villain, and the female patient as parturient damsel-in-distress. Before turning to Smellie's *Treatise* in detail, it is necessary to establish the parameters of the picaresque and romance modes. It is also necessary to tease out some strands of the cultural code that readers would have brought to the *Treatise*—i.e., to examine the role and character of the man-midwife as he was perceived in Georgian Britain that caused Smellie's works to resonate.

## The Picaresque

The picaresque and the romance modes are two common and interrelated narrative forms, often used together in many works of literature. Critic Ulrich Wick distinguishes between the these two modes by suggesting that *the essential picaresque situation*—the fictional world posited by the picaresque mode—is that of an unheroic protagonist, worse than we, caught up in a chaotic world, worse than ours, in which he is on an eternal journey of encounters that allow him to be alternately both victim of that world and its exploiter. By way of contrast, I would say that the *essential romance situation*— the fictional world posited by the romance mode—is that of a heroic protagonist in a world marvelously better than ours in which he is on a quest that confronts him with challenges, each ending in a moral victory leading toward a final ordered and harmonious cosmos. [6]

Picaresque and romance act as a sort of yin and yang, one a pessimistic vision of travail and failure, the other an optimistic tale of hope and success against all odds. Wicks goes on to suggest that these two seemingly opposite modes are often combined. Picaresque tales are often hybrids whose protagonists enjoy the chaos of the fallen reality they are trying to escape yet yearn for the order of a moral universe.[7] In early picaresque tales, the picaro often ended as ignonimously as he began in life, sometimes telling his tale as an act of penance in prison or while awaiting the gallows. However, in eighteenth-century British picaresque novels, the picaro often got his wish for a happy ending, and novels like Tobias Smollett's *Roderick Random* (1748) and Daniel Defoe's *Roxana* (1724) had shifted the traditional picaro's origins from the gutter to the genteel parlor.[8]

The basic characteristics of the picaresque mode can be boiled down to three categories. First, the picaro (or occasionally picara), who generally tells his own story, is traditionally a rogue, an outcaste, who tricks his way up and down Fortune's Wheel, on bottom perhaps more than he is on top. His misdeeds are usually more knavish than criminal, done out of necessity rather than maliciousness. He is a master of disguise, changing appearance and identity as needed.[9] By the eighteenth century, the picaro had risen from his humble origins, and, like the knight of chivalric (or gothic) romances, he was often of noble or genteel birth. Denied his birthright, his ramblings are his quest to regain it.[10] Second, the picaro's story is loosely episodic, held together mostly by the presence of the picaro himself.[11] This episodic structure enables a third aspect of the picaresque, a panoramic view of society with "a vast gallery of human types who appear as representatives of the landscape."[12] The picaro's journeys take him into different social settings, from the peasant's hut or seedy tavern to the posh parlors and boudoirs of the elite, as well as various locales in between. Furthermore, disconnected adventures allow for a constant expansion of the story that pushes back the final end point of the picaro's dilatory journey to build narrative tension.[13]

Obviously, unlike *Roderick Random* or *Roxana*, Smellie's *Treatise* is not fiction. Volume I was not a collection of entertaining stories, but rather a collection of classroom lectures and narrative examples of the lessons taught. It presented the "theory" of midwifery. Divided into four "books," the first explained female anatomy before and during pregnancy; the second, common diseases of women during pregnancy; the third, the onset and various types of labors; and the fourth, advice on postnatal care. The "art" of midwifery was expounded in Volume II, "A Collection of Cases and Observations," and Volume III, "A Collection of Praeternatural Cases and Observations." These volumes were collections of case histories meant to illustrate the principles Smellie lays out in Volume I and were not intended to be read continuously. Nevertheless, as narratives, they lend themselves to a literary reading. Thomas Laqueur has argued that novels and case histories, as "humanitarian narratives," share many qualities, including the amassing of details, "the personal body… as the locus of pain…[and] the common bond" between reader and character, and "the lineaments of causality and human agency" that make "ameliorative action…possible."[14]

Even in its own time, Smellie's case histories were noted for their literary character, which contemporary critics and modern scholars alike have often attributed to the editorial (or possibly co-authorial) skills of Tobias Smollett.[15] Competing man-midwife John Burton (widely believed to be the basis of *Tristram Shandy*'s (1759) Dr. Slop) enviously attributed Smellie's greater success to the quality and style of his prose, insinuating that Smollett had more of role than simple editor: "Had I the Talents of the ingenious Writer of that Book [*Peregrine Pickle* (1751)], what a pathetic Harangue might I here make on the Usefulness of critical Skill in Language in these Cases?"[16] What Burton saw as a fault, scholar Robert Erickson sees as the strength of the *Treatise*: "Smellie was a true artist with as deep a reverence for the truth as he saw it as that other mid-eighteenth-century master of verisimilitude, William Hogarth."[17] For Erickson, Smellie's style, and other writers' lack thereof, accounts for Smellie's longstanding popularity.

The case histories recount Smellie's nearly forty years of practice in Scotland and London, from both his private practice amongst those who could pay—the wealthy and well-to-do—and from his teaching practice in which he recruited London's poorest to act as living laboratories in exchange for free medical care during labor and lying-in.[18] Like a picaresque tale, the case histories offer a panorama of London society, from the boudoir of the Lady to the garret and basement corners of the beggar-woman. Moreover,

each case history is a tightly compressed vignette. Successively presented, the case histories create an "episodic rhythm"[19] that gives a narrative feel to the whole and makes the archetypal man-midwife (Smellie) the central character. Similar to a picaro's quest for respectability, Smellie tried to establish the man-midwife's character as honorable and upright, yet his readers might see long established links between men-midwives and roguishness. In Smellie's tale, the man-midwife had his happy ending by reaching genteel respectability, like other picaros in eighteenth-century British novels.

## Man-Midwife as Picaro

As discussed above, the picaro in the eighteenth century was typically a knave, often of gentle birth, but denied his birthright, in a quest for respectability during which he engages in misdeeds and acts of disguise in order to achieve his ends.  It is a short step from the literary rogue to the perceived character of the man-midwife. Men-midwives were often criticized as rogues for three main reasons: First, they operated outside the normal medical profession, as neither wholly surgeon nor physician. Second, their usurpation of a traditionally female practice led to accusations of sexual impropriety. Finally, they were often involved with the illegal dissections that were winked at by the authorities but remained the terror of the lower classes. In the following sections, I will explore the three characteristics—quackery, rakishness, and dissection—that made the man-midwife a picaro.

### Man-Midwife as Quack

Traditionally, men-midwives were surgeons, called in during a difficult labor to manually or surgically manipulate the fetus in a last-ditch effort to save a woman's life. Unfortunately, this usually meant using a blunt hook or crochet to perform a craniotomy (the practice of fracturing the fetal skull to remove the brain), sometimes on a still-living baby. Although alternatives to the hook such as podalic version—turning and delivering the baby by the feet—became more common in the seventeenth century, men-midwives were still seen as harbingers of death of either baby or mother or both.[20]  They were so feared, according to Edmund Chapman, "that many unhappy Women have chosen to *Die*, or at least stay to the very last Extremity, rather than call for our Assistance."[21]

Beginning in the seventeenth century, some men began specializing in obstetrics, offering themselves as primary attendants to the exclusion of the female midwife. Most notable of these were the Chamberlen family, who kept their use of the forceps a secret. By the 1720s, their secret was out, and many others were adopting the technique.[22] Typically called man-midwives or accoucheurs (after the French), more fanciful titles were offered as alternatives to disassociate male from female practitioners. John Maubray preferred "andro-boethogynist," while Edward Baynard suggested "midman," neither of which entered into popular parlance.[23] Midwife and critic of male practitioners Elizabeth Nihell suggested "pudendist" as the proper title, since medical specialists usually assume the name of the part they "take under their protection."[24]

This new specialty was not welcomed by the medical establishment. According to Roy Porter, "Man-midwifery was a branch of 'quackery' particularly unscrupulous because...with their intrusive and infected forceps, their labours were 'usually fatal.'" Indeed, "[s]o ignominious was this cowboy trade that when [William] Hunter disenfranchised himself from the Company of Surgeons, he found that, on joining the College of Physicians, he was ineligible, as an *accoucheur*, for the fellowship."[25]

Traditionally, physicians did not get their hands dirty by actually touching patients. That was left up to the lower order of surgeons. Rather, physicians relied upon patients' own accounts and upon visual appearances to make diagnoses. However, as educational centers like the University of Edinburgh and the Hôtel-Dieu in Paris began emphasizing anatomical instruction for both physicians and surgeons and as private anatomy schools in London gained in popularity, the divisions between the two branches gradually eroded.[26] By titling his *Treatise* the *Theory and Practice of Midwifery*, Smellie pointed to the duality of obstetrics—that it both engaged in *Theory*, the intellectual province of physicians, and *Practice*, the manual art of surgeons.

Theory was one of the qualities that set men-midwives apart from female practitioners. A standard plaint of midwifery treatises of the era, whether they were written for female or male practitioners, for a high or low audience, was that female practitioners were dangerously ignorant of their business. In the cheap print text, *Aristotle's Compleat and Expereinc'd Midwife* (1731), attributed to William Salmon, the author claims he has learned the secrets of childbirth by being called to labors because of "either the Unskilfulness of the Midwife, or the Hardness or Difficulty of the Woman's Labour." He goes on to state that it is "a Disparagement" to midwives if they have to call in male practitioners, even if it is for the safety of the patient.[27] John Burton scathingly blamed midwives' incompetence for male entry into the field: "*as the Frequency of the (almost innumerable) Evils which daily befel the Women and their Infants during Labour, by the Ignorance and Mismanagement of the Female-Midwives, first put Men upon applying their Study and Assistance...."*[28]

William Buchan, in his *Domestic Medicine* (a general home medical guide rather than a midwifery treatise) similarly weighed in on the incompetence of midwives. Women

> are often hurt by the superstitious prejudices of ignorant and officious midwives.... [N]o women [should] practice midwifery but such as are properly qualified. Were due attention paid to this, it would not only be the means of saving many lives, but would prevent the necessity of employing men in this indelicate and disagreeable branch of medicine, which is, on many accounts, more proper for the other sex.[29]

Even in 1812, American physician Samuel Jennings repeated the centuries-old complaint: "When it is granted that there are some women skilled in the art of *Midwifery*, the known liberality of the ladies will indulge me in a declaration that most of those who make pretensions to this important profession are exceedingly ignorant and self-conceited."[30] Eleven years later, another American physician rejoiced that midwives were permanently extirpated from Boston, he hoped for good.[31] By this point in history, the established discourse maintained as fact that centuries of reform and educational efforts had barely affected midwives, making it necessary for men to dominate the field in order to protect mothers and babies.

Despite some men-midwives' claims that ousting female midwives was absolutely necessary for the continuation of the species, their insurgence into the profession was not left uncriticized. Frank Nicholls, in his *Petition of the Unborn Babes to the Censors of the Royal College of Physicians in London* (2nd edition, 1751) argued that laws needed to be made to protect mothers and babies from the "Hooks, Pincers, and other bloody Instruments" of the men-midwives.[32] As Cody points out,

> Critics lampooned men-midwives as half male, half female in both name and mannerisms, emphasizing their category-crossing status as a 'heteroclite', a 'hermaphrodite', 'amphibious', 'a vile poisonous fruit', a 'manifest Absurdity!'"
> ... It implies a Thing, that is neither a "Man," nor a "Wife, but a "MID" both!—
> "Man-Midwife," must consequently be a Monster in Nature!!!'....[33]

To illustrate this theme, Cody refers to the frontispiece of the anti-man-midwife tract *Man-Midwifery Dissected, or Obstetric Family Instructor* (1793), which

Fig. 1.1: This bifurcated image of a midwife and a man-midwife satirizes the new masculine profession as unnatural and dangerous. A "man-midwife" (male obstetrician) represented by a figure divided in half, one half representing a man and the other a woman. Colored etching by I. Cruikshank, 1793. Courtesy of the Wellcome Institute.

depicts a bifurcated individual and scene (Figure 1.1). The left side of the central figure is that of a well-dressed man, holding forceps and standing in a bare shop in front of an orderly row of bottles and fierce, oversized, midwifery instruments hanging from hooks. On the right, the figure is a matronly woman, holding a pap-spoon, standing in front of a cheerful fire in a paneled, carpeted room. On the whole, the woman's side looks much more welcoming than the stark room of the man-midwife. Clearly, the profession was better off in the matron's capable hands.

Men-midwives were nominal outlaws as well as professional outsiders. In addition to being a professional "hermaphrodite," Smellie faced legal challenges when he began teaching classes in London. His school was not only outside the medical establishment but outside parish law as well. Smellie and his students hired poor women to act as living laboratories for their studies in exchange for free medical care, and often food and fire, during labor and the lying-in month. They made no distinction between the married and unmarried poor, but treated anyone willing to make the exchange. The parish, however, had a vested interest in making sure illegitimate children were not born within its borders in order to avoid having to provide charitable support for them. Smellie's former student Mr. Ayers remembered that, in 1747, Smellie and his students "were obliged to smuggle our patients, on account of the barbarity of the church-wardens."[34] The patient in this case was delivered on a bed of "a little straw laid in a cold garret"; they couldn't risk moving her to more comfortable accommodations for fear the parish wardens would forcibly drive her from the parish.[35] A year later, Smellie reported a case in which twenty-eight students, mostly from the navy and army, convened upon one poor woman's abode. Suspicions about such a large number of men inside the room of a laboring woman caused an angry mob to gather. Upon receiving word they had called the parish authorities, Smellie rushed the delivery, breaking the infant's thigh. On hearing that a living child was delivered, the mob dispersed, as did Smellie and his students. However, he left "one of the eldest pupils" to take care of the child. The student "was at great pains in attending it frequently; but the child was lost by the carelessness of a drunken mother."[36]

Smellie was not alone in coming into conflict with the parish authorities. Two of the five London lying-in hospitals admitted unmarried women, causing regular legal battles to rage between the proprietors and the parishes until Parliament forged a compromise "in 1773 permitting hospitals to accept unmarried women only if they provided security to the parish to cover the maintenance of the child in settlement disputes."[37]

## Man-Midwife as Rake

Much of the criticism leveled at man-midwifery was at the profession's potential for sexual impropriety. Nicholls, for instance, went on to suggest that not only were the lives of the unborn and their mothers at stake, but so was their mothers' chastity. Men-midwives "treat our Wives in such a manner, as frequently ends in their Destruction, and to have such Intercourse with our Women, as easily shifts itself into Indecency, from Indecency into Obscenity, and from Obscenity into Debauchery."[38] In the frontispiece to *Man-Midwifery Dissected* (Figure 1.1), the lowest shelf behind the man-midwife is labeled, "This shelf for my own use," and the bottles on it are labeled, "Love Water," "Cantharides," "Eau de Vie," and "Cream of Violets"—aphrodisiacs to assist in his seductions of patients.

The potential for sexual impropriety had long been recognized as a danger posed by all medical men.[39] Man-midwifery, with its technique of "touching," could only stoke such fears to new heights. Touching, the insertion of a finger into the vagina to determine pregnancy and/or the stage of pregnancy or labor, was a controversial technique frequently satirized as a lascivious action dangerous to the sanctity of marriage. One such satire, S. Hooper's 1773 print *The Man-Midwife* (Figure 1.2), depicts a sour-looking husband being forced

*The MAN-MIDWIFE, or FEMALE DELICACY after MARRIAGE:*
Addressed to Husbands

Fig. 1.2: Another satire of man-midwifery that highlights its sexual danger. Interestingly, the wife's female companion (possibly her mother) seems intent on helping the scene of seduction and adultery to occur. A male-midwife suggestively examines an attractive pregnant woman, as her disgruntled husband is led out of the room by a servant. Line engraving, 1773. Courtesy of the Wellcome Institute.

away from the scene of his wife's gynecological examination. One of the man-midwife's hands is suggestively up the woman's skirts and the other rests behind the small of her back. Her arm is around his shoulders as they gaze into one another's eyes. On a chair near the couple, a cat kills a bird, while above the door is a picture of a bull being led to slaughter: the husband knows he is being cuckolded and can do nothing about it.[40]

Medical writers did little to calm such fears. Someone coming across Jean-Louis Baudelocque's instructions that touching should first be practiced on cadavers and then on "women not pregnant, in great number,"[41] or Smellie's explanation that the area between the vagina and clitoris, which he called "the *Fossa magna* or *Navicularis*" was "for the direction of the *Penis* in coition, or of the finger in touching, into the *Vagina*," would rightly be alarmed.[42] Suggesting that the female body was designed to be sexually penetrated is unsurprising, but in this context, equating sexual penetration with the medical technique of touching should have been. The indecorum was not lost upon the medical establishment. Alexander Hamilton, professor of midwifery in Edinburgh, admonished his male students not to engage in "*officious touching* at the beginning of labor" of this "exceedingly irritable" area, designed to "render the sensation *in coitu* more exquisite," because of the risk of "inflammation and tumefaction."[43] It is hard to tell if the professor is cautioning against injuring or arousing the laboring woman.

Contemporary critics were quick to pick up on such rhetorical slippage. Phillip Thicknesse attacked touching and the impropriety of man-midwifery. He argued that no man could visually or manually examine a woman, even during labor, without becoming aroused or able to resist indulging his lusts.[44] Men were the passive victims of an irresistible female sexuality unless they carefully girded themselves against temptation.[45] Thicknesse's primary target and source of evidence of sexual impropriety was Smellie's *Treatise*. Other critics such as Francis Foster in *Thoughts on the Times* (1779) and Elizabeth Nihell echoed Thicknesse's accusations against Smellie in particular and man-midwifery in general.[46]

According to Michel Foucault, the "steady proliferation of discourses about sex" was accompanied by an increasing sensitivity to the language used by and the identities of those who communicated about sex.[47] Indeed, all midwifery guides from the era reveal anxiety about maintaining modesty and morality while at the same time being informative and comprehensive. There was always the chance that the texts would fall into flippant hands that would put the explicit descriptions and figures to misuse.[48] Henry Bracken, in *The Midwife's Companion* (1737), for instance, prays that his description of intercourse "may not, at any Time hereafter, fall into the Hands of the lascivious or wanton Libertine; guard it…O divine Architect! from such unhallow'd Lips."[49]

One strategy for preventing this outrage was to euphemize the discourse by coining specific medical terms for the organs in question, privileging knowledge of the female body to the educated male. Descriptors for anatomical parts gradually became more Latinate over the course of the century as medicine professionalized. For instance, "vagina," Latin for "sheath," did not come to into standard medical usage with its current meaning until 1700. It was decades before it replaced the vernacular "neck of the womb" entirely in medical writings, and presumably it took even longer to enter the common parlance outside the medical world.[50] Thus, Bracken uses "neck of the womb" interchangeably with "vagina," which he glosses as "sheath." Similarly, he glosses "penis" as "Man's Yard."[51] By Smellie's day, "vagina" and "penis" could be used without glosses.[52]

The emphasis on the pelvic bones was another discursive strategy for downplaying the potential for prurience. Beginning midwifery treatises with the "well-formed Pelvis," as does Smellie's, served two purposes. First, it distinguished the male doctor from female midwives by advertising his superior anatomical knowledge. Doctors understood how babies' heads and mothers' pelvic bones worked in conjunction—or failed to work. Midwives, it was claimed, did not. Second, medical men wanted to downplay the potential erotic frisson in anatomizing female genitalia. Most doctor-authored midwifery treatises of the era echoed Smellie's privileging of the pelvis, and someone opening one with prurient intent would be sorely disappointed to find over half of the anatomy section dedicated to the skeleton. While Smellie dedicated an entire chapter on the pelvic bones alone, he devoted substantially fewer pages to all the organs and wet tissue—internal and external—that one normally thinks about as involved in birth. Even the uterus and ovaries were subordinated to the pelvis.

This is not the case in traditional midwives' books. While teaching midwives about anatomy was stated in these books as a primary goal, that anatomy meant the soft organs of generation, and usually those of both sexes. Midwives were consulted in all matters of sexual health, from conception to delivery, and for neonatal care. A good midwife needed to understand the secrets of sexual intercourse and conception to advise her patients on how to promote or retard fertility; thus, she needed explicit knowledge of the workings of the parts of generation. Nicolas Culpepper began his popular *Directory for Midwives* (1651), which stayed in print throughout the eighteenth century, by declaring "I began first at the Principles, namely; the Anatomy of the Vessels dedicated to Generation; for above all things I hold it most fitting, That Women (especially Midwives) should be well skil'd in the exact Knowledge of the Anatomy of these Parts." He includes anatomical descriptions for the external and internal reproductive organs of both sexes, beginning with those of the male.[53] Other lay manuals such as the various versions of *Aristotle's Masterpiece* and *The Compleat Midwife* follow suit. The first chapter of the first English midwifery text by a woman, Jane Sharp's *The Midwives Book* (1671) concerned itself with "A brief description of the Generative parts in both sexes; and first of the Vessels in Men appropriated to procreation."[54] A belief in a homogeneity between the reproductive organs of the sexes underlay these texts: ovaries and testes are both stones that concoct seed; penises and clitorises (and vaginas to a lesser degree) were all erectile organs with analogous functions. The clitoris was perceived as a small, imperforated penis crucial for successful conception: "The Clytoris [sic] is a sinewy and hard body, ful [sic] of spongy and black matter within, as the side-Ligaments of the Yard are, in form it represents the Yard of a Man, and suffers erection and falling as that doth; this is that which causeth lust in Women, and gives delight in Copulation, for without this, a Woman neither desires Copulation, or hath pleasure in it, or conceives by it."[55]

Books produced early in the eighteenth century were more likely than later books to replicate the vivid visual descriptions and earthiness of those from the previous era. John Maubray, who dedicated the first half of his treatise to a discourse on God, Nature, Man, the mysteries of conception and other philosophical quandaries, declares "the *External Parts of GENERATION...* are generally so well known, that I would not so much as mention them, out of *Modesty*, were it not, that, I presume some *young MIDWIFE* may find something in the ensuing *Description* worth her singular *Notice*." He went on to describe the appearance of various external parts, comparing, for instance, the labia with "Pullet's Gills" and giving a long description on the changes these parts undergo during intercourse to add "to the *Charms* of *COPULATION*."[56]

However, as men entered the field and began writing for each other instead of writing to instruct midwives, they became increasingly reluctant to provide explicit detail on "the Generative parts." As the century wore on, most anatomical descriptions found in midwifery books could be described, in Foucauldian terms, as the revelatory medical gaze that pierced the opacity of the flesh and made the invisible interior visible.[57] Most male-authored midwifery treatises typically consisted of a long, detailed chapter on the pelvic bones, followed by a shorter one on reproductive organs in which, in topographical fashion, the anatomist takes the reader from the outside in, traveling quickly past the outer sexual organs by providing their Latin names and locations to the vagina and uterus, which are then treated in more detail. The chapter on anatomy in Smellie's *Treatise* follows this path: "The *Mons Veneris* is situated at the upper part of the *Pubis*, from which also begin the *Labia pudendii*, stretching down as far as the lower edge where the *Froenum laborium* or *Fourchette* is formed...."[58] At a glance, there seems to be no erotic woman inhabiting the text. She is merely a collection of parts, denoted by Latin names, measurements, locations. Titillation seemed to have given way to empirical detachment.

The apparent clinical detachment of midwifery treatises, however, actually eroticized their subject in subtle ways. Smellie, for example, expected his students to develop a sort of x-ray vision that would enable them to imagine the movement of pelvic bones hidden beneath the flesh of their patients. He instructed the reader to imagine the well-formed pelvis inside of "a woman... reclined backwards, or half-sitting, half-lying."[59] This exercise should be repeated upon every patient the practitioner attended. Furthermore, Smellie invited students to imagine the unseen living interior of female bodies engaged in sexual intercourse: "In coition, the *Uterus* yields three or four inches to the pressure of the *Penis,* having a free motion upwards and downwards, so that the reciprocal oscillation which is permitted by this contrivance, increases the mutual titillation and pleasure."[60] It is not a far stretch to assume that the young medical student would make the cognitive hop and imaginatively populate the textual peep show. In fact, Burton took issue with Smellie's description of the uterus moving during coitus: "I will not here enter into any Debate with you upon the Matter of Fact or Propriety of your Expression, but shall only observe, that to move the Uterus four inches higher than *its usual Situation,* will require a Man of *extensive Abilities;* but it requires no great Capacity to know that it is the Friction on the Clitoris, that increases the Pleasures in the Female, to which this *Oscillation* of the Uterus can no way contribute, therefore their *mutual Pleasure* cannot be *thereby* promoted."[61]

Smellie is famous for turning the female body into a machine, "reduce[d] to the principles of mechanism"[62] both conceptually and in the fabrication of his artificial mother machines, so lifelike some students raved they could barely tell the difference between the machines and real women (Figure 1.3).[63] The conception of bodies and body parts as machines in motion connects midwifery treatises to the materialist philosophies espoused in many libertine works. As Margaret C. Jacob explains, "materialists…attempted to narrate a new universe composed solely of atomized, animate bodies in motion, mechanisms driven by the law of pleasure. The universe of the bedroom created by the materialistic pornographers stands as the analogue to the physical universe of the mechanical philosophers."[64] Atomized, anatomized (female) bodies in motion make up the bulk of midwifery treatises outside of, and in tension with, individuals mentioned in case histories. Disembodied pelvises, vaginas, uteri, and clitorises fill the pages in much the same way as they do in contemporary erotica such as *A New Description of Merryland* (1741), which described female genitalia as a mythical land, whose latitude and longitude are unfixable. For a visual depiction, the author Thomas Stretzer directed the "curious Reader to a Map of MERRYLAND…published some Years ago by the Learned Mr. [François] *Moriceau* [sic], who was a great Traveller in that Country, and surveyed it with tolerable Exactness"—referring to French accoucheur François Mauriceau's influential midwifery treatise, *Traité des maladies des femmes grosses* (1668).[65] Clearly, Stretzer saw connections between his sophomoric bawdry and medical writings. The topographical survey cinches the connection by making manifest the geographical metaphor implicit in the idea of an anatomical atlas. Throughout much of the tract, Merryland is the

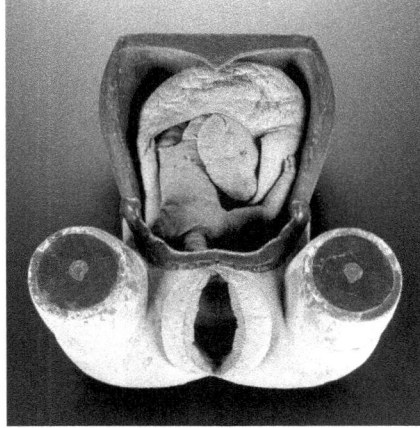

Fig. 1.3: An eighteenth-century
obstetric phantom. Although not
one of Smellie's, his were likely very
similar. Credit: Eighteenth-century
obstetric phantom, Italian. Full view,
graduated matte black perspex background. Science Museum, London.

mons veneris itself, "a naturally wet and fenny land"; the vagina, a "Canal," is
the site of all the country's "traffick"; while the uterus is the country's "Great
Storehouse."[66] However, Stretzer, much like the obstetric writers he satirized,
was unable to maintain a reified, dissected female body. Strategies for policing
the erotic potential of obstetrics, such as coining a specialized vocabulary
and attempting to divorce parts of the body from both their functions and
from the human consciousness perceiving their sensations, failed to produce
the veneer of respectability and modesty medical men craved. In fact, these
strategies more or less fueled fears that men-midwives were wolves in periwigs
bent upon seduction.

## Man-Midwife as Necrophiliac

An association with illegal dissections was the third mark against men-
midwives in the popular imagination. Dissection held an ambiguous place in
Enlightenment medicine. On the one hand, anatomical knowledge was thought
to be a crucial foundation in medical education. On the other, desecration of
the body, even of a felonious one, violated religious interdictions against the
violation of the to-be-resurrected corpse. Even if their objections were not
motivated by religious reasons, people still resented the arrogance of medical
men who violated graves and desecrated deceased loved ones with impunity.
The quest to understand the mechanical body, and perhaps even to find
the bodily seat of the soul, led medical men to perform illegal dissections.[67]
Materialist philosophy underlay the attempts to discursively separate body from

mind and flesh from organ. Descartes's separation of body from mind left an indelible mark on Enlightenment thinking, even if he was often repudiated or ridiculed by the thinkers themselves.

Though largely ignored by the authorities, the anatomist's knife was an object of fear and loathing among common people, felons included.[68] Legally, the Royal Company of Barber-Surgeons received six criminal corpses a year on which to perform dissections, but after its split into two companies, the Barbers and the Surgeons, "the new Company of Surgeons was temporarily homeless" until 1753.[69] With or without a dissecting theatre, the offerings of the Company of Surgeons were not enough to meet the demands of medical students. Private courses in anatomy, analogous to the ones in midwifery offered by Smellie and other practitioners, stepped in to fill the gap. William Hunter opened his private anatomy school in London in 1746, a wildly successful venture visited by luminaries the likes of Adam Smith, Edmund Burke, and Edward Gibbon. Hunter promised a body for each student, creating a massive demand that could not be filled by legal means, even after the dissection of all felons was legalized in London in 1752.[70] Most of the bodies used in the classroom were obtained by Resurrectionists (professional grave robbers) under the auspices of William's brother John, the master anatomist and surgeon.

Anatomy schools were not the only game in town. Many medical men, men-midwives amongst them, dissected bodies whenever the opportunity arose, and often without the permission of the deceased's family. Irish surgeon Fielding Ould used dissections as a novel excuse for the lack of literary polish in his treatise: "The candid Reader must not expect to find, either Purity of Stile [sic] or Elegance of Expression, in this Undertaking; and I hope he will criticize more tenderly on it, when I confess, that I spent that Time which others employ in their Improvement in polite Literature, in a more laborious Manner; namely in the Dissection of human Bodies."[71] The bodies dissected came, presumably, from patients who died while under his care or the care of close colleagues, as they did for many practitioners. In 1761, Charles White reported he was forced to stop dissecting one Betty Riggs, who died of pneumonia while six months pregnant, with the arrival of "her friends."[72]

Dissection held an ambiguous place in the popular imagination. It was the last stage of cruelty in William Hogarth's *The Four Stages of Cruelty* (1751), but it was also increasingly considered necessary for medical progress. Despite these negative associations, medical practitioners were expected to have participated in dissections, and they openly discussed even illegal ones in their treatises. Even midwife Sarah Stone claims to "have seen several Women open'd," though she argues all the anatomical training in the world could not have prepared her for her business without having served a six-year apprenticeship with her mother.[73]

Dissection had apparently become routine, albeit still feared and hated. However, people still occasionally resisted. American statesman and poet Francis Hopkinson, in *An Oration Which Might Have Been Delivered to the Students in Anatomy on the Late Rupture Between the Two Schools in This City* (1789), used the specter of a vengeful mob as reason enough to quell the antagonism between Philadelphia Drs. Foulke and Shippen and their respective students after animosity between the two parties boiled over into public scandal.[74] The mob was more than an empty threat—Dr. William Shippen, who also taught midwifery, was only one physician whose house had been attacked by angry mobs.[75] Despite its ostensible purpose as a call to the end of hostilities, the bulk of Hopkinson's satirical poem is a gruesome depiction of the anatomist engaging in interracial necrophilia. The anatomist speaker of Hopkinson's poem falls in love with consumptive "Brown Cadevera" for her skeletal charms.[76] After her death, he exultantly exhumes her body, boils and scrapes her bones, and rearticulates her skeleton with wire. Then, enthralled,

> Oftentimes I sit and contemplate her charms,
> Her nodding skull and her long dangling arms,
> 'Till quite inflam'd with passion for the dead
> I take her beauteous skeleton to bed—
> There stretch'd, at length, close to my faithful side
> She lies all night a lovely grinning bride.—[77]

Hopkinson took the hint straight from the writings of medical men in which images and descriptions of the dissected female body was often tinged with desire. Critics of dissection accused anatomists of loving their work a little too much. They saw a connection between anatomists' excitement at discovering the secret workings of the human body with sexual excitement. While sexy might seem a far cry from the decaying, bloody remains on a dissection table, anatomists were quick to presume the copulative activity of the dissected woman from what they saw in her dead body. Thus, anatomists believed that the presence of *corpora lutae* (the scars ovulation leaves on the ovary) in virgins was evidence of masturbation;[78] by the same token, John Burton assumed that women with "the greatest Number of Branches of Nerves from the Intercostals"—something he could only determine through dissection— would experience "agreeable Sensation in the Clitoris" when having their nipples "tickled" and would also enjoy breastfeeding more.[79]

Men-midwives' ability to control their lusts were suspect even when handling dead bodies. Still, Smellie made clear that the anatomical knowledge he was spreading came from corpses. Opening the body of a pregnant woman, or one who had recently delivered, was considered an especially momentous occasion as it offered rare insight into the mysteries of life. Smellie divulged, "I have assisted in opening several women who died after delivery...."[80] He explicitly referred to the anatomist's "cut" into uterine flesh, the vessels made visible by "nice injections" and "subtle injections."[81] The illegal and quasi-legal dissections of parturient women culminated with the production of magnificent anatomical atlases (explored more fully in Chapter Two) such as Smellie's *Sett of Anatomical Tables* (1754) or Hunter's *The Gravid Uterus* (1774), with its exquisite depictions of chubby babies so lifelike one could almost imagine lifting them, crying, from the cadaverous wombs entombing them. The medical engravings of dissected mothers and fetuses are often hauntingly, disturbingly beautiful. As Thomas Denman, whose work will be explored in more detail in Chapter Three, said of his engravings of "abortions," "It must...be allowed, that in the generality of these things are preserved for their beauty, or as matters of curiosity, rather than of use."[82]

## Smellie's *Treatise* and the Picaresque

Violation of social and cultural codes marked the man-midwife as an outsider. Engaged in women's work, he violated accepted gender roles. This, in turn, presented him the opportunity to violate the marital bed. Searching for the secrets of life, he violated graves and the bodies of the dead. He operated outside the confines of the Faculty, the law, and propriety. So how is the unsavory character of the man-midwife related to the respected, trusted, fashionable accoucheur like William Hunter, the chosen birth attendant of London's leading ladies and Queen Charlotte herself? On the one hand, successive generations of men-midwives were able to intervene efficaciously in difficult childbirths, resulting in a growing acceptance of the field. Accoucheurs like William Hunter cut a noticeable figure in Georgian society, and this visibility led to broader acceptance. On the other hand, the ultimate ascendancy of the man-midwife can also be traced to the influence that texts like Smellie's *Treatise* had on the opinion of the medical field as a whole. In other words, not only did the man-midwife win the war of public opinion through deeds and actions, but also through words and arguments.

The explosion of man-midwifery textbooks was not simply to meet the expanding demands of students, as most authors claimed. They were also written to counter the accusations and criticism leveled against male practitioners. As Keller explains, it is valuable to read midwifery manuals "as rhetorical constructs, as public performances offered for commercial consumption, intended not so much to instruct as to promulgate certain images and identities of practitioners."[83] These texts present a self-image of the man-midwife as heroic. William Smellie, a key figure in this debate, influenced all subsequent writers on the topic. Moreover, he stands at the juncture of change in the profession, at the transition from emergency practitioner to primary care attendant in the birthing room. His *Treatise* registers the anxiety about "honour of the profession" and the role of the man-midwife.[84] Smellie is presented as the archetypal accoucheur, on a quest to save women and babies and to rescue the profession from undeserved calumny.

## The Quest for Patrimony

Like all heroes, especially those of uncertain background such as those found in picaresque tales, the hero-accoucheur needed a pedigree. In the Preface and Introduction to the first volume, Smellie laid out a historical lineage for his students and himself in which he contrasts the dark ages of midwifery when it was "altogether in the hands of women" to the growing light male physicians and surgeons have shed upon it over the centuries.[85] Smellie began with Hippocrates, "because all the succeeding authors, as far down as the latter end of the sixteenth century, have copied from his works the most material things relating to the diseases of women and children, as well as to the obstetric art."[86] Hippocrates was the father of medicine; if he was also the father of man-midwifery, men were justified in their intrusion and hostile takeover of this female profession. Smellie emphasized this lineage on the course completion certificates he gave out: fully half the page was covered by a bust of Hippocrates. Although Smellie's lineage was promulgated by many of his students who went on to teach midwifery, others were not so certain of the purity of the pedigree.[87] Elizabeth Nihell called Smellie's history a "legend"[88] and later nineteenth-century obstetricians, needing to create a complete break with the past, deposed Hippocrates as patriarch, relying instead on the legacy of eighteenth-century icons like Smellie himself.[89] The hero-accoucheur might make large claims about his family tree, but like any other picaro, his claims were doubted as the fabulous tales of a rogue bent upon trickery.

Unsurprisingly, Smellie dismissed the possibility of a matriarch, discounting all ancient female practitioners because "none of their writings are extant, and the accounts given of them are mostly fabulous and foreign to our purpose"—namely to establish a historical lineage and precedent for man-midwifery.[90] Smellie intended to establish a line of begats, a direct lineage from Hippocrates to the present day that demonstrated historical precedence for the development and use of obstetrical instruments. The summaries of the ancients detailed their practices of craniotomy, fetal dismemberment, and other horrific techniques, setting up a favorable comparison to the modern, humane forceps. "Modern" midwifery was dated to sixteenth-century France, when Ambrose Paré pioneered footling delivery and Paris's Hotel-Dieu opened a lying-in ward for the indigent. There, the successes of male practitioners "got the better of those ridiculous prejudices which the female sex had been used to entertain."[91]   However, in England, advancements in midwifery were held up by writers like Nicolas Culpepper and William Salmon (to whom he attributed *Aristotle's Masterpiece*) and the selfishness of the Chamberlen family, who kept the forceps secret. The hero-accoucheur had a long patrilineage, obscured through the machinations of unscrupulous men who preyed on female superstitions. He may have been an outsider, but that was through no fault of his own, for he was worthy of his patrimony—professional inclusion within the Hippocratic medical establishment—and through his efforts in the lying-in chambers of the women of England (and later America), he would regain it, even if he was forced to engage in trickery to do so.

In the discursive space of the *Treatise*, the quest for this patrimony of medical respectability ranked with equal importance with the task of saving women and children. Smellie interleaved lessons about the state of the profession throughout his opus; moreover, focused on the exigencies of difficult labors and post-partum and neonatal care, Volume III ends not with a final word about gynecological or pediatric care, but with "Cases and Example for young practitioners to shun errors, and ement [sic] the harmony betwixt male and female practitioners." Men-midwives who could not conciliate female midwives and nurses were bad men-midwives, the true villain of the story and the antagonist of the hero-accoucheur.

However, the hero-accoucheur also faced one final challenge—the most obvious one—Death. Smellie revealed that he began his journey to perfect the forceps and midwifery instruction because the typical methods of podalic version, the fillet (a flexible piece of whalebone with a cord attached), or at the last resort, the crochet, too often meant the "loss of children, which gave [him] much uneasiness."[92] Yet Smellie maintained a stoic attitude toward death, which "would sometimes happen, even to the best and most careful practitioners."[93]   Such an attitude was a necessary defense mechanism in a world that did not practice sterilization of medical equipment nor understand how infections spread. If Smellie's *Treatise* can be read as a picaresque tale, as I am arguing it can, Death is the equivalent of the ups and downs of Fortune that spins the picaro about despite his dogged efforts to climb the ladder of success. Like Fortune, Death was frequently beyond the control of "even to the best and most careful practitioners," yet the reputations of accoucheurs, by and large, depended upon their ability to defy death in the uncertain space of the lying-in chamber.

## Smellie as Archetypal Accoucheur

The picaresque mode features a roguish hero telling his own episodic story about his ups and downs on the wheel of fortune. These traits are evident in Smellie's tale. Largely a first-person account of his successes and failures in midwifery, it was offered not merely as idiosyncratic and personal, but as model of progress from ignorance to enlightenment. Smellie explained, "I have given this short detail of my own conduct, for the benefit of young practitioners, who will see, that, far from adhering to one original method, I took all opportunities of acquiring improvement, and cheerfully renounced those errors which I had imbibed in the beginning of life."[94] The *Treatise* created a phallocentric mythos that would have had a powerful, subconscious appeal for young men on the cusp of professional life. The male obstetrician hero, armed with education and ever-better instruments, was bent on saving all parturient damsels-in-distress from their worst enemies—themselves and other "ignorant" women—to triumph over death and the calumny of the masses. His success would bring honor to his nation in the form of new citizens and scientific advancement.

The transmutation of Smellie's personal story into an archetypal model required the creation of a collective male voice. The two *Collection of Cases* achieved multivocality through the inclusion of letters and cases from Smellie's correspondents, many of whom were former students. In stark contrast to the first-person activities of the case histories, Volume I displayed a grammatical confusion of pronominal and verbal constructions. Throughout much of the volume, the grammatical presence of the accoucheur remains hidden through convoluted and contorted constructions of the passive voice. Reading it the first time, I could not help but wonder why an accomplished novelist like Tobias Smollett permitted such bad writing to escape his editorial eye. Upon reflection however, I realized that downplaying the subject/actor actually created a collective male voice, subsuming Smellie's experience into the collective experience of the Hero-Accoucheur whose physical presence is typically signaled only by his hands, employed as tools, and separate from the watchful control of the grammatically-absent physician. To give just one example, the instructions on delivering a woman suffering from hernia are entirely in passive voice:

> In order to prevent or remedy this accident, **let** the *Os externum* **be** gradually **opened** with the hand, which **being introduced** in the *Vagina*, **shall raise** the child's head, so as to suffer the intestine **to be pushed** above it by the assistance of the other hand, which presses upon the outside: in this manner both hands **may be used** alternately, till the purpose **be effected**; or should this method fail **to reduce** and **retain** the intestine, the child **must be delivered** with the forceps, or turned and brought by the feet....[95]

In this example, the passive voice hides the presence of the operator using his hands to "reduce" and "retain" —to physically handle—the female body until it submitted to his imperative will. Moreover, the use of the jussive "let" positions the physician as the director in a drama of parts, hiding in the wings, but watching and commanding the players. If his hands fail on stage, he could replace them with his mechanical hands, the forceps.

The masculine self, separate from his body, could maintain an aloofness from the struggling, bared flesh of the woman his hands manipulated. The jussive also creates a sense of immediacy and identification with the text. Medical students and young practitioners could project themselves into the action, imaginatively taking Smellie's magisterial role in the unfolding medical drama. However, the lack of consistency in voice and person limits this effect. Passive voice occasionally gives way to active voice, and the grammatical person constantly shifts. Aside from the occasional slip into first-person narrative, certain passages are written to "you," while others are to an inclusive "we." The rhetorical thrust behind this pronominal shifting was to provide emphasis to certain passages. Although Smellie was generally content to leave his male readers as an unspoken presence within the text, occasionally he admonished them with a direct "you," typically during explanations of procedures he felt were crucially important to master correctly. For example, when explaining where to cut the umbilical cord, Smellie exhorted, "run the scissars [sic] as near as possible to the root of the blades, else the *Funis* will be apt to slip from the edge, and **you** will be obliged to make several snips before **you** can effect a separation: at the same time guard the points of the scissars [sic] with **your** other hand."[96] Similarly, "In order to deliver the *Placenta*, take hold of the navel-string with the left hand, turning it round the fore and middle fingers, or wrapping it in a cloth, that it may not slip from **your** grasp; then pull gently from side to side, and desire the woman to assist **your** endeavour...."[97] Both of these procedures were considered potentially life and death matters for child and mother respectively. Smellie broke out of the collective voice into direct address in order to underscore their importance.

By and large, however, the *Treatise* maintains a collective masculine presence. The use of "we" united Smellie with his male readers, and most, if not all, male midwifery practitioners, often as a defensive gesture against the calumnies of the general public and the complaints of female patients and attendants. For example, although the sections on "touching" in Book Three of Volume I are mainly written in passive voice that conceal the agent, an articulated male collectivity appears in two interesting places. First, in reviewing which finger(s) to use while "touching," Smellie asserted, "By some **we** are advised to touch with the middle finger, as being the longest; and by others, to employ both that and the first; but the middle finger is too much encumbered by that on each side, to answer the purpose fully, and when two are introduced together, the patient never fails to complain."[98] Here, Smellie rhetorically placed himself with the students as recipients of an ineffective tradition with no clear solution—the technique that yields the most information for the practitioner was also the one most unacceptable to the patient—leaving the "we" to work together to find a way to balance professional and patient needs.

Similarly, a united "we" must defend against "clamorous" attendants and the anxiety and complaints of the laboring woman, too "impatient to wait the requisite time" during a lingering delivery. "[W]e must endeavour to surmount by arguments and gentle persuasions [these complaints]; but if she is not to be satisfied, and strongly impressed with an opinion, that certain medicines might be administered to hasten delivery, it will be convenient to prescribe some innocent *Placemus*, that she may take between whiles, to beguile the time and please her imagination...."[99] Male practitioners had to guard against being weakened into unmanly capitulation by women's pleas for hastened labors.[100] Knowing that their brothers-at-arms were united with them in shunning the use of drugs and instruments precipitously could perhaps shore up their resolve in the face of the most importunate of the "fair sex."

"We" could also be used to distinguish good from bad men-midwives. The sections in Volume I on the forceps contained a medley of voices and persons. The controversy is introduced in passive voice that grammatically removed Smellie and his students from the controversy. They were neither the calumniators nor the faulty practitioners:

A general outcry hath been raised against gentlemen of the profession, as if they delighted in using instruments and violent methods in the course of their practice; and this clamour hath proceeded from the ignorance of such as do not know that instruments are sometimes absolutely necessary, or from the interested views of some low, obscure, and illiterate practitioners, both male and female, who think they find their account in decrying the practice of their neighbors. It is not to be denied, that mischief has been done by instruments in the hand of the unskillful and unwary....[101]

Smellie, however, becomes a grammatical presence inserted between this former group and the "judicious practitioners" evidently included in the "we": "**I** am persuaded, that every judicious practitioner will do every thing for the safety of his patients before he has recourse to any violent method, either with hand or instrument; though cases will occur, in which gentle methods will absolutely fail."[102] Smellie, with his experience, served as the barrier protecting the "judicious" from the "low, obscure, and illiterate." Thereafter, shunning the bad, the inclusive "we" provides instructions on forceps use. For example, "**We** must determine when **we** ought to wait patiently for the efforts of nature, and when it is absolutely necessary to come to her aid. If **we** attempt to succour [sic] her too soon, and use much force in the operation, so that the child and mother, or one of the two are lost, **we** will be apt to reproach ourselves for having acted prematurely..." and vice versa if "we" wait.[103] "We" are the only ones qualified to reproach "ourselves." No one else, including the woman or her family, were qualified to make complaints against "we" men-midwives.

The passive voice and confusion of pronouns are dropped from the succeeding volumes of case histories. Instead, a more engaging active "I" recounts Smellie's experiences over his forty-odd year practice. Nevertheless, it is likely that the reader identification so carefully constructed in the first volume was meant to be carried over into the two volumes of case histories. Already primed to see himself as Smellie, the reader would readily identify with the "I" of the cases. As Pam Lieske notes, "There is an immediacy and urgency to [Smellie's] story, as if he wanted his readers to peer over his shoulder and see firsthand exactly what he experienced moment by moment"—as his students undoubtedly did in practice.[104] Moreover, the inclusion of case histories borrowed from other male authors and letters from former students seeking approval and advice constantly reinforced the male collectivity that helped establish professional standards by continuing the division between "we" good accoucheurs and "they" bad ones. Some letters display good or promising practices while others prompt chastisement from Smellie. Letter writers of the first sort were named, while those of the second got a mere initial to protect their identities (but likely not from members of Smellie's student coterie). Writers of the letters, and the reader of the cases, undoubtedly wanted to be identified with the former category, the archetypal Hero-Accoucheur.

## The Hero-Accoucheur

In Volume II, Smellie reminisced about why he decided to leave his general surgical practice in Scotland to travel to London and Paris to learn to use the forceps before embarking on his mission to improve them and obstetrics instruction by opening his own London school. This trip down memory lane occurs at the end of a case featuring a primigravida 40-year-old woman who would not "permit[ ] [him] to examine" her because of the "artful insinuations of the midwife, who terrified her with dreadful accounts of instruments," and whose baby died during labor.[105] Smellie assured the reader that had he been allowed to use the forceps, he could have saved the child. The midwife's machinations reminded him of "the first year of my practice, when I was called to lingering cases…occasioned by the imprudent methods used by unskillful midwives to hasten labour…. [O]n such occasions, without knowing the steps that had been taken, I have been told that the patient had been in severe labour for many hours, and sometimes days, and that now I was called to prevent her from dying with the child in her belly."[106] However, it was not maternal deaths that made him seek to improve his practice, but rather he wanted "to avoid this loss of children, which gave [him] much uneasiness," so he requisitioned "a pair of French forceps" made "according to a draught published in the Medical Essays by Mr. *Butter*."[107] Finding these unusable, and after reading the recently published "treatises of [Edmund] *Chapman* and [William] *Giffard*," Smellie travelled to London, where he "saw nothing was to be learned" and then to Paris where he was again disappointed, this time by the crudeness of the mannequin, or mechanical mother, used in forceps teaching (Figure 1.3).[108] Convinced he could do better, Smellie set about devising more realistic dolls and improving the design of the forceps. He also sought the advice and accepted the correction of eminent practitioners. Vigilant self-improvement, cooperation with "brother accoucheur[s]," and shunning "false ambition" were key traits of those who wished to be a hero-accoucheur.[109]

Smellie's practice remained primarily an emergency one even after he relocated to London and began specializing in midwifery. Over 60% of the case histories related were emergencies, featuring some complication with the labor that precipitated Smellie being called not a moment too soon and sometimes a moment too late.[110] In recounting these situations, he presented himself as heroically saving the day. Sometimes this meant quietly remonstrating with the midwife to correct her bad practices, but frequently Smellie described himself as fighting a tireless battle with the female body in which he was exhausted and sometimes even injured. The case histories vividly describe Smellie's actions, creating a sense of immediacy and urgency as if the reader were there in the room, watching or helping Smellie in his efforts to deliver a woman of a child. It would be impossible to analyze such a great number of cases in any detail; instead, I will quote extensively from a representative case to display the vivid detail, the intrepid efforts, and the heroic posturing typical of the case histories at large.

Smellie and his students had been called by a midwife to a "watchman's wife." The arm of the baby presented, and the midwife

> had tried different methods to make the child (as she ignorantly imagined) withdraw up its hand into the womb and change itself into the natural position; dipping its hand into a bason [sic] of cold water, and also in vinegar and brandy; but finding these trials fail, she had recourse to the last remedy, before any assistance from a man practitioner was thought necessary: she directed the woman's husband to take hold of her legs over his shoulder, and lift up her body three times, with her back to his, and her head downwards.[111]

After all these expedients failed, whose ludicrous inefficacy was meant to contrast with Smellie's enlightened practice, the midwife turned to Smellie for assistance, who agreed not only to deliver the woman, but to pay for her lying-in if he could bring his students to watch the delivery. Apparently this was a satisfactory arrangement because in the next paragraph, his students are present and helping with the delivery:

> Finding I could not keep the patient in a firm position, when on her side, I had her turned to her back, with her breech to the bed's feet; two of the gentlemen sustained her legs; her head was supported by lying in the midwife's lap; the midwife was seated on the bolster at the head of the bed, to keep her firm in that position, and restrain her arms, so as to prevent her hands from pulling at the assistants or me, in time of the operation.

As the arm of the child was but little swelled, I easily introduced my left hand below it, into the *Vagina*; then pushing up the shoulder, insinuated my hand betwixt the breast and the right side of the *Uterus*; but finding, after several strong efforts, that I could neither raise the shoulder higher, nor push my hand sufficiently up to come at the feet, I altered her position in the following manner.

Observing that the midwife kept the woman's head and shoulders too high, I made her sit further up on the bed, that they might lie lower; but my hand and arm being by this time cramped and wearied, with working in a hurry, I was obliged to withdraw both, and rest a little. Considering that my other hand could not, in this position of the woman, reach the legs of the child…I turned her to her knees and elbows, and had her supported in that posture by the assistants, on the bed.

I then insinuated my right hand, and gradually stretched the contracted Uterus, when I found the feet were turned up to the breech at the *Fundus*. I now endeavoured, with all my strength to push farther up, so as to make more room to take hold of the legs but the woman being strong, and struggling incessantly, we could not keep her in that position so that all my efforts to bring them down, proved abortive.[112]

Smellie had the woman again laid on her back and restrained, but this time with bedding under her backside to raise her "breech" and lower her head and shoulders before resuming the manual manipulation: "My left hand being now pretty well recovered from the former fatigue, I introduced it as at first, and at last reached up to the *Fundus Uteri*; I now brought down one of the legs and delivered the child, with the assistance of the noose…. The child was alive; the mother recovered; and the *Placenta*, being loosened in time of operation, followed the delivery."[113] Smellie's promise of paying for the lying-in care proved fortunate for the mother since "She continued weak for three or four weeks, and complained of great pains in the Abdomen and neighboring parts…."[114] Smellie did not overtly connect his medical interventions with her pain and "the danger from a violent inflammation of the Uterus" that he feared.[115]

In recounting the case, concern about professional reputation is given equal rhetorical weight as the successful postpartum care. Indeed, Smellie even momentarily doubted his decision to become an instructor:

As this was one of the first difficult cases in which my pupils were allowed to attend, after I began to teach midwifery, I was really afraid, in time of operating, of being foiled, and suffering reproach, for pretending to teach others, while incapable of delivering so strong and so well formed a subject....Although...I had been called to many such cases, yet I was never more fatigued. I was not able to raise my arms to my head for a day or two after this delivery; and one of the gentlemen, who was present, being of a delicate constitution, was so much afraid, that he resolved never to venture on the practice of midwifery.[116]

Through these revelations about his insecurities about his abilities and his concern with self-image and reputation, Smellie indicated the character he thought a man-midwife should have. The hero-accoucheur must not be "delicate," fearful, or squeamish, like the student who dropped out after this case; he also must assume a calm, unflappable demeanor and persevere in his efforts, despite his own pain or exhaustion or the obvious agony and distress of the woman he is delivering. Death and loss of reputation would be the inevitable result. Pain was not an excuse for failure. Even transparency and honesty about practices could fall sacrifice in the quest for a successful outcome.

## The Trickster-Accoucheur

Deceptions occur frequently in the *Treatise*. Smellie taught students to disguise their instruments with leather wrappings and in pockets and themselves with feminized garb, which was mocked by Nihell has "their Margery [i.e. homosexual] field uniform."[117] He taught them to administer placebos to quiet women and their families, to withhold information from the woman and her family, and, most disturbingly for a present-day reader, to conceal the injuries they caused to women and children during labor. The hero-accoucheur was often a trickster who sometimes had to disguise himself, his tools, and his deeds.

Famously, Smellie instructed young practitioners to hide the forceps in their "side pockets" and from thence "the blades ought to be privately conveyed between the feather-bed and the cloaths [sic], at a small distance from one another, or on each side of the patient...by which means he will often be able to deliver with the forceps, without their being perceived by the woman herself, or any of the assistants."[118] Presumably, his followers heeded and passed on his advice. Pennsylvanian Elizabeth Drinker reported that Shippen, who had trained with Colin MacKenzie, a former head pupil of Smellie's, had carried his obstetrical instruments in his side pocket when he thought he would need to use them to deliver her daughter in a difficult labor.[119] However, as many of the next generation of men-midwives advocated more openness as the correct way to reduce women's fears of instruments. Denman, for instance, would demonstrate "upon one of my knees, all that I intended to do with the *forceps*."[120] Instrumental deliveries remained a frightening prospects, but nearly a century of their public use had somewhat dissipated their terrors.

According to Smellie, men-midwives were not merely to conceal the forceps, but they should also disguise them with leather wrappings intended to make them appear "simple and innocent" to women who associated man-midwives and their instruments with death.[121] In much the same way, the trickster-accoucheur should conceal his tempered masculine steel beneath a feminized garb. By adopting feminized attire, the hero-accoucheur could, like Achilles, hide among the women and gain admittance into the lying-in chamber.[122] Smellie preferred "the genteel and commodious…loose washing night-gown" instead of the "sleeves and apron…necessary in hospitals [because] in private practice it conveys a frightful idea to the patient and female spectators."[123] Smellie's clothes were mocked by Nihell, who suggested he add "pink and silver ribbons" to complete the ensemble, suggesting a gender hybridity captured in the "Man=Mid=Wife" print (Figure 1.1).[124]

As a trickster, the hero-accoucheur did not merely conceal his instruments and himself. He also concealed information that he thought was dangerous from the laboring woman and her family. Sometimes Smellie did so to protect the woman or child. For example, he typically chose to conceal the impending arrival of a twin "lest the woman should have been uneasy."[125] He also hid situations like nearby fires from the laboring woman under the belief that such anxiety would retard the labor and possibly kill the infant. Moreover, he concealed information if the knowledge of it could be damaging to him. For instance, in a lingering or tedious labor, he never told the mother if the baby was still alive because he "had learned by experience, that if the child is mentioned to be alive, and afterwards perishes in the birth, the mother grieves, and imagines it is lost by the unskillfulness of the practitioner."[126] Maternal feelings and professional reputation were presented as being of equal weight when deciding what information to share with patients.

As questionable as these choices might seem to a present-day audience, they pale in comparison with what we would identify as Smellie's malpractice.[127] If Smellie broke an infant's bone or tore a woman's perineum or her uterus, he would keep this knowledge from the patient and her family and instruct the nurse or midwife to do the same, to avoid "mak[ing] the patient uneasy, and giv[ing] her [the nurse] much trouble."[128] A simple rip of the perineum does not seem that bad of a deception. However, when Smellie hid mistakes like feeling the cervix "tear on the left side" despite expecting it to be fatal, or more alarmingly, when he secretly chose to "snip" the cervix with scissors in an attempt to deliver an impacted fetus, resulting in the woman's death, it seems more like outright fraud.[129] Moreover, Smellie taught such practices to his students.[130] One, whose name Smellie concealed, reported back to his former preceptor that during a recent case, he had felt a ruptured uterus when he attempted to deliver the placenta. "Mr.—" reported, "According to your prudent advice, I spoke nothing of the matter, but pronounced her a dead woman, and she accordingly expired in less than six hours after."[131] Like Smellie, this student sought to protect his reputation by hiding his possible culpability in the woman's death.

On numerous occasions, Smellie admitted to concealing severe injuries to infants.[132] In one Scottish case, the patient's "husband, and some of their friends" begged him to prescribe "remedies to procure barrenness" after the second pregnancy that Smellie had been forced to terminate with the crochet because the woman had a severely distorted pelvis.[133] Smellie dismissed their request as old wives' tales, telling the husband the best solution would be to call him at the beginning of labor. The husband followed Smellie's advice, and Smellie was able to deliver the third child alive, but broke its arm. However, he "neglected at that time to examine if all the limbs were sound. The father calling on me about three months after, told me, that although I had brought him a fine girl, yet he had been punished for his desire of not having children, for she had not the power of her left arm."[134] While he did (futilely) attempt to correct his mistake, Smellie did not bother to disillusion the father about the cause of the injury.

The woman had at least three more pregnancies (including an additional one delivered by Smellie), all of which ended when the attendant surgeon was forced to kill the child. If Smellie had not dismissed traditional medicine (including medicines found in classical writers like those he cited as historical precedents), he might have prescribed various known organic emmenagogues and abortifacients—birthwort, tansy, pennyroyal, sage, savine, rue, and other herbs and resins—to this couple as birth control. Emmenagogic and abortifacient herbs were staples in the midwife's arsenal. Sharp, in *The Midwives Book,* suggests, in addition to an eagle's stone, that the midwife use "Any of these herbs half a dram in powder drunk in white-wine...viz of Bettony, or Sage, or Penny-Royal, Fetherfew or Centory, Ivy-berries and leaves, or drink a strong decoction of Master-wort, or of Hyssop in hot water" to hasten the delivery of a child, living or dead.[135] Smellie dismissed such simples as the inefficacious, dangerous, and "ridiculous opinion[s] of the vulgar."[136] Instead he condemned that couple to the repeated pain and horror of hopeless, dangerous labors. He was no more merciful to other women to whom he prescribed "harmless" placebos to "amuse" and "beguile" them and their families.

Many critics have interpreted Smellie's dishonesty and trickery as misogynistic gloating. Cody suggests that "What has disturbed Smellie's critics the most is how he reported triumphing over mothers by hiding knowledge from them."[137] Lieske echoes this complaint, arguing that such deception displayed a lack of empathy and in fact were acts of "demonization" and "infantilization" of the mother.[138] Helen King argues that Smellie's consistent concern for patients "should make us question recent analyses of Smellie in which he is held responsible for exploitation of the poor, and the 'virtual silencing of indigent women.'"[139] While he often infantilized women, time and again Smellie expressed deep empathy for patients and admiration at the bravery and stoicism of some. Nor was it only medical practitioners he coached to lie. When "called by the friends of a young woman in *Park-Street*, who had been delivered of her first child by her aunt," a midwife with whom they were angry because of a perineal tear, he defended the midwife: "such things" he said, "would some times happen, even to the best practitioners." To the woman, who was afraid that "this misfortune would cool [the] affection" of her husband, Smellie counseled her to "keep the secret, and he would know nothing of the matter."[140]

The triumphal tone apparent in Smellie's *Treatise* has less to do with misogyny than with a man who feels he has succeeded at his life's calling. He had improved midwifery, trained legions of male and female practitioners, and had elevated the reputation of the profession. Smellie wanted his students to succeed, to become hero-accoucheurs like himself, and concealment and deception were occasionally a means to that end. He taught them to hide the forceps to protect themselves from the "calumnies and misrepresentations [of those] who are apt to prejudice the ignorant an weak-minded against the use of any instrument." This precaution was necessary because if "unforeseen accidents… afterwards happen to the patient," then "the whole misfortune [would be blamed upon] the innocent operator."[141] Such precautions were necessary even when instruments were not used. When a fatal mistake occurred it "was kept secret" "[i]n order to avoid reflections" that could destroy a practitioner's career and bring dishonor to the profession as a whole.[142]

Why then bring such cases to light in the *Treatise*? Smellie wrote for the benefit of the profession, whose members could learn from each other's mistakes. He did not seem to envision being read by outsiders, not even by a midwife like Nihell—who professed horror that men could get away with what she called murder by citing "occult causes" as the reason for the woman's or child's death—much less the mothers she claimed read all the books on pregnancy they could.[143] There was no way for Smellie to predict that changes in medical ethics and standards of malpractice would eliminate the protective veil of secrecy surrounding medical practitioners' errors. Rather, concealment was a legitimate technique for medical heroes, just as it was for the heroes of myth and romance.

## Midwife as Companion and Helper

All early modern romantic heroes needed a squire—a sidekick that sees them through the hard times and the flush. Don Quixote had Sancho Panza, Roxana had Amy, Lady Arabella had Lucy, Roderick had Strap; even Dorcasina had Betty.[144] The hero-accoucheur had the properly trained midwife or nurse. Far from wanting to eliminate female practitioners, Smellie wanted to demote them from independent professionals to subordinate helpers.

Although Smellie certainly decried midwives and nurses he perceived as "ignorant" and "officious," by and large his depictions of them were positive. Out of the 198 case histories in which midwives are mentioned, over half (101) featured positive depictions of midwives. Add the 18 cases in which Smellie used one of "his" midwives that number reaches to 60%. Of the remaining 79 cases, just under half (37) depicted midwives either neutrally or with only mild criticism. Only 42, or 21% of the total cases, depicted midwives in a clearly negative light. Often in cases with multiple midwifery practitioners present, the midwives come off much better than some of the male practitioners.

Of course, this begs the question what qualities Smellie described as belonging to a "good" midwife, and the simple answer would be one who called him at the very first inkling difficulty in labor, and who acted as an assistant and adjutant to the accoucheur. Bad midwives were those who "fatigued" the patient, relied on their own "self-sufficiency," and resented the intrusion of male practitioners. The best midwives, undoubtedly, were the ones trained by Smellie himself. According to Wilson,

> the midwife had an immense utility for [men-midwives who used forceps at midcentury,]: she could take care of the slow tedium of normal labour, while also…acting as a rapid conduit to bring [their] own services into play when

required…. What the forceps dictated—both as practical reality and, reaching still further, male ambition—was not the replacement of the midwife, but rather a new equilibrium between midwifes and male practitioners.[145]

In order to achieve this change, midwives needed to be taught to respect man-midwives and to defer to their greater skill and knowledge.

The depiction of midwives in the *Treatise*, therefore, is meant to illustrate how to properly handle them. Men-midwives should never berate or belittle their female competitors but instead "ought to make allowance for the weakness of the sex, and rectify what is amiss, without exposing her mistakes." Such gentle conduct would "operate as a silent rebuke upon the conviction of the midwife; who finding herself treated so tenderly, will be more apt to call for necessary assistance on future occasions, and to consider the accoucheur as a man of honour, and a real friend."[146] The apparent patronizing misogyny should not be over-emphasized for Smellie thought faulty male practitioners should be corrected in the same way. In the case histories, Smellie modeled this behavior and attitude for his students. He included cases in which he met and overcame the resistance of midwives through politeness and the quiet display of superior skill. King suggests that

We should… understand…Smellie's studied politeness to midwives as a shrewd move on his part in order to win their confidence and to gain more cases, learned from the time when a man-midwife would rarely be pre-booked, and needed good relationships with midwives so that they would recommend his name if an emergency developed, sometimes remembering his help from cases a few years before.[147]

This fact was made this abundantly clear in the cases included in the final collection.

Previously, I suggested that the last section of the third volume, "Collection XLIX: Cases and Example for young practitioners to shun errors, and ement [sic] the harmony betwixt male and female practitioners," was the take-away, the most important lesson to be learned. In the first, the story of Mr. W, it was the timely intervention of a nurse who recognized the faulty practices of the male attendants that saved the patient. In the third, a Dr. C embarrassed a midwife who had called him for assistance by openly accusing her of tearing the patient's perineum. Later, when "the same accident to a much greater degree happened to himself…. [t]he midwife heard of [it], on which she hunted him out, and attacked him every where upbraiding him with being guilty in reality of what he had villanously [sic] and falsely laid to her charge."[148] In the fourth case, the accoucheur's abuse of midwives "frightened many...from calling in men practitioners.... This the midwives have acknowledged to me in private, when I expostulated with them for not calling me sooner."[149] The lessons of these three cases seem to be for male novices to trust skilled and experienced female practitioners, to rebuke privately lest ye be rebuked in turn, and to treat midwives gently in order to gain their trust, their recommendation, and their business. If treated correctly, midwives would be invaluable "squires" for the hero-accoucheur.

Achieving this type of relationship with midwives meant the accoucheur must gain their trust through a studied display of respect and diplomacy. Smellie repeatedly demonstrated these skills in the cases he shared. In the final case of this collection, Smellie was presented as a King Solomon arbitrating between two quarreling midwives:

> I was one night called very late to a woman of my acquaintance, in the neighbourhood. I was not a little surprised when I came into the room, to hear two women scolding one another in a ferocious manner, and ready to come to blows. As they did not know of my being sent for, my appearance surprised and silenced them for the present. I soon found they were two midwives of my acquaintance. I said nothing, but spoke to the patient who was in bed. The midwife that was sitting at the bedside desired me to take a pain [vaginally examining the patient during a labor pain to determine the dilation of the cervix], saying she would yield her seat to me; but to no midwife in *London*.... I then desired the two midwives to go into the next room, where I heard both their complaints. One had been bespoke; but was engaged when sent for, on which the other was called. I again went to the patient, told her she was in a very good way, and asked which of them she chose for her midwife. She said the one who was bespoke, for she was afraid of the other. I made them acquainted with this decision, and advised her that came first to yield, because if any accident should happen she would be blamed, and I told her she should be paid for her trouble. Thus ended the contest, and both were pleased.[150]

Here, Smellie exemplified the polish and accomplishments of the hero-accoucheur. He was called in, not for a medical emergency, but to settle a quarrel between midwives. He ascertained the safety and comfort of the patient. He spoke no harsh words and stayed above the fray. Because he had cultivated respect for himself in the midwives, they acknowledged his superior skill and willingly used him to arbitrate their case. And because there was no medical emergency, Smellie respected the midwives' turf and did not take over the birth. He stepped on no toes, ruffled no feathers, and it is probably safe to assume that all three women involved—the patient and both midwives—were willing to call for his assistance in the future.

## Man-Midwife as Villain

Rather than the female midwife, the real foil for the hero-accoucheur is the faulty male practitioner, whom Smellie occasionally styles a "pretender"[151] — loaded language coming from a Scot in the 1750s—the Jacobite rebellion of 1745 and its brutal defeat at the Battle of Culloden were still fresh memories. In her discussion of Scottish practitioner John Maubray's use of similar language, Cody suggests he did so to reassure his audience that he was "a good loyal supporter of the Hanoverians."[152] Smellie, a Country Whig, seemed to follow a similar tack. He studiously avoided mentioning his roots, generally referring to Scotland as simply "the country." There is only one direct reference in the *Treatise* to the recent Jacobite rebellion and even this is distanced from Smellie by being in a letter from Mr. Pierce and paraphrased in third person instead of a direct quote. The letter shared the case of a woman who gave birth to a deformed fetus, apparently missing part of its skull. The tragedy was attributed to her having been "grievously frightened with thinking on Lord *Lovat*, who was that day to be beheaded" when she was two months pregnant.[153] Her husband had gone to the execution, a scaffold had collapsed, and a neighbor misinformed the woman that her husband had been killed. The text leaves it unclear if it was her fright at Lord Lovat's real or at her husband's supposed death that caused the deformities; as a result, it seems to suggest that even in death, the rebel Scottish peer, and by extension all Jacobites, could wreak havoc on the nation by destroying the next generation. Furthermore, labeling bad men-midwives "pretenders" aligned them with Jacobites and their malpractice with treason.

Treasonous accoucheurs brought shame to the profession by exhibiting the worst qualities of the worst midwives; moreover, these negative qualities led the men to use rashly, and often fatally, the instruments to which women were denied access. Smellie frequently used the same terminology for faulty practitioners of both genders, lumping accoucheurs and midwives into one "ignorant" and "self-sufficient" lot. However, contemporary misogyny gave an excuse for midwives—they were only weak women after all. The same sexist standards held male practitioners doubly blamable. These men not only practiced bad, often lethal, medicine, they became womanish and emasculated by their practices. Such men brought dishonor to the profession and needed to be eliminated much more urgently than midwives. The *Treatise* offered two means to achieve this goal: censure and (re)education.

Smellie claimed he shared his correspondents' failures "as so many beacons to caution others from falling into the same errors and mistakes in the course of practice."[154] Undoubtedly this was his main goal; however, public shaming of the offenders also seemed to be a function of some of the letters. Although the same discretion with men as with women midwives was practiced—correcting them only privately and withholding their names in the *Treatise*—faulty male practitioners, unlike midwives, were more individualized and given identifying markers, making the censure of them more personal and public. Many were identified with an initial, often coupled with the first letter of the town in which they practiced. Former students were identified as such. Moreover, they were often subjected to the further mortification of having Smellie's chastisement published after their letter. Surely enough information was provided to readily reveal at least some of their identities to the first generation of readers and enough to allow later ones inclined to research to make educated guesses. Even without such hints, identification is still sometimes possible. King surmised that the "surly," "forbidding," midwife-abusing practitioner ready to force labor upon a woman he had drugged into an opium stupor was none other than William Douglas, one of Smellie's earliest critics. The case in the *Treatise* seems to be a more detailed version of a case over which the two argued in a vitriolic pamphlet war in 1748.[155]

Incorrigible offenders like Douglas gave man-midwifery a bad name. Judging from Smellie's treatment of Douglas, one might surmise that since such fellows could not be reasoned with, they should be exposed as frauds to other members of the medical profession, driven away from patients, and exposed publicly albeit with a veil of quasi-anonymity. However, young offenders were to be treated differently. The case given immediately before the Douglas one functions as a parable of a former student gone astray, but reclaimed to "the honour of the profession."[156]

After attending one course of Smellie's lectures but not choosing attend actual labors, Mr. W had "gained reputation from being called to assist midwives…in preternatural cases; but this being the first time of his being bespoke to attend by himself, he was at a loss how to manage his patient in a natural case."[157] In recounting the event, Smellie took care to point out all of Mr. W's mistakes. To begin with, he disdained "attend[ing] the labours, imagining every thing in midwifery trifling," displaying a negative attitude toward the profession that extended to its female practitioners, causing him to fail to heed the advice of "the nurse, a sensible woman, who had been many years in that business."[158] Hubris caused Mr. W to spurn his would-be trusty assistant, much as Smollet's eponymous, over-proud hero, Roderick Random, spurned the friendship of his boon companion, the lower-class Strap, after Roderick had achieved some social success. And like Roderick, Mr. W. soon repented of his snobbery.[159] Acting like an "ignorant midwife," Mr. W fatigued the patient by trying to rush the labor. As a final faux pas, after the family called a second man-midwife, "who by art and cunning had got a name amongst the lower sort of patients," these "self-sufficient" "obstetric adversaries" get into a heated argument before (and with) the female attendants and the family.[160]

When would-be heroes slip up, it is often the sidekick who must come to the rescue. This story is no exception. The nurse convinced the husband to "call an old practitioner." As chance would have it, Smellie happened to be walking by the house at just that moment. A truly British hero, Smellie ordered everyone a soothing cuppa, after which he listened to "the different parties, both male and female." Setting all to rights, he corrected the two accoucheurs privately and agreed to superintend when Mr. W delivered the woman.[161] Both men, grateful for his "friendly behavior in this case, by which they were prevented from exposing their ignorance," returned to both Smellie's lectures *and* "public labours."[162] Thus, Smellie's diplomacy enabled him to reclaim two straying accoucheurs before they had hardened into "ignorant pretenders" to the lasting disparagement of the profession.

## Parturient Damsels-in-Distress

The *Treatise* described the female body as the discursive field on which the hero-accoucheur was to rescue the honor of the profession from calumny and obloquy. Intimate knowledge of that field was crucial for success. The description of the female body began with the "well-formed pelvis," the ideal female pelvis which Smellie calibrated down to a fraction of an inch. For the mechanical-minded Smellie, the solidity of bone undoubtedly made it seem more reliable than frail flesh. Bones, lasting long after flesh decayed, were more easily identifiable, their functions more readily understood than the mysteries of living organs. The female pelvis could function as a signifier of sexual difference and as an anchor from which sense could be made of the uncertain female body. After all, the pelvic bones "restrain[ed]" that ever-changing cipher of female mutability, the vagina, "as if with a bridle."[163] However, within the female body, even bones become frangible and unreliable. Pelvises might be rickety and ill-formed, and the hero-accoucheur had no certain way of determining the case.

Female appearances could not be trusted. Much as Jonathan Swift's "Beautiful Young Nymph Going to Bed" (1731) used prosthetics to conceal her time- and disease-ravaged body,[164] "tall stately women" might conceal rickety malformed pelvises, and "decrepit women" might conceal ones perfectly formed.[165] Women were physically unreliable; childhood mismanagement exacerbated the problem. Rickety pelvises were formed, according to Smellie, from ill children "sitting on stools or the nurse's knees" and decrepitude was caused by "mismanagement in their dress, lying too much on one side, and other accidents" during a girl's early adolescence.[166] This seemed to imply that girlhood, like the birth process itself, should be managed by men—physicians and fathers—or properly trained women because girls (and mothers) were physically damaged when left to follow irrational tradition or the whims of fashion.[167]

If the solidity of bones was a delusive mirage, female genitalia were a frightening *terra incognita*. A vein of fear about mutability and unknowability coupled with an urgent need to fix the female subject runs throughout Smellie's description of female genitals. This underlying fear of the feminine is perhaps best revealed in the description of the Fallopian tubes and ovaries. In fact, the *Treatise* describes the female body as divided against itself. Whereas in the past these tubes were often described as resembling trumpets, by the mid-eighteenth century, medicine had styled them "the *Fimbria* or *Morsus diabolii*... [that] resemble a hand with membranous fingers, which is supposed to grasp the *Ovum* when ripe and ready to drop from the *Ovarium*."[168] The oviducts, like a bridal chamber, contained awaiting semen, "conveyed [there]...by some absorbing or convulsive power."[169] Turgid with arousal, the Fallopian tubes diabolically reach out, "firmly grasp the ripened Ovum," (a reluctant bride) and hold it for down for penetration. Once invigorated by forced impregnation, the zygote (to use the current terminology) "swims" into the uterus to be implanted.[170] Inside of a woman's body, imperceptible fingers devilishly gripped (*morsus diabolii*) an unseen ovum, impregnated, no one knew how, by male semen and implanted into the waiting uterus.

The uterus itself was fraught with uncertainty. While the ancients' wandering womb had largely been dismissed as a fairy tale, fear remained that the uterus might dangerously shift positions during parturition, no doubt fueled by fears of prolapsed uteri and vaginas, too common ailments of the period. Smellie instructed his students and his patients to carefully bind the abdomen to hold the uterus in place. Failure to do so could be fatal.

The fragmentation of the female body extended to the birth process.[171] Smellie described birth as a contest of wills between a woman and her body, and one that women ultimately were too weak to win without help. Smellie maintained that the fetus was passive during birth, in opposition to many writers who claimed that an active child birthed itself from the body of its passive mother.[172] Birth was initiated by irritation of the "nervous fibres" of the cervix. At the beginning of labour, the woman was an active agent, "sqeez[ing] her *Uterus*" "to alleviate" the "uneasy sensation" caused by her cervix, which then dilated.[173] Ultimately, however, she was too weak to bodily deliver on her own. She was "unable to continue this effort for any length of time, from the violence of the pain it occasions, and the strength of the muscles being thereby exhausted and impaired."[174] Thereafter the accoucheur took over the birth, placing the laboring woman under his supervision and control.

Women were the field of action on which the hero-accoucheur operated. The diversity of the homes they inhabited creates one of the picaresque elements of the case histories. In the eighteenth-century, medical practitioners primarily came to patients, treating them in their homes. Smellie followed this pattern. Instead of setting up a private lying-in hospital as did several midwifery instructors including Richard Manningham and John Leake, Smellie treated the poor in their own homes, even if that was merely the corner of an attic on a straw pallet. Moreover, while Smellie has been primarily identified with his teaching practice and London's poor on whose bodies he taught, over 80% of the cases provided in Volumes II and III in which Smellie acted in a medical capacity come from his private practice in London and in Scotland. Out of these, he identified a few patients as "gentlewoman," but the economic status of most was left unremarked. They presumably came from the middling ranks of society. As a result, Smellie's text, like that of a picaresque novel, presents a panorama of Georgian society through the private spaces of women's bedrooms. One goes on a journey from Scottish heaths and farmhouses to London, where one travels from the slums of Gin Alley, with its starving beggar women selling ballads, to Windmill Street, future home of William Hunter's anatomy school, with its brewery and young ladies' academy, to the fashionable West End where ladies read each other "odd romantic tales" and played cards during their lying-ins.

Smellie's case histories carefully record multiple markers of class: poor women were sometimes starving and beaten; middling women sometimes became injured or ill from doing business during the latter months of pregnancy; wealthy women road in coaches and journeyed to the country to drink asses' milk when ill. Nevertheless, Smellie also radically leveled class.[175] All of his patients shared the mutable, weak female body described in the first volume of the *Treatise*. High or low, pampered or beaten, all were too weak to deliver on their own. In order to rescue them, they needed to submit to his direction and will; those who did not risked theirs and their infants' lives.

Only a small number of patients (around 6%) in the case histories resisted Smellie's treatments in some way. That number is not necessarily reflective of the reality of his interactions with his patients. We have no way of knowing how he chose which cases to include and which to exclude to get a real sense of how many women resisted his treatments. It is likely that he shared the cases exhibiting patient resistance for the same reason he shared some cases in which he made (often fatal) mistakes: as warnings to the young practitioners he expected to read his book. They needed to be aware that not all women would follow their directions nor allow them to touch their bodies, or, even if they did get permission from the woman or her family, that the woman would not cooperate by holding still and might need to be restrained by her attendants, and even when cooperative, pain might make restraints necessary.

Smellie held women who failed to cooperate with him as culpable for their own deaths and those of their children. One woman, who "had been used to take opiates," for example, repeatedly refused to let him physically examine her during labor, demanding that he prescribe her opiates for the pain instead. When she did deliver, Smellie was unable to resuscitate her child. He blamed the death of her child on "her timorous disposition, in consequence of which she refused all assistance at the latter end of labour."[176] Here was a woman who refused to submit to Smellie's ministrations, who refused to see him as the hero-accoucheur, instead insisting that, as a paying patient, he defer to her demands. However, Smellie chose to present her actions as fearful rather than as dismissive of his authority.

As a hero-accoucheur, it was Smellie's duty to try to rescue unsubmissive women from themselves. For instance, when he was called to a country woman come to London to have her child, she refused to lie in bed and was "quite unmanageable." Her subsequent illness during her lying-in came to no surprise to Smellie, who nevertheless carefully doctored her back to health.[177] In Volume II, he presented a pair of cases in which the women had refused to exercise and had failed to lace tightly enough to hold their uteri in place. The first obeys Smellie's advice and began exercising and lacing. She and her child lived. The second "acted in diametrical opposition" to his advice. She and her child died.[178]

Nevertheless, most women seemed to have submitted to Smellie's intervention into their labors, or at least to have not resisted enough to warrant comment. The women whom Smellie admired most were the ones who "endured…with great fortitude" and "courage."[179] These were women who calmly submitted to his ministrations, no matter how painful and tedious. On the one hand, it is possible to interpret his admiration for patients' stoicism as admiring them for being most like his silent obstetrical machines. The more quietly courageous and passive the woman, the more actual labor replicated the pretend labors performed in the front of the lecture hall. However, Smellie also admired the woman who "behaved with great courage, and assisted with all her strength by forcing down every time I desired."[180] Smellie had taken over the birth—*he* was the one laboring, she assisting *his* efforts. Nevertheless, she was not quite reduced to pure automation. Dolls could not offer assistance or play any active role in the simulated birth. Moreover, his admiration of her courage reveals his recognition that she did not have to obey him. She could have refused and resisted his efforts. Instead, she played the part of the damsel-in-distress to his hero-accoucheur, following his directions and letting him rescue her from the danger she posed to herself.

The *Treatise* described women as having weak, mutable bodies that were unable to labor and deliver living children without male assistance. The *terra incognita* of female flesh could never be sufficiently explored and mapped by medical men. Their investigations could never provide enough knowledge to ward off Death, the wild card haunting the picaresque world of the *Treatise*. Female patients became parturient damsels-in-distress, in need of rescue by the hero-accoucheur, even if they failed to realize it. These (ideally) submissive damsels were in danger from "ignorant" midwives and male "pretenders" using outdated, dangerous medical practices. Parturient damsels needed to be protected from themselves and from villainous practitioners by men-midwives like Smellie and by the midwives and nurses whom he had trained act as assistants. Moreover, Smellie sought to rescue the honor of the profession from its bad reputation. In Georgian society, men-midwives stood accused of quackery, effeminacy, and sexual predation. They were also associated with illegal dissections and other nefarious medical practices. Smellie wrote his *Treatise* to educate young practitioners and the general public about proper practice, demeanor, and behavior. He used it to showcase himself as the archetypal hero-accoucheur, a picaresque outsider on a quest to claim his professional patrimony and to bring honor and respect to his chosen profession.

# Endnotes

1    Wilson, *The Making*,124-25. See also Richard B. Sher, *The Enlightenment and the Book* (Chicago: University of Chicago Press, 2006), 92.

2    Samuel Bard , *A Compendium on the Theory and Practice of Midwifery* (New York, 1808), 8. Bard's work will be explored in more detail in Chapter Four. Part of the wide availability may have been its relative cheapness: All three volumes plus the tables could be had for 12 shillings (around $70 today) in Edinburgh in the 1780s. See the book advertisements of C. Elliott in the back of Alexander Hamilton's *Outlines on the Theory and Practice of Midwifery* (1784). Current prices were calculated using the retail price index calculator on the website *MeasuringWorth.com* , http://www.measuringworth.com/calculators/. Accessed on 02/15/2018.

3    Wilson, *The Making*, 124-29; 164. For more information on the medical marketplace and London medical teaching, see Susan C. Lawrence, *Charitable Knowledge* (Cambridge: Cambridge University Press, 1996)

4    Smellie, *A Treatise on the Theory and Practice of Midwifery* Vol. I (London, 1752). (Birmingham: Classics of Medicine Library, 1990), iii. Hereafter Vol. I. I have chosen to use this facsimile edition and editions of Volumes II and II from *Eighteenth Century Collection Online* rather relying upon Alfred H. McClintock's edited editions (1877-78) because I found McClintock's edits contrary to my purposes.

5    Keller, *Generating Bodies*, 156-65.

6    Ulrich Wicks, "The Nature of Picaresque Narrative: A Modal Approach," *PMLA* 89.2 (1974): 242, italics in original.

7    *Ibid*. See also Lars Hartveit, *Workings of the Picaresque in the British Novel* (Oslo, Norway: Solum Forlag A/S, 1987).

8    See Birgit Öllerer-Einböck, *The English Picaresque Tradition* (Saarbrücken, Germany: VDM Verlag, 2008), 239; Hartveit, *Workings* ,41.

9    See Wicks, "The Nature," 244-45; Hartveit, *Workings*, 13-16; Öllerer-Einböck, *English Picaresque*, 3-7.

10   See Öllerer-Einböck, *English Picaresque*, 238-9; Hartveit, *Workings*, 41.

11   See Öllerer-Einböck, *English Picaresque*, 11.

12   *Ibid* 245.

13   For more on the early modern use of *dilatio* to build narrative tension, see Patricia Parker, *Literary Fat Ladies* (London: Methuen, 1987), 11-12.

14   Thomas Laqueur, "Bodies, Details, and the Humanitarian Narrative." In *The New Cultural History*. Eds Aletta Biersack and Lynn Hunt (Berkeley: University

of California P, 1989): 177-78.

15   See Wilson, *The Making*, 124; Pam Lieske, "Configuring Women: William Smellie's Obstetrical Machines and the Poor," *Studies in Eighteenth Century Culture* 29 (2000): 66; Robert A. Erickson, "'The books of generation': Some Observations on the style of the British Midwife Books, 1671-1764." *Sexuality in Eighteenth Century Britain*, 87-88; R. W. Johnstone, *William Smellie* (Edinburgh: E & S Livingstone, 1952), 39; Lewis Mansfield Knapp, "More Smollett Letters" *Modern Language Notes* 48.4 (1933): 246-47. Knapp suggests that William Hunter was also involved in editing Smellie's *Treatise*. For another contemporary accusation of Smollett's editorship see Phillip Thicknesse, *Man Midwifery Analysed Or, The tendency of that indecent and unnecessary practice detected and exposed.* (London, 1790).

16   John Burton, *A Letter to William Smellie, M. D* (London 1753), 10.

17   Erickson, "The Books of Generation," 87.

18   In a "Configuring Women," Lieske argues that Smellie's use of poor women dehumanized and silenced the poor women whom he recruited. See pp 78-80. While Lieske makes some good points, as Helen King suggests, Lieske may be too harsh in her assessment that Smellie lacks all empathy with the women whom he treated. See also King, *Midwifery*, 77.

19   Wicks, "The Nature," 244.

20   Ambrose Paré worked in the Hôtel-Dieu in the sixteenth century and wrote a treatise on midwifery which was translated into English in 1612. Despite a century of popular use some people continue to view podalic version with as much mistrust as the hook. In Volume III, Smellie recounts a case in Scotland during the mid 1720s (he doesn't give a precise date), in which the family, the midwife and a man-midwife oppose Smellie and a third man-midwife who want to turn the fetus to deliver. The woman dies of a hemorrhage undelivered (180-83).

21   Edmund Chapman, *A Treatise on the Improvement in Midwifery*, 3rd ed., (London 1759; First edition 1737), xviii, italics in original.

22   See Roy Porter, "A Touch of Danger," *Sexual Underworlds of the Enlightenment* (Manchester: Manchester University Press, 1987), 215; Adrian Wilson, "William Hunter and the varieties of man-midwifery," *William Hunter and the Eighteenth Century World* (Cambridge: Cambridge University Press), 342-46. Forceps were not the only tool that spurred on men to specialize in midwifery. Wilson makes the case that the fillet, promoted by Hendrick van Deventer was equally important. See 79-87.

23   See Wilson, *The Making,* 107-08.

24   Elizabeth Nihell, *An Answer to the Author of the Critical Review, for March, 1760, Upon the Article of Mrs. Nihell's Treatise on the Art of Midwifery* (London 1760), 17.

25   Roy Porter, "William Hunter: a surgeon and a gentleman." *William Hunter and*

*the Eighteenth-Century Medical World*, 10. Italics in original.

26   See Roy Porter, *Cambridge Illustrated History of Medicine* (Cambridge: Cambridge University Press, 1996), 77; 221-23. King suggests that man-midwifery itself contributed to the erosion of boundaries between the three medical branches. See King, *Midwifery*, 21-22; 80.

27   [William Salmon], *Aristotle's Compleat and Experienced Midwife* (London 1731), ii-iii.

28   John Burton, *An Essay Towards A Complete New System of Midwifry* (London 1751), ix, italics in original.

29   William Buchan, *Domestic Medicine* 7th ed. (London 1781), 582. Unless otherwise noted, all references will be to this edition.

30   Samuel Jennings, *The Married Lady's Companion, or Poor Man's Friend* ( New York 1812), 98.

31   *Remarks on the Employment of Females as Practitioners in Midwifery by a Physician* (Boston 1820).

32   [Frank Nicholls] *Petition of the Unborn Babes* (London 1751), 6. See Cody, *Birthing the Nation*, 181-183 for more information.

33   Cody, *Birthing the Nation*, 206.

34   Smellie, *A Collection of Preternatural Cases and Observations in Midwifery* Vol. III (London 1764), 91. Hereafter, Vol. III.

35   *Ibid*, 91; see also Cody, *Birthing a Nation*, 50-51; 59.

36   Smellie, Vol. III, 456-57.

37   Cody, *Birthing a Nation*, 283-4; See also Wilson, *The Making*, 145-54; and Philip Rhodes, *Doctor John Leake's Hospital* (London: Davis-Poynter, 1977): 39-44.

38   [Nicholls], *Petition*, 6.

39   See Porter, "A Touch of Danger," 209-10.

40   For additional discussion of this print, see Cody, *Birthing the Nation*, 207-08.

41   William Dewees, *An Abridgement of Mr. Heath's Translation of Baudelocque's Midwifery; with notes by William P. Dewees*, (Philadelphia 1807), 142.

42   Smellie, Vol. I, 92, italics in original.

43   Alexander Hamilton, *Outlines of the Theory and Practice of Midwifery* (Philadelphia 1790), 45, italics in original. Hamilton wrote two textbooks, one for his male pupils (*Outlines*) and one for his female ones (*Treatise of Midwifery*, 1781).

44   Thicknesse, *Man Midwifery Analyzed*, 7-9.

45   For a discussion on the belief in female sexual voracity see Clare Lyons, *Sex Among the Rabble* (Chapel Hill, NC: University of North Carolina Press, 2006), 162-64; 251-52.

46   See Porter, "A Touch of Danger," 219-20; Cody, *Birthing the Nation*, 186-89; Jean Donnison, *Midwives and Medical Men A History of the Struggle for the Control*

*of Childbirth*. 2nd Ed. (London: Historical Publications, 1988), 28-33; Richard W. Wertz and Dorothy C. Wertz, *Lying-In: A History of Childbirth in America*. Expanded Edition. (New Haven, CT: Yale University Press, 1989), 55-56.

47  Michel Foucault, *The History of Sexuality*, Vol. 1. Trans. Robert Hurley (New York: Vintage, 1990), 18-20.

48  See Erickson, "The Books of Generation," 74.

49  Henry Bracken, *The Midwife's Companion* (London 1737), 10.

50  See Thomas Laqueur, *Making Sex* (Cambridge, MA: Harvard University Press, 1990), 159-160.

51  Bracken, *The Midwife's Companion*, 10-11.

52  However, there had been no decision as to what to call the opening of the uterus. Smellie uses "os tincae" or "os internum" interchangeably; it's not until the 1780s that the modern "cervix" comes into use. See Thomas Denman, *An Introduction to the Practice of Midwifery* (London 1788). The terminological shift is made manifest in an America medical student's annotations of his textbook by his Edinburgh professor, Hamilton's *Outlines on the Theory and Practice of Midwifery* (Edinburgh 1784). In a note on page 46, near a section discussing the anatomy of the uterus, he began to use the old terminology, but crossed it out in favor of the new: "Dr. Smellie's mistaken in his Plates—he has made the Os Tin Cervix Uteri too long—it is of the same Length as the Fundus." Copy held *COP*.

53  Nicolas Culpepper, *A Directory for Midwives* (London 1656), 3.

54  Jane Sharp, *The Midwives Book* (London 1671). Ed. Elaine Hobby (Oxford: Oxford University Press, 1999), 13.

55  Culpepper, *A Directory*, 22.

56  John Maubray, *The Female Physician* (London 1724), 183-85, italics in original.

57  Michel Foucault, *The Birth of the Clinic*. Trans. A. M. Sheridan Smith (New York: Vintage, 1994), esp. 6-9. 87-93.

58  Smellie, Vol. I, 91, italics in original.

59  Smellie, Vol. I, 77.

60  Smellie, Vol. I, 102, italics in original.

61  Burton, *A Letter to Smellie*, 68, italics in original.

62  Smellie, *A Collection of Cases and Observations in Midwifery*. Vol. II. (London 1754), 212. Hereafter Vol. II.

63  See Lieske, "Configuring Women," 66-75; Bonnie Blackwell, "*Tristram Shandy* and the Theatre of the Mechanical Mother," *ELH* 68.1 (2001): 81-133; King, *Midwifery*, 17-18; 133-37; Cody, *Birthing the Nation*, 171-72; Wilson, *The Making*, 125-27; Johnstone, *William Smellie*, 25-29. The body-as-machine metaphor has persisted in obstetrics and gynecology. See Emily Martin, *The Woman in the Body* (Boston: Beacon, 1992), 27-67; Amanda Carson Banks, *Birth Chairs, Midwives*,

*and Medicine* (Jackson: University Press of Mississippi, 1999), xv-xxiii and 79-123; *The Business of Being Born*, Dir. Abby Epstein (Barranca Productions, 2008).

64    Margaret C. Jacob, "The Materialist World of Pornography," *The Invention of Pornography* (New York: Zone Books, 1993), 164. See 157-202, esp. 159-65.

65    [Thomas Stretzer], *A New Description of Merryland* (London 1741), 269. Excerpted in *When Flesh Becomes Word* (Oxford: Oxford University Press, 2004). Mauriceau's treatise was translated into English in 1673 by forceps practitioner Hugh Chamberlen and saw many subsequent reprinting in the eighteenth century. For more on geographical metaphors in erotic and medical writing see Harvey, *Reading Sex,* 179-85; Paul-Gabriel Boucé, "Chthonic and Pelagic Metaphorization in Eighteenth-Century English Erotica." *Tis Nature's Fault.* Ed. Robert Purks Maccubbin (Cambridge: Cambridge University Press, 1985), 202-16; Darby Lewes, *Nudes from Nowhere* (Lanham: Roman & Littlefield, 2000), 130-133; Marcia D. Nichols, "A Colonial Man of Science: Imperial Fantasy in *Merryland*" in *Expanding Worlds: Travel Narratives, the New Science, and Literary Discourse*, ed. Judy A. Hayden. (Burlington, VT: Ashgate, 2013), 143-60.

66    [Stretzer], *A New Description*, 265-8.

67    See Roy Porter, *Flesh in the Age of Reason* Ed. Simon Schama (New York: Norton & Co., 2003), 84-87; Keller, *Generating Bodies*, 125-55, esp. 128-31.

68    See Wendy Moore, *The Knife Man* (New York: Broadway, 2005), 31-43; Michael Sappol, *A Traffic of Dead Bodies*, (Princeton: Princeton University Press, 2002); Ruth Richardson, *Death, Dissection and the Destitute*. 2nd ed. (Chicago: University of Chicago Press, 1987).

69    Moore, *The Knife Man*, 26. In addition to private courses attended by medical students, other entrepreneurs sought a wider, non-medical audience among the virtuosi and other interested spectators and offered lectures featuring public dissections of humans and animals and vivisections on animals with a theatrical rather than practical bent. Additionally, wax figures and drawn depictions of dissected bodies were displayed to anybody willing to pay the admission price. See Anita Guerrini, "Anatomists and Entrepreneurs in Early Eighteenth-Century London." *Journal of the History of Medicine* 59.2 (2004): 219-34; King, *Midwifery*, 135-35.

70    See Porter, "William Hunter," 22-26.

71    Fielding Ould, *A Treatise of Midwifery, In Three Parts* (Dublin 1742), 4.

72    Charles White, *Treatise on the Management of Pregnant and Lying-in Women* (Worcester, MA 1793), 174-75.

73    Sarah Stone, *A Complete Practice of Midwifery* (London 1737), xv.

74    Francis Hopkinson, *An Oration which might have been Delivered to the Students in Anatomy on the Late Rupture Between the Two Schools in This City* (Philadelphia 1789).

Sappol reads this poem as placing dissection as "medicine's defining practice"—the lynch pin to professionalizing efforts. See Sappol, *A Traffic*, 44-47.

75    In 1788, a mob became enraged at seeing anatomical preparations at the Columbia College medical school, attacked the school and nearby buildings, including Dr. Samuel Bard's house. The militia had to be called to suppress the riot. New York did not soon recover from the tumult. As late as 1819, a medical student wrote home to complain that the governor had placed a guard around the potter's field to keep the graves from being robbed for anatomy lessons. See Moses Champion to Reuben Champion, New York, Feb. 7, 1819, Moses Champion Letters; Misc Mss Box 1, folder 32; *CUHS*; John Brett Langstaff, *Doctor Bard of Hyde Park* (Dutton & Co: New York, 1942), 162-3; Betsy Copping Corner, *William Shippen, Jr.* (Philadelphia: American Philosophical Society, 1951), 102-03; Sappol, *A Traffic*, 105-110.

76    Hopkinson, An Oration, 11. Most of the bodies dissected in nineteenth-century America were those of the disenfranchised working poor—African Americans, Irish and other immigrants, etc.—snatched from potters fields or African-American burial grounds. See Sappol, *A Traffic*, 35-36, 124.

77    *Ibid*, 15.

78    Burton, *An Essay Towards*, 10-11.

79    See Laqueur, *Making*, 184-85; Sappol, *A Traffic*, 201-07, 217-34; Nora Doyle, *Maternal Bodies: Redefining Motherhood in Early America* (Chapel Hill: University of North Carolina Press, 2018), 86-110.

80    Smellie, Vol. II, 17.

81    Smellie, Vol. I, 98.

82    Thomas Denman, *A Collection of Engravings, Tending to Illustrate the Generation and Parturition of Animals and of the Human Species* (London 1787), Plate V. At the time, the word "abortion" could refer to either a spontaneous miscarriage, especially one happening between the fourth and seventh months, as well as the deliberate destruction of a fetus through herbal/medicinal or surgical means. Denman clarified that his drawings depict "spontaneous" abortions. See Chapter 3 for more on Denman.

83    Keller, *Generating Bodies*, 164.

84    Smellie, Vol. III, 485.

85    Smellie, Vol. I, ii.

86    *Ibid.*, iv.

87    King argues that Smellie created Hippocrates as the first man-midwife in order to give male obstetrics credibility in the medical establishment. See King, *Midwifery*, 85-99.

88    Nihell, *A Treatise on the Art of Midwifery* (1760). *Eighteenth-Century British Mid-*

*wifery*, Vol. 6. Ed. Pam Lieske (London: Pickering & Chatto, 2008), 59.

89    See King, *Midwifery,* 68-70.

90    Smellie, Vol. I, iii.

91    *Ibid*, lv.

92    Smellie, Vol. II, 311.

93    Smellie, Vol. III, 456.

94    Smellie, Vol. II, 313-14.

95    Smellie, Vol. I, 156, emphasis added; italics in original.

96    *Ibid*, 230, emphasis added; italics in original. Smellie's sense of urgency concerning tying the navel cord likely arises from near-fatal mishaps in this department. See Volume II, 340-43.

97    *Ibid*, 232 emphasis added; italics in original.

98    *Ibid*, 180, emphasis added.

99    *Ibid*, 224, italics in original.

100   See King, *Midwifery,* 78.

101   Smellie, Vol. I, 241.

102   *Ibid*, 241, emphasis added.

103   *Ibid*, 245, emphasis added.

104   Lieske, "Configuring Women," 66.

105   Smellie, Vol. II, 309.

106   *Ibid*, 309-10.

107   *Ibid*, 311. Italics in original.

108   *Ibid*, 311. Italics in original.

109   Smellie, Vol. III, 136 and 250.

110   In the majority of the remainder, it is unclear if Smellie had been called or if he had been bespoke.

111   Smellie, Vol. III, 203-04; this is Case III from Collection XXXIV, Number II.

112   *Ibid*, 204-05.

113   *Ibid*, 206.

114   *Ibid*, 206.

115   *Ibid*, 206.

116   *Ibid*, 207.

117   Nihell, *A Treatise*, 144. See also Lieske, "Configuring Women," 79; Cody *Birthing the Nation*, 189.

118   Smellie, Vol. I, 264.

119   See Jane B. Donegan, *Women and Men Midwives: Medicine, Morality and Misogyny in Early America.* (Westport, CT: Greenwood, 1978), 79.

120   Thomas Denman, *Aphorisms on the Application and Use of the Forceps and Vectis* (Philadelphia, 1803), 14, italics in original; See also King, *Midwifery,* 138-39.

121  Smellie, Vol. I, 209.

122  When Smellie came across a young practitioner wearing what he considered a ridiculous garb, he gave him "friendly advice private" (Vol. II, 227), and he took the time to mock his old enemy William Douglas's outfit for being both "forbidding" and "greasy" (Vol. III, 486). Douglas is not named in the case itself; however, King identifies that this must have been Douglas, as the story seem to be about the same incident debated in the pamphlet war between Douglas and Smellie in 1748. She speculates that Douglas had died (as had Smellie) by the publication of the third volume, freeing Smellie (or Smollett) to divulge more (damaging) details than had been shared in the earlier pamphlets. See King, *Midwifery*, 110. For additional treatments of Smellie's sartorial advice, see Cody, *Birthing the Nation*, 189-91; Donegan, *Women and Men Midwives*, 82; Lieske, "Configuring Women," 78.

123  Smelllie, Vol. I, 338.

124  Nihell, *Treatise*, 143.

125  Smellie, Vol. III, 336.

126  *Ibid*, 164. See also Collection XXX, Case II. In this case, after feeling the baby "move its tongue and lower jaw," Smellie decided to "not [to] mention [that it was alive] to the mother, that she might not be overwhelmed with anxiety, in case it should be afterwards still-born" (Vol. II, 444).

127  Smellie's contemporary and rival John Burton accuses Smellie of malpractice in his *Letter to William Smellie*; however, by this he meant a more literal translation of bad or dangerous practices, such as the positions Smellie would place women in and his forceps techniques. See King, *Midwifery*, 100-09.

128  Smellie, Vol. III, 381.

129  Smellie, Vol. III, 119; Smellie, Vol. III, 271.

130  Though I do not pretend this or the following list of cases are complete, for other instances of uterine rupture, see also Collection XXI, Number III, Case VI; Collection XXXIII. Number II, Case IX; Collection XXXV, Numbers VIII, Case X and Case XVI; Collection XL, Number I, Cases VII and VIII; For pirenal tears see Collection XI, Number II, Case V; Collection XVII, Number I, Case VI; Collection XXVII, Number II, Cases IV and IX; Collection XXVIII, Cases I and IV; Collection XXXI, Case X; Collection XXXV, Case IV; Collection XL, Number I, Cases I, III, IV, and VI; and Collection XLIX, Number II, Case II.

131  Smellie, Vol. III, 387.

132  For other injured infants, see also Collection XVI, Number I, Cases II and III and Number VI, Case I; Collection XXII, Number I, Case I and Number II, Case III; Collection XXVII, Number II, Case IX; Collection XXVIII, Number

II, Case IV; Collection XXXIII, Number II, Case XIV; Collection XXXIV,
Number II, Case X; Collection XLV, Number II, Case I and Number III, Cases
I, II, and III; and Collection XLVI, Number II, Case I.

133   Smellie, Vol III, 221. Although I write here as though the couple were unani-
mous in seeking birth control, it is entirely possible that the woman herself did
not choose to attempt to control her fertility out of religious or cultural convic-
tions about its immorality.

134   *Ibid*, 222.

135   Sharp, *Midwife's Book*, 152-53. According to John M. Riddle, who has compared
emmenagogue and abortifacient herbs cited in traditional and classical sources,
many still in use today in both contemporary traditional societies and in pockets of some Western nations, with current Chinese and Indian research that
indicates many have active properties that could be used as effective, though
far from failsafe, birth control. (Many more remain to be studied). However,
physicians during the early modern period seemed to have largely forgotten or
suppressed the use of herbal contraceptives and abortifacients. Most of these
herbs were ejected from official pharmacopeia in the eighteenth century, though
evidence suggests they remained on apothecary shelves. See John M. Riddle,
*Eve's Herbs* (Cambridge, MA: Harvard University Press, 1997), esp. 167-205.;
Susan Klepp, *Revolutionary Conceptions* (Chapel Hill, NC: University of North
Carolina Press, 2009),179-200.  See also Angus McLaren, *Reproductive Rituals*
(London: Methuen & Co., 1984),73-87. McLaren doubts the efficacy of the
herbals and focuses instead on *coitus interruptus*, condoms and other measures.

136   Smellie, Vol. III, 221.

137   Cody, *Birthing the Nation*, 188.

138   Lieske, "Configuring Women," 78.

139   King, *Midwifery*, 112.

140   Smellie, Vol. III, 379, italics in original.

141   Smellie, Vol. I, 273.

142   Smellie, Vol. III, 386.

143   Nihell, *Treatise* 70, 159-62.

144   Miguel de Cervantes, *Don Quixote* (1615); Daniel Defoe, *Roxana* (1724); Charlotte Lennox, *The Female Quixote* (1752); Tobias Smollett, *Roderick Random* (1748);
Tabitha Tenney, *Female Quixotism* (1801).

145   Wilson, *The Making*, 100-01.

146   Smellie, Vol. I, 449.

147   King, *Midwifery*, 75.

148   Smellie, Vol. III, 491.

149   *Ibid*, 492.

150  *Ibid*, 492-93, italics in original.

151  *Ibid*, 419.

152  Cody, *Birthing the Nation*, 156-60; see also Wilson, *The Making*, 130-31; 161-63.

153  Smellie, Vol. III, 353, italics in original.

154  Smellie, Vol. II, ii.

155  King, *Midwifery*, 109-110. The case appears in Smellie, Vol. III, 486-90.

156  Smellie, Vol. III, 485.

157  *Ibid*, 482.

158  *Ibid*, 482-83.

159  Smollett, *Roderick Random*, 126.

160  Smellie, Vol. III, 483-4.

161  *Ibid*, 484-8.

162  *Ibid*, 486.

163  Smellie, Vol. I, 92.

164  Jonathan Swift, "A Beautiful Young Nymph Going to Bed," *Jonathan Swift: The Complete Poems*. Ed. Pat Rogers. (New Haven: Yale University Press, 1983): 453-55.

165  Smellie, Vol. I, 81-82.

166  *Ibid,* 82-83.

167  Josephine M Lloyd, in "The 'Languid Child' and the Eighteenth-Century Man-Midiwife," *Bulletin of the History of Medicine* (2001), suggests that Smellie also helped pioneer pediatrics with his concern for neonatal healthcare.

168  Smellie, Vol. I, 97, italics in original.

169  *Ibid*, 115.

170  *Ibid*, 117.

171  Metaphors of fragmented, divided female bodies have continued to dominate medical writings. See Martin, *The Woman*, 15-24.

172  See Keller, *Generating Bodies*, 69; 118-119; 175.

173  Smellie, Vol. I, 118-19, italics in original.

174  *Ibid*, 119.

175  This shared physicality of all women likely helped to naturalize the construction of a middle-class subjectivity in other realms of discourse mapped out by Nancy Armstrong in *Desire and Domestic Fiction: A Political History of the Novel*. (New York: Oxford University Press, 1990). This point will be returned to in Chapters 3 and 4.

176  Smellie, Vol. II, 229-31.

177  Smellie, Vol. III, 394-95.

178  Smellie, Vol. II, 121-23.

179  Smellie, Vol. III, 197.

180  Smellie, Vol. II, 201.

# Chapter Two

## Anatomizing "an Hairy Monster": William Smellie's *A Set of Anatomical Tables*

Willllliam Smellie's *A Sett of Anatomical Tables, with Explanations, and an Abridgement of the Practice of Midwifery With a View to Illustrate a Treatise on that Subject, and Collection of Cases* (1754) had as large an impact on obstetrics and the creation of a medicalized female body as the hero narrative found in his monumental *Treatise of Midwifery* explored in the previous chapter.[1] Originally printed in a massive portfolio format, the *Tables* went through two editions during Smellie's lifetime, printed in 1754 and again in 1761; after his death, new editions appeared on both sides of the Atlantic and other medical writers rifled the *Tables* for choice illustrations to enliven their own publications. The *Tables* remained a source of inspiration and illustrations well into the nineteenth and twentieth centuries.

The *Set of Anatomical Tables* are an anatomical atlas depicting the gravid uterus at various stages of pregnancy and labor in 39 plates, engraved by Charles Grignion from the original sketches of Peter Camper, Jan Van Rymsdyck, and a third unnamed artist (possibly Smellie himself).[2] In the previous chapter, I argued that, in the *Treatise*, Smellie attempted to stablize the unstable *terra incognita* of the female body. To continue the metaphor, his grand anatomical atlas was the map outlining the shifting boundaries of that body.

Feminist scholars have commented upon the implicit violence against the maternal body found in these images. Ludamilla Jordanova cites Smellie's *Tables* as an eighteenth-century medical example of "representational violence... which invites readers and viewers to collude with sexually aggressive fantasies and practices." Taking Table 16 as her example, she notes that the unusual angle creates "a shocking and violent effect" and that its depiction of forceps usage "contained its own form of implicit violence" by evoking the forceps debate of the day.[3] In a similar vein, Andrea K. Henderson argues that Smellie's plates, with their focus on pelvic bones, created a mechanistic view of childbirth that envisioned women "as a machine—and an oddly inactive and poorly constructed one at that."[4] The title of the chapter in which Roberta McGrath analyzes Smellie's work, "Doll Machines and Butcher Shop Meat," implies that Smellie depicted the maternal body as fleshy versions of his teaching phantoms—headless, limbless torsos issuing fetuses through mechanical pelvises. She agrees with Henderson's assessment, placing Smellie's work in a tradition of "geographies of the female body" stretching from the drawings and engravings of the eighteenth century to the photography, stereoscopy, and radiography of the early twentieth. She suggests, "the illustrations in each atlas represented part of an argument about the way in which women's bodies should be seen at the particular historical moment when generation was beginning to decline and reproduction had yet to emerge."[5]

What were the ways of seeing women's bodies as argued by eighteenth-century medical atlases? Do they tell us to see women as passive victims of sexual violence? As machines?  How did contemporary viewers understand the images? Originally, the *Tables* were meant to be read in conjunction with the *Treatise*, and Smellie consistently directed the reader of the atlas back to the *Treatise* and particular case histories. In the *Treatise*, Smellie instructed his students to employ a kind of X-ray vision to imagine the bodily interior of living women. His atlas was meant to enable this type of imaginative medical gaze while reading about and practicing midwifery. This was likely a two way street: contemporary readers would look at images in the atlas, remember the details of the cases that they illustrated, and imagine the interiors as belonging to the bleeding, crying, struggling, laboring women they had read about. Contemporary readers would approach Smellie's *Tables* with a sort of double vision. On the one hand, they would know they were viewing the dissected bodies of corpses; on the other, as a kind of visual synecdoche, the images were illustrations of living women. However, textual reference could not prevent the images from being interpreted in multiple ways. Additionally, the proliferation of small-format versions of this polysemous atlas increasingly distanced the images from the *Treatise* itself.

Moreover, medical illustrations were not the only cultural reference that a contemporary viewer would have in mind. Naked female bodies were the subject of art as well as bawdy writings and drawings. Readers of the *Tables* and other anatomical atlases brought with them a pre-existing cultural lexicon or code for interpreting nudes. The refined, artistic body and the bawdy body each had well established representational conventions by the mid-eighteenth century. These readers would be confronted with elements—pubic hair, labia, and other genital organs—that moved medical drawings like Smellie's away from artistic conventions and into the realm of contemporary bawdry and pornography.

Atlases are scientific "working objects" that form a "collective empiricism" for scientists. Atlases trained scientists on "what is worth looking at, how it looks, and…how it should be looked at."[6] In effect, atlases help create a sense of the "normal." Concepts of the "normal," according to Foucault, are used to police and regulate deviations from a standard.[7] This normalizing function has implications for perceptions of the female body and female sexuality. By including elements that had long been the province of bawdry, the atlas images discursively eroticized and classed the bodies depicted. Additionally, the presence of pubic hair partially undermined the attempt in the *Treatise* to stabilize permeable female flesh (an attempt echoed by much of Western Art): instead of presenting a passive, contained, universal Woman, design elements and textual references in atlas constantly threaten to differentiate and sensualize her. Furthermore, if anatomical atlases influenced the way readers interpreted the female body, Smellie's had a much wider influence than most of these massive tomes. British and American printers whittled the expensive portfolio into a relatively cheap octavo format that was widely available in the Anglo-Atlantic world, and many of his tables were used to illustrate the *Encyclopedia Britannica*. In fact, images from Smellie's atlas continued being used throughout the nineteenth century. Before I turn to Smellie's *Tables*, however, it is necessary to take a broader look at the changing artistic conventions of medical illustrations and eighteenth-century bawdry to place the *Tables* in a historical context.

## Historical Anatomies

The United States National Library of Medicine's *Historical Anatomies on the Web* is a digital collection of selected images from anatomical atlases from the fourteenth through the nineteenth centuries from Europe, the Middle East and Asia. The Introduction to the website announces itself as a "digital project designed to give Internet users access to high quality images from important anatomical atlases in the Library's collection." It emphasizes that the images provided are selections, and not whole books, chosen "for their historical and artistic significance, with priority placed upon the earliest and/or the best edition of a work in NLM's possession."[8] Nevertheless, the website provides a peripatetic tour through the changing historical and cultural representations of the human body.

Fig. 2.1: An *ecorché*, or flayed man, from Table 36 of Bernardino Genga's *Anatomia per uso et intelligenza del disegno* (1691). Courtesy of the National Library of Medicine.

Browsing through the images taken from European atlases, it becomes apparent that, until the eighteenth century, most early anatomists posed their specimens in positions taken from classical art.[9] The bodies, mostly male, stand or kneel like macabre versions of Greco-Roman or Renaissance statuary— magnificent, monumental, and flayed. For example, Table 36 of Bernardino Genga's *Anatomia per uso et intelligenza del disegno* (1691) shows a flayed man standing before an Arcadian landscape (Figure 2.1). His mouth is open, left hand raised, right pointing to the ground, as if he went on declaiming without his skin. Notably, despite his lack of skin, his armpits and pubis are haired— male bodies were often depicted as having hair in one or both locations as were male nudes in art.

Female bodies, on the other hand, are coy Venuses, often supine and inviting.[10] Those depicted in the work of Charles Estienne, *De dissectione partium corporis humani libri tres* (1545), for instance, recline or sit spread-eagled on a birthing chair, coyly inviting the viewer to examine their genitals or abdominal cavity (Figure 2.2). Occasionally they were depicted standing, like the woman in Table 2 of Govard Bidloo's *Ontleding des menschelyken lichaams* (1690) (Figure 2.3). She stands, one leg slightly raised, giving her body a dainty S-curve and making her seem a bit off-balance. Smiling softly, she holds back her garment,

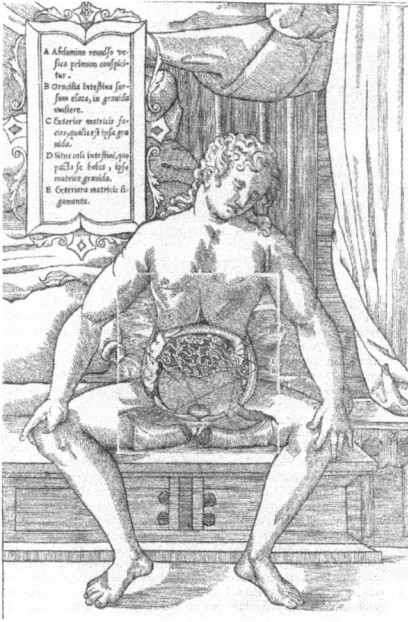

Fig. 2.2 (left): An image depicting female reproductive organs from Charles Estienne, *De dissectione partium corporis humani libir tres* (1545), pg. 267. Courtesy of the National Library of Medicine. Fig. 2.3 (right): A woman in a classical pose from an anatomical atlas by Govard Bidloo's *Ontleding des menschelyken lichaams* (1690), Table 2. Courtsey of the National Library of Medicine.

inviting the viewer to examine her pelvic area. Near her right foot lies an overturned urn, its dark cavity a yonic reminder of what remained unseen.

Bidloo's Venus is a prime example of the ways medical illustrations borrowed from the conventions of the female nude in Western art, which typically presents a sexually inviting woman, made immature and unthreatening through her lack of body hair. Traditionally, Western art has sought to control representations of female sexuality. According to Lynda Nead, "one of the principal goals of the female nude has been the containment and regulation of the female sexual body. The forms, conventions and poses of art have worked metaphorically to shore up the female body—to seal orifices and to prevent the marginal matter from transgressing the boundary dividing the inside of the body and the outside, the self from the space of the other."[11] Hair is marginal matter, exuding from the hidden interior of the body. As such, as Galia Ofek contends, it must "be carefully monitored in order that the symbolic body may retain its internal order and hierarchy."[12] Removal of body hair, including that of the pubis, was one means of shoring up and containing the leaky female body. It was a visual declaration of its subordination to male artists and viewers.[13] The hair on a woman's head remained presentable because, though it evoked the hair of the pubis, her sexuality remained "implicit rather than explicit...keep[ing] the art/contemplation coupling intact and ... maintain[ing] the conventional polarity of art and pornography."[14] Along with urns like the ones in Bidloo's and Estienne's engravings, a woman's mane of hair served as a symbol of her genitalia.[15]

The convention of removing body hair from the female nude was largely obeyed even in depictions of the dissected female body. While there were a few exceptions—for instance, the woodcut illustration found in the English edition of Mauriceau's treatise mentioned in Chapter One (which perhaps accounts for the reference to it in *A New Description of Merryland*)—the convention holds true in the monumental atlases. To return to Estienne, the women's viscera are exposed, breaking down the boundaries between external and internal (Figure 2.2). These bodies teeter on verge of obscene—"the body without borders or containment...."[16]    Nevertheless, their hairless vulvas are a last bastion of containment, offsetting their exposed interiors and sensual poses through the removal of the most recognizable reminder of their sexual maturity. According to Nead, "The nude is precisely matter contained, the female body given form and framed by the conventions of art. But when these conventions fail to contain the connotations of the female sexual body...the image is judged to have gone beyond the bounds of art, and is unpresentable."[17] Dissected female bodies were presentable because they continued "to contain the connotations of the female sexual body," through the removal of the signs of sexual maturity. Moreover, the exposure of the uterus signaled scientific mastery over this most mysterious of female organs.

Browsing through the *Historical Anatomies on the Web* site, it soon becomes apparent that a major change in the depiction of the female body takes place in the eighteenth century: the pubic hair that had so carefully been avoided in accordance with the conventions of art began to be represented.[18] Compare, for instance, Bidloo's Table 56 (Figure 2.4) with one from Smellie's *Tables* showing a similar pose (Figure 2.5). While Bidloo gave a faint nod to the dissected woman's sexual maturity by darkening her mons veneris with crosshatching, he placed her at an angle that draws attention away from the woman's genitals and toward the revealed fetus. Smellie's image, in contrast, is straight on. Nearly at eye-level, the woman's vulva is the secondary focal point, drawing the eyes away from the looming dark mass of the pregnant uterus. On it, each pubic hair is individually delineated. If the perspective is that of a man-midwife, then the female body is triply exposed—not only have the bedclothes and garments that would have veiled the female body been

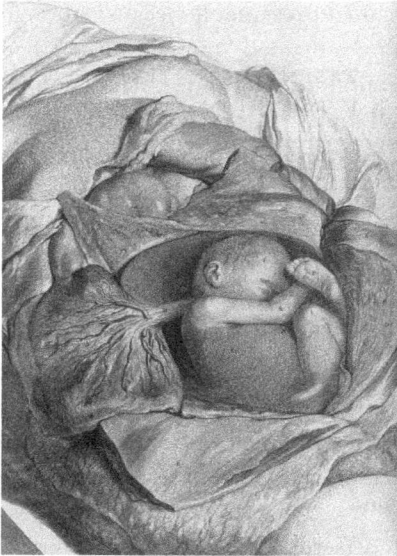

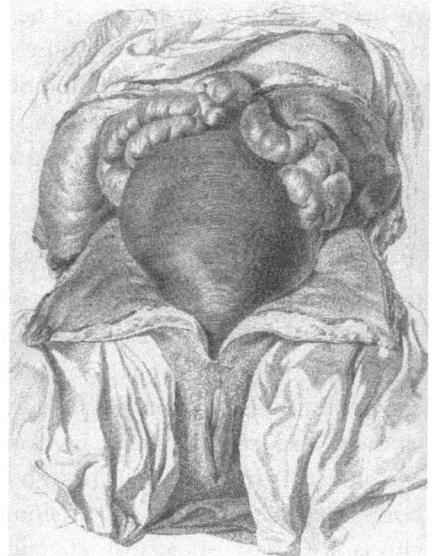

Fig. 2.4 (left): A dissected pregnant woman, displayed at an angel that keeps the focus on the fetus rather than the woman's vulva, from Govard Bidloo's *Ontleding des menschelyken lichaams* (1690), Table 56. Courtesy of the National Library of Medicine.
Fig. 2.5 (right): While the uterus is still the focus of this dissected female abdomen, the front angle makes the vulva a secondary focal point. From William Smellie's *A Sett of Anatomical Tables* (1754), Table 7. Courtesy of the National Library of Medicine.

removed, in addition, the dermis has given way to reveal uterine mysteries. Interestingly, in Bidloo's image, the woman's head and arm are distinctly covered with a sheet, while Smellie's appears to be headless and armless. The woman's sex and reproductive capacity—her sexuality in an inclusive sense that encompasses all her sexual functions (copulative, reproductive, and maternal)—rather than the fetus are the focus of Smellie's image. However, even images that depicted (nearly) whole women kept attention on the sexual body by evoking bawdy conventions. Jacques Fabian Gautier d'Agoty depicted a whole woman and a whole man in his life-sized *Anatomie generale des viscères* (1752) (Figures 2.6 and 2.7). While the man is fully dissected and looks away from the viewer, the standing woman boldly faces the viewer, her coy glance inviting him to examine the secrets of her half-dissected body: D'Agoty chose to leave undissected her head, shoulders, breasts, right arm and mons veneris with its thick bush of hair—all highly eroticized areas of the body—juxtaposing them with the blood and muscle normally hidden beneath skin. It is a depiction of a strip tease continued beyond mere nudity.[19]

A fine line separated the medical from the bawdy or pornographic in

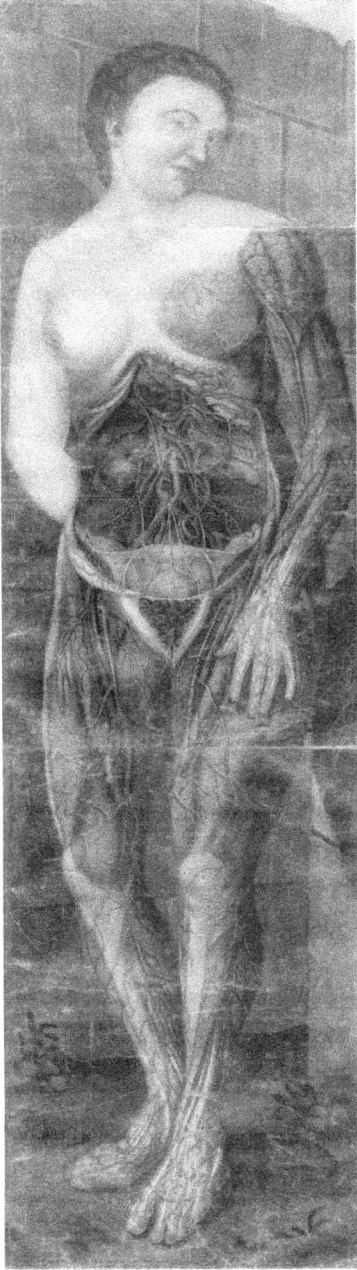

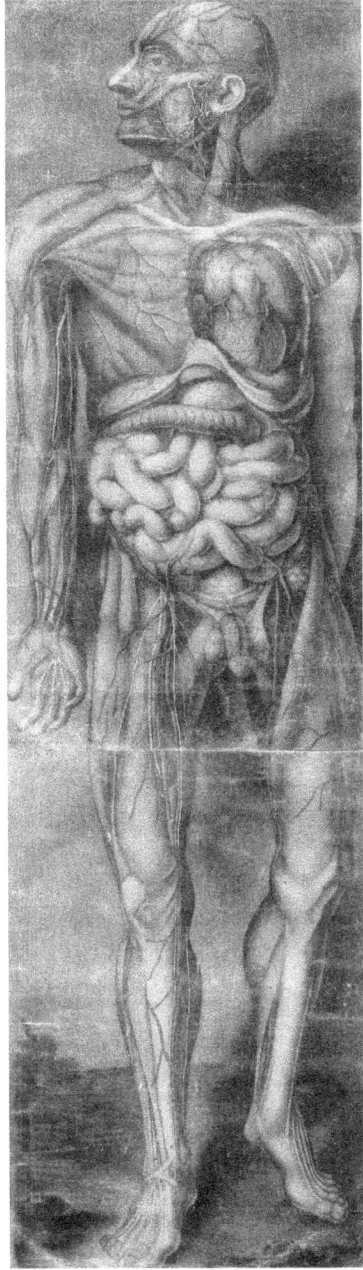

Figs. 2.6 and 2.7: The presentation of these male and female figures differ dramatically. From Fabian Gautier d'Agoty, *Anatomie generale des viscères* (1752). Courtesy of the National Library of Medicine.

the eighteenth century. Many bawdy books assumed a veneer of medical respectability and many legitimate medical books were put to uses other than as guides to healing. From our vantage point, it is often difficult to distinguish to which category a book originally belonged. What should we make of French doctor S.A.D. Tissot's popular anti-masturbation tract *Onanism* (1758), for instance? It rails against masturbation, but its lurid stories and letters surely had prurient appeal for many readers.[20] Anatomical displays were another area which blurred such distinctions. Anatomists dissected in front of any man willing to pay the admission fee, not merely medical students.[21] In Philadelphia, the curious could get a glimpse of naked female torsos at the Pennsylvania Hospital 30 years before the first nude painting went on display. Beginning in 1762, the Pennsylvania Hospital charged a dollar admittance for non-medical Philadelphians to view the soft-focus peach and blue oil drawings Van Rymsdyck made for Charles Jenty's anatomical atlas, *Demonstrations of a Pregnant Uterus* (1758).[22]

In addition to the more legitimate medical displays, London provided access to carnivalesque ones. Waxworks shows, purporting to be educational displays, flourished in there. Models of the "parts of generation" of women were a main attraction, as were preserved fetuses and, at one show, the life-size figure of a chained-down pregnant woman, meant to mimic a vivisection to display the circulation of blood.[23] Europe abounded with life-size wax pregnant women displayed for educational and entertainment purposes. McGrath argues that these "waxen medical 'venuses'" were an "antecedent for pornography.... [T]hese animated, almost life-like mannequins resemble closely what would become the standardised pose of the pornographic model. These early models suggest a sexualised female body that the observer, presumed male, might penetrate."[24] At least one eighteenth-century writer agreed. The anonymous poem "Adollizing" (1748) tells the story of Clodius who is "rebuffed" by the cold Clarabella. Not to be thwarted in his desires, the ingenious Clodius constructs "a Doll, by new mechanic aid/ As big as life" that exactly resembles Clarabella, down to "A tuft of hair" placed "On the arch'd mount, just o'er the cloven part" (which he cleverly lined with sponges).[25] Although we have no evidence that any usable sex dolls actually existed,[26] clearly someone looked at the wax venuses and envisioned the possibility. Life-sized models were not the only size for sale. Ivory miniatures with removable abdomens and organs were sold as private table-top spectacles.[27] Some of these languishing venuses lay with legs open, granting the viewer the sight of their meticulously carved labia. Such figurines were part of a large market for erotic objects, prints, and books in the eighteenth century.

## All Cats are Grey

The inclusion of pubic hair in medical figures and drawings, on the one hand, was part of the hyperrealism in vogue in medical illustration in the eighteenth century, a point to which I will return. On the other, it linked medicine with the conventions and tropes of bawdry and pornography. Excluded from art, pubic hair was extolled in erotica. As Karen Harvey points out,

> women's pubic hair was important in erotica. First it was regarded as one of the most noticeable aspects of female genitalia and the only female protuberance, thereby indicating the sex of women's bodies…. [P]ubic hair was a crucial sign of sexual maturity in a genre deeply concerned with reproduction….the concerns of the erotic genre served to bolster its status as a sign of sexual maturity and fertility. What in science and medicine indicated sexual difference took on quite a different meaning in erotica.[28]

Pubic hair was an important indicator of female sexuality. Not only did its emergence indicate puberty, but it also indicated the humoral temperament of a woman. According to traditional medicine, the body contained four humors (blood, phlegm, black bile, and yellow bile) that corresponded to the four elements (air, water, earth, and fire respectively). Moreover, blood and yellow bile were hot, while phlegm and black bile were cold. Every person had all four humors and balance was needed to maintain health; nevertheless, one or more humors tended to predominate, creating a person's constitution (sanguine, phlegmatic, melancholic, or choleric). In this cosmology, heat caused the humoral body to excrete hair. In men, who were naturally hotter than women, this resulted in a beard. Most women (as well as most non-European males according to many contemporary thinkers) were too cold to produce facial hair. To measure their temperament, one had to consult a hirsute barometer found a bit lower: Too little pubic hair meant that a woman, while she may be fertile, would not enjoy copulation. Too much, she would be lascivious and infertile.[29] The ideal, according to one anonymous poet, was a *mons veneris* "but thinly hair'd,/It not too bushy, nor too bald appear'd."[30]

The hair-covered *mons veneris*, the triangle of a woman's sex, was (and is) the most recognizable sign of the female genitals. As such, pubic hair was often used synecdochically for them. Bawdy poems and stories frequently alluded to the privates through references to hairy animals. Although the cony-cunny pun was perhaps the most common one, cats, birds, and deer were all contrived into similar allusions as were a variety of architectural, agricultural,

Fig. 2.8: The central woman's mons veneris
has hair, but her labia does not. From [Jean
Baptiste Girard], *Thérèse philosophe* (1748)
by Jean-Baptiste de Boyer d'Argens. Public
Domain.

and topographical metaphors.[31] In all variations, written erotica spotlighted the "bush." For example, in a two-poem collection sold as *Little Merlin's Cave* (1737), the first poem describes genitalia as a cave, with "Shrubs and Bushes all without"; in the second poem, they become "an Hairy Monster Often found under Holland," that is "Hairy when old, and bald when young" and "has Mouth, Lips, Beard, but has no Eyes, Nor Teeth, altho' it often bites."[32] In "Advice on Choosing a Mistress," Benjamin Franklin famously quipped that "in the dark all cats are grey," to suggest that, when it came to coitus, pleasing tactility was more important than visual beauty[33] while Fanny Hill fears that the state of her pubic hair will give away her infidelity to Mr. H——.[34] In *The Merry Muses of Caledonia*, the collection of improved-upon folk songs Robert Burns prepared for a select group of friends, the Scottish bard paid homage to pubic hair in many poems. In some like "Yellow, Yellow Yorlin" or "Ken Ye Na Our Lass Bess," Burns metaphorically transformed the woman's genitals into a goldfinch and a "magpie's nest" respectively. In others, the hair became grass, and the male speaker must "mow," a favorite euphemism for coitus.[35]

Most often, however, Burns used plain language—the poems in the collection are full of hairy "cunts," and that hair is desirable. The female speakers in "Johnie Scot," at a loss of how to "get a coat to Johnie Scot,/ to make the laddie braw," hit on a plan to "twine" their "cunt hair" to accomplish the deed.[36] In fact, the lack of pubic hair was reason to mourn. The speaker of "Nae Hair On't" "grieves" and flies into "a passion" upon discovering that "on [his bride's] cunt there grows nae hair." The speaker expected that his wife would exhibit the signs of sexual maturity, suggesting that he did not marry a pubertal girl. It angered him that her "cunt was out o' fashion," indicating that he believed her baldness natural and she, therefore, promised to be a tepid lover.[37] Nevertheless, the joke is upon the speaker—likely his wife had shaved her pubis to get rid of crabs or had lost the hair during treatment for venereal disease. To trick him, she might have opted to wear a merkin, a pubic hair wig often worn by prostitutes in similar plights who could not afford to have their wares go out of fashion.

In common with artistic conventions of the day, two-dimensional visual erotica evinced some reluctance to depict a hirsute pubis. Naked breasts and bodies, often engaged in sexual acts, abounded; however, these works typically positioned the female body to shield her privates from view. In bawdy prints and illustrations that did give an unimpeded frontal view of naked women, exaggerated labia signified their sex. Illustrations in editions of *Thérèse philosophe* (1748), *Histoire de Dom Bougre* (1741), *Memoirs of a Woman of Pleasure* (1748) and even the works of the Marquis de Sade, the white, hairless labia of the women starkly contrast with the bushy crown of their montes venerum (Figure 2.8). Together, the labia and pubic hair were considered veils of modesty, "call'd Pudenda (from the Shamefacedness that is in Women to have them seen)."[38] Women who revealed their genitals to men who were not their husbands lost all "natural" modesty. They became in essence public women—prostitutes, in other words—who lacked the proper femininity on which masculine respect was based. The taboo against revealing female genitalia was deeply engrained in eighteenth-century society and extended to medical practitioners, who were not allowed to visually examine their female patients' bodies. Even in childbed, forceps deliveries had to be accomplished blind on paying clients.

In bawdy writings, pubic hair, while *speakable*, remained *unrepresentable* except in the most licentious erotic art. It becomes all the more striking that medical men, who were actively engaged in seeking professional respectability in the mid-eighteenth century, chose that time to begin including explicit illustrations to accompany written descriptions of anatomy. The medical profession in the mid-eighteenth century still suffered from disrepute; this was doubly so for the man-midwife, whose specialization, as discussed in Chapter One, opened him up to accusations of sexual predation. On the one hand, Enlightenment ideals held realistic visual representation as a universal language that could reveal Truth. On the other, Lucienne Frappier-Mazur suggests that plain words are turned into obscenity when they are placed in an unexpected context.[39] It follows, then, that female pubic hair, although realistic, would have seemed unexpected and out of place in medical atlases. It would have seemed obscene. Thus, this trend was an odd choice for a profession that was seeking to raise its public opinion. At the very least, these medical atlas makers' scientific reputation came at the expense of those of their female patients whose torsos and abdomens were immortalized in the atlases.

## Erotic Medicine

Enlightenment thinkers desired a universal language, one that could surpass boundaries of nation and tongue to reveal a greater truth unsullied by imperfect translation. Engraved visual images seemed to fulfill this need by realistically depicting images that needed no interpretation.[40] However, that did not mean that images were unmediated. Rather, "the atlas makers were united in the view that what the image represented, or ought to represent, was not the actual individual specimen before them but an idealized, perfected, or at least characteristic exemplar of a species or other natural kind."[41] Medical atlases strove to construct realistic illustrations of the interior and exterior of the human body that often included every observable detail—every pore, every gobbet of fat, every ligament, creating "a verisimilitude so relentless that it becomes hyper-realism."[42] Nevertheless, medical men and the artists they employed could not escape from encoding social beliefs and understandings of the body, gender, class, and race into these drawings. Instead of revealing some universal truth, the images in medical atlases are ideologically loaded, informed by and informing the ways men and women understood their bodies.

The images found in medical atlases were highly constructed: the surgeon first dissected the body, posing it to demonstrate whatever organ or feature was to be immortalized. An artist like Van Rymsdyck would then draw it to the author's specifications; next an engraver would translate the original artwork into a printable medium before handing the plates off to a printer. For the handful of colored atlases produced, after printing, the images would be returned to an artist for coloring.[43] Then on to the bindery and the bookseller. In this process, the author (the surgeon or physician whose name appeared on the title page) worked in close collaboration with all the artists involved to create images which conveyed his vision of the organs that were the focus of his atlas. As a result, distinctive differences amongst atlases emerge. For instance, scholars frequently juxtapose Hunter's *Gravid Uterus* with Smellie's *Anatomical Tables,* noting the careful rendering of the texture of skin, fat and muscle in Hunter's in contrast to the preponderance of bone in Smellie's.[44] Despite such differences, however, after mid-century most anatomical atlases featuring female genitalia included pubic hair, even when doing so added nothing to the anatomical value or realism of the image.[45] Whatever the medical merit, the inclusion of pubic hair eroticized the anatomized female body.

This eroticization was a marker of class. The presence of pubic hair made the image "vulgar," i.e. of the lower classes and not in the realm of genteel art. The exposed "pudenda," moreover, indicated that woman's lack of shame or modesty—modesty and shame were deeply class-inflected qualities, whose presence marked the good-breeding of the woman who exhibited them. Hence, men-midwives were not permitted to look at the genitals of their paying, middling and upper class patients. Nor would the bodies of these patients typically have been available for dissection or preservation. Rather, that lot fell to the poor charity patients, whose class would have made them sexually vulnerable just as it made them vulnerable to the activities of the Resurrectionists. By denying the female cadaver "modesty," the pubic hair depicted in these images would remind viewers that poor women were the source of these images.

The rest of this chapter will be focused on William Smellie's *Anatomical Tables* for four reasons. First, Smellie's *Tables* was explicitly produced for medical students instead of wealthy collectors as were most other atlases. Second, Smellie's work highlights the fiction of realism of the genre: though the images are purportedly *in media res*, instead of being drawn during a dissection, Smellie and his artists arranged body parts to create macabre still lives. Third, several line-drawings, or cartoons, far removed from the hyperrealistic aesthetic of the genre are included. Finally, Smellie's *Tables* had an enormous reach geographically and demographically, staying in print well into the nineteenth century in small, cheap octavo editions printed in London, Edinburgh and the United States.

## Smellie's *Set of Anatomical Tables*

Unlike most of the atlases created by his contemporaries, who produced collector's items, Smellie designed his explicitly for "*the improvement of the young Practitioner… to illustrate what I have taught and written on the Subject.*"[46] Having the drawings engraved and published added the visual element that, as a substitute lecture hall, his textbook lacked. Smellie had employed a variety of visual teaching aids in the classroom. In addition to the mechanical mother device discussed in the last chapter, he had used the original twenty-six drawings by Van Rymsdyck as well as a variety of wet and dried preparations for classroom demonstrations.[47] The wet preparations included fetuses and body parts, some sealed in jars and others in open vats of some preserving fluid, most likely

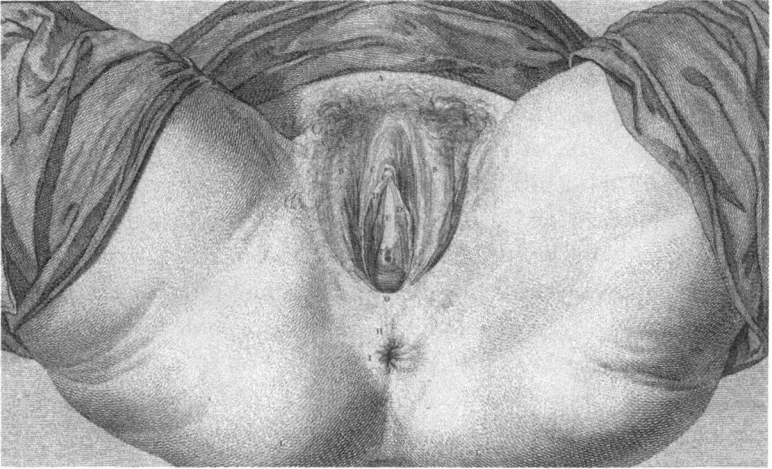

Fig. 2.9: This image of what might be termed the classic pornographic pose, was actually drawn from a section of a human cadaver preserved in alcohol. From William Smellie, *A Set of Anatomical Tables* (1761), Table 4. Courtesy of the Library of the College of Physicians of Philadelphia. Except for along the upper edge, the frame has been cut out of the photograph.

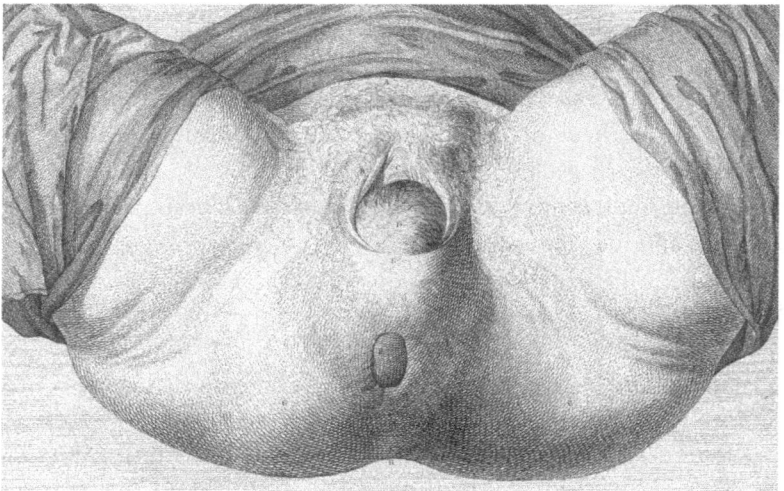

Fig. 2.10: This image, which appears to be showing a crowning fetus, would have been created by someone pushing a fetal doll through the preserved human torso. William Smellie, *A Sett of Anatomical Tables* (1754), Table 15. Courtesy of the National Library of Medicine.

alcohol, that could be taken out and handled by his students.[48] Smellie chose specimens from this latter category as models for his atlas.

While at least one the figures in the *Tables* was undoubtedly taken from the dissection of a pregnant woman (Table 7 [Figure 2.5]), most were drawn from parts of women and fetuses set up in particular poses to demonstrate a particular presentation or delivery technique. In the Preface, Smellie explains that *"The greatest part of the figures were taken from Subjects prepared on purpose...."*[49] Peter Camper elaborated on this process in his journal:

> Dr Smellie...was the first person I saw, as also his figures, drawn by Rymsdijk, but not all from real life. The children are placed in pelves of women, the children themselves looked natural, but the other parts were copied from other preparations.... On Tuesday I drew for Smellie, and checked precisely the position of the heads that are wedged.... Friday, 21st I drew for Dr. Smellie and with the forceps delivered from a corpse a head in the transversal position wedged with the ear against the os pubis.... Thursday, 27th. I again experimented with Dr. Smellie on a corpse, delivered with forceps and made careful drawings and profiles. Then we sawed this body in two, which enabled us to see inside very well....[50]

Smellie and his artists set up compositions as a painter sets up still lives. They took prepared female body parts and preserved fetal corpses and posed them to demonstrate the different techniques and positions Smellie taught in his lectures and writings. Moreover, they "experimented" with the bodies. The female corpse had become quite literally an obstetric phantom, giving birth strictly through the efforts of the male accoucheur. Further, the details of the women's bodies were added from "other preparations," indicating that while the fetuses were individuals, the "mother" depicted was a composite of various women whose bodies came into Smellie's possession after their deaths.[51]

The pretense of life-in-death reaches its peak in the *Tables* in Tables 4 and 15. These are companion images, showing the same view of the female pelvic area, with the woman apparently on her back, her legs spread and raised. Drapes over the truncated torso and stumps of the thighs provide an illusion of wholeness. The focal point of Table 4 (Figure 2.9) is the vulva. Its labia and clitoris appear plump, possibly even in a state of arousal. The pose itself could just as convincingly be from the perspective of a lover as a physician or surgeon and the image captured mid-coitus instead of mid-dissection. Table 15 (Figure 2.10) appears to be the same body, only here, a

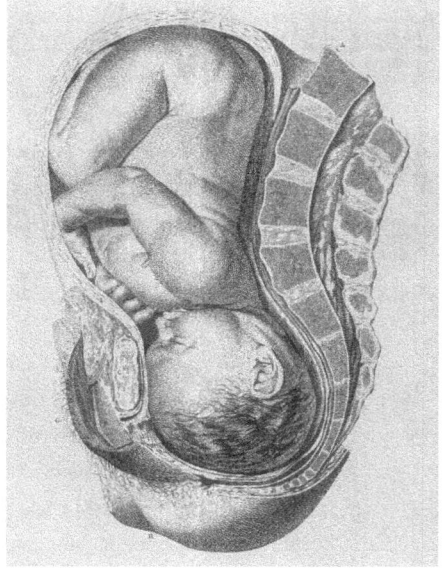

Fig. 2.11: The spine and pubic hair
might act as guideposts to this
anatomical image. From William
Smellie, *A Sett of Anatomical Tables*
(1754), Table 20. Courtesy of the
National Library of Medicine.

baby's head crowns, while the perineum and anus painfully stretch. If one only
looked at the images without reading the explanations, he might be fooled
into thinking he was seeing images of the beginning and end of generation
drawn from life. Turning to the explanation, however, the reader discovers
that "this [is a] Draught from one of the preserved Subjects which I keep
by me, in order to demonstrate these parts in the ordinary Course of my
Lectures."[52] Extrapolating from Camper's journal, the dynamism of Table 15
was created by inserting a preserved fetus into the vagina and pressing it out
in a simulation of birth. Table 4, on the other hand, is clearly the work of
artistic imagination—what was in reality a desiccated, bloodless hunk of flesh
was imagined to be the genitalia of a seemingly living woman. This was not
a disinterested image, but a hegemonizing act of desire, similar to the poems
and stories that also imagined female genitals waiting for a sexual embrace.

Interestingly, in the prospectus for subscribers, Smellie sought to distance
himself from the type of artificiality described by Camper. In it, Smellie
averred, "In each plate the child is represented in its own *Uterus*, the forepart
of which is cut off, in order to exhibit the inside view, together with the size
and situation of the *Foetus*."[53] Smellie sought to reassure potential subscribers
about the *realism* of the drawings by rhetorically granting the fetus property
rights to its mother's body. In stating "the child is represented in its own
Uterus," Smellie alleged that the drawings were taking during dissections, i.e.
taken from "life." This truth claim—that the drawings are an unmediated

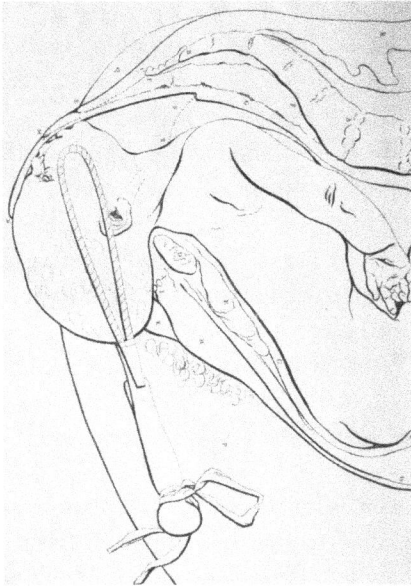

Fig. 2.12: It is difficult to understand why pubic hair appears in this cartoon of a forceps delivery. From William Smellie, *A Set of Anatomical Tables* (1761), Table 19. Courtesy of the Library of the College of Physicians of Philadelphia.

glimpse into the process of birth—was meant to appeal to an Enlightenment audience seeking universal truths.

Whereas a present-day audience might find the sheer dynamism of the figures unbelievable, Smellie was more concerned that a contemporary one would not find his images detailed enough. He apologized for "*avoiding however the extreme Minutiae, and what else seemed foreign to the present design; the situation of parts, and their respective dimensions being more particularly attended to, than a minute anatomical investigation of their structure.*"[54] Anatomical investigations were extraneous to the stated purpose of creating a learning aid for young obstetric practitioners. Minutia, the finer details like the texture of clammy skin or sliced muscle, would have to be sought elsewhere. Usefulness trumped curiosity, so it would seem. Only those parts important in childbirth would be illustrated— including the clitoris and its attendant structures, the labia, the mons veneris, and pubic hair.

Except for the labia (which sometimes swell during pregnancy and were therefore widely believed to be able to obstruct the birth), none of these parts appear to have any bearing on childbirth, pubic hair least of all. Their inclusion served what purpose?

The aesthetic of realism is an obvious answer. These structures are present, and therefore must be represented. Nevertheless, the exclusion of "minutiae," meant these body parts were not rendered in much detail. They are dark masses, differentiated by varying etching techniques. Looking at each separately without the guide letters and explanations, one would often be hard put to identify just what was represented on the page. Here is precisely where pubic hair comes into play. The labia and the mons veneris, when present, are always indicated by a halo of hair (that sometimes fails to actually connect to the body). Pubic hair kept the viewer orientated, acting as a pole by which one could get one's bearings. Table 20 (Figure 2.11), for example, shows a female corpse prepared by Van Rymsdyck. The image depicts the spine and parts of the pelvic bones, one hip and thigh, and half of the genitals: the vagina (labeled E), the labia minora and majora (labeled F and G respectively). The pregnant uterus and fetus rise from the flattened plane of the maternal body. The presence of pubic hair in this image help make sense of the image by clarifying external from internal organs.

Four of the figures (Tables 17, 19, 26, and 34) in the Tables are cartoons—simple line drawings without the subtle shadings to give them depth and detail. Partial, cross-sectioned bodies are mere outlines, strangely angled; thus, the fetus is the only easily identifiable item. Table 19 (Figure 2.12), for instance, is disorienting. The baby seems to lie amongst a bewildering array of curves. In the cartoons such as this one, pubic hair is a crucial lodestone guiding one's way through the atlas. The stylized hair is easily recognizable; the open, wavy curlicues of hair at one side of the body create a visual contrast with the closed curves of the spine on the other. Identification of these two poles helps make sense of the image: the woman's back is arched and her knee would be just beyond the lower right edge of the page. According to the explanation, the reader, with the life-size folio laid out before him, should imagine the woman as "on her side with her Breech a little over the side or foot of the Bed, her Knees being likewise pulled up to her Belly, and a Pillow placed between them…."[55] The bed, the knees, the belly, and the pillow—the woman herself—have all disappeared, leaving a mere trace of her left hip like a fossil on the page. The poles of spine and pubic hair orient the viewer, helping him distinguish back from front as he interpreted the intersecting lines and mysterious ovoid structures. Although oriented by the hair and spine, without the additional guide letters and explanations, that would still have been a daunting task. If H was not labeled as "mons veneris," nothing about it would distinguish it from the labia. They are both merely curved lines with an aureole of curlicues.

The textual explanation refers the viewer to Collection 25 of Volume II, a set of twelve case histories from Smellie and his pupils in which forceps were used during delivery. In all of these cases, the women were languishing near death, in some cases simply from a difficult labor, but in others from poverty and hunger or from mental anxiety from the recent loss of husbands. When the viewer imagined the woman lying on her side, he could choose to envision her as a poor, unmarried woman lying on a pallet, and himself full of philanthropic pity. Or, he could imagine her as a young, grieving widow in better circumstances, and himself full of protective solicitude sure to be rewarded by her gratitude. In the interplay of texts, the fossil-like drawing in the atlas becomes mnemonic device for the would-be hero-accoucheur as he learned his role as the rescuer of parturient damsels-in-distress.[56]

Examining the lines and letters of Table 19, the non-sequential X placed near a small circle stands out. Here X marks the *corpus cavernosum clitoridis*—the internal erectile tissue that engorges with blood when the external clitoris (I) is stimulated. This internal portion of the clitoris is included in some of the drawings of forceps delivery (though not all), without explanation beyond identification. Although no explanation is given why purely copulative organs integral "to the present design" of illustrating childbirth for obstetric students, extrapolating from his cautions about the nearby bladder (E), perhaps they are included it as an organ the accoucheur should be careful not to puncture when employing the forceps.

While such inclusions might lend an air of realism to anatomical images, they also subtly eroticized them. The clitoris was well known for being women's "seat of pleasure," singular in its function and increasingly problematic in medical discourse. While in the seventeenth century, female orgasm was widely believed to be necessary for conception, this theory was thrown into doubt in the eighteenth and was largely believed to be completely debunked after Lazzaro Spallanzani successfully artificially impregnated dogs in the late eighteenth century, although there continued to be hold-outs for the old theory into the nineteenth century.[57] The means of conception was hotly debated, and while Smellie claimed he would stay out of the fray in the overview of theories he provided in Volume I of the *Treatise*, his frequent inclusion of the clitoris and its erectile tissue suggests otherwise.[58] Their presence acts as a subtle visual argument for their continued importance in generation and childbearing.

Pubic hair also seemed to serve a similar function. In addition to acting as a visual guide, it was an eroticizing element that signaled a woman's fertility. Pubic hair was an indicator of a woman's humoral temperament, providing invaluable information about her potential for fecundity and ardor. As discussed above, in bawdry, a woman's bush was an object of admiration and desire. Lovers frequently extolled the beauties of their mistresses' bush; even in less panegyric writings, pubic hair, often clothed in a variety of metaphorical forms, remained the major signifier of female genitalia. Its inclusion in medical drawings brought them in line with the conventions of contemporary erotica.

The amount of hair depicted in Smellie's *Tables* suggests this assessment is not far from the mark. Not only is the hair stylized, but its strategic placement indicates artistry more than realism was at play. Eighteenth-century medical men wished to create "an unmediated gaze based on purely scientific interest through "the lack of any artificial, ornamental framing device."[59] Yet elements within the images like drapery (such as that in Tables 4, 7, or 15) and pubic hair created internal framing devices. The pelvises in the atlas are, in the words of a bawdy poet, "but thinly hair'd,/It not too bushy, nor too bald appear'd": they are never thickly furred, nor does the hair ever obstruct the viewer's gaze of the various parts. Rather, the hair is like decorative trimming—like fringe on clothing designed to attract the eye. It seems to function as a frame, drawing the eye into the sexual organs. Moreover, many of the images are actually contained in black line frames. By directing the gaze, frames "alter the status of the image from simple to special object; the realm of art is held within the frame."[60]

For example, in Table 4 (Figure 2.9), a series of concentric framing devices keeps the eye focused the vaginal opening placed at the center of the page. First is an actual line frame, reminding the viewer that the object inside is "special," that it deserves his especial attention and concern. (Except for along the upper edge, the frame has been cut out of the photograph of the Table included in this chapter). Next, the drapery keeps the eye from straying to the implied rest of the body, directing it to the displayed sexual organs. Then wisps of hair surrounding the vulva draw the eye into it. The vulva itself is a series of light and dark concentric curves that ultimately end at the vagina. Additionally, the vagina is the center point of an implied vertical line running from the dark flower of the anus, through the vagina, clitoris, preputium where the labia minora meet and, strangely, a part in the hair on the mons veneris. These design elements focus the eye on the woman's sex and the actual frame complicates claims of scientific detachment of the image by bringing it into the realm of art. Other medical atlases, such as Hunter's *The Gravid Uterus*, appear more neutral because they lack frames. Some of the later octavo reprints of Smellie's *Tables* are missing the frames as well. Works like those of Samuel Bard or John Aitken avoided the *in media coitus* of Table 4 by only including images of free-floating vulvas, but whether the separation of sex from body created a sense purity of purpose or if it merely heightened its specialness (and frisson), would be hard to decide.[61] Illustrations like these reified and eroticized the female body as much as bawdy song or story. Perhaps more so, as medical atlases were imbued with an authority and solemnity that bawdry lacked.

Anatomical atlases and medical writings of the eighteenth and nineteenth century reveal marked tensions and contradictions in their approaches to the human body. Race and class were two of the most salient and controversial ways of distinguishing among humans. While some theories underscored the essential sameness of people, others became increasingly convinced that race and class brought with them innate, unchangeable negative characteristics. For example, Scottish Enlightenment thinkers like David Hume, Adam Ferguson and Henry Home, Lord Kames, each promoted theories of embodied racial inferiority in their influential essays and books.[62] By the nineteenth century, American doctors like James Marion Sims touted the inferiority of raced/ classed women—slave women and indigent Irish—on whom he experimented to perfect medical techniques for elite white women—those closest to the ideal in this schema.[63] Anatomical atlases like Smellie's were polysemous, attempting, on the one hand, to construct the ideal, universal "Woman"; on the other, their details were reminders of the underclass origins of this "Woman."

Medical authority takes on a disquieting cast to the modern reader when Table 4 is viewed in conjunction with the cases histories of Collection II that the explanation cross-references. These histories are all concerned with "abnormal" genitals and the ways in which medical men could surgically bring them into line with the "normal" represented in Table 4. Four of the cases describe operations to cure imperforate hymens.[64] Two other cases of the collection describe the excision of elongated labia minora. Elongated labia minora were often associated with non-European women, such as South African "Hottentots" or supposed tailed inhabitants of Borneo. For instance, "the Hottentot Venus," a South African woman named Saartjie Baartman, was put on display in 1810 and poked and prodded by European virtuosi intent on discovering the secrets of her large buttocks and elongated labia minora—if they were a "natural" veil of modesty with which uncivilized women were endowed or if they were "the products of female artifice." After her death, Baartman's preserved genitals were on display at the Musée de l'Homme well into the twentieth century. She was finally repatriated and buried in 2002.[65]

Thus, the primitive labiaplasties described in the *Treatise* and in other midwifery writings could have had racial undertones.[66] Surgery to make a woman's or girl's genitals conform to European "norms" could have been a radical means to assure that British women's bodies were semiotically civilized. In any case, large labia minora were not the only part subject to excision. While

Smellie did not refer readers to cases of clitoridectomy, other midwifery writers did, recommending the removal of the clitoris to cure chronic masturbation (believed to be the primary cause of large clitorises).[67] Table 4 normalized a particular image of the female genitals. In much the same way pornography fuels the market for vaginoplasty and labiaplasty today,[68] this Table could be used as a standard by which practitioners and the public at large could decide if a woman or girl needed to undergo painful sexual reconstructive surgery.

Contradictory ideas about female sexual desire circulated in the eighteenth century. Men of science and medicine, eager to naturalize gender roles, were quick to attribute modesty or chastity to female animals. "Madame Chimpanzee," an ape on display in mid-century London, was touted for her table manners and modesty.[69] Famed surgeon and anatomist John Hunter (younger brother to William) decided that

> It would appear that the female is not so desirous for copulation as the male. We find in most animals, if not in all, that the male always courts the female; that she requires being courted to give her desires, otherwise she would not have them so often. Lord Clive's zebra is a strong proof of this. When she was in heat, they brought a common male ass to her, but she would not admit his addresses. Lord Clive ordered that the male ass should be painted similar to the female zebra; and this being done, she received him very readily. In this curious fact we have instinct excited by mere colour; for we cannot suppose that she reasoned or judged of the male for herself, as she never could have seen herself so perfectly. Colour had so strong an affect in the present case, as to get the better of everything else. But the male did not require this; [she] being an animal somewhat similar to himself was sufficient to rouse him.[70]

What we would attribute to the zebra's reluctance at forced mating with a strange species, Hunter attributed to an inborn *female* lack of sexual desire. He denied females agency in choosing a mate. Instead females are subrational creatures, fooled by gaudy appearances. The implications for women are plain—they too lacked desire and agency, and were easily fooled by marvelous appearances. This same lesson was driven home to women in seduction novels, the pages of which are littered with the fallen, pathetic corpses of women foolish enough to rely on their own faulty reason, hoodwinked and betrayed by asses in flashy technicolor disguises.

Yet not all medical men and natural historians were ready to make such an unequivocal statement. In their lectures and textbooks, these men typically acknowledged that stimulation to the clitoris produced sexual pleasure and that both men and women were desirous of coitus. However, they tended to manifest discomfort with the subject. Often the tension was resolved through equivocation. This was the strategy employed by Benjamin Rush, who explicitly coded desire as masculine, yet implicitly acknowledged the possibility of female desire. Rush lectured:

> We have now brought the *sexes* to that period in which they are prepared to propagate their species—This period takes place from 14 in the *female*, and 18 or 20 in the *male*, and continues 'til the venereal appetites decline. Marriage appears to be a wise institution of nature to prevent the abuse of the venereal appetites, for as there are no particular reasons in which *mankind* abstain from embraces, as there are in the brute creation, *he* would soon destroy himself by the excess of desire and embrace…. This desire *between the sexes* is congenial with their nature, and there is no *man* who has not at one time or another felt the venereal impulse…. I before observed that there was no period in *manhood* that did not prompt to the venereal appetite—It is an happiness to the *human* race, that this appetite is so deeply seated, that no time nor pain can eradicate it. If it was not naturally interwoven with *our system*, from the care and anxiety attending the rearing of an offspring, *poor people* would never marry. To prevent the male from using unnatural embraces, woman was formed for his companion and partner in care, as an outlet of this natural stimulus. The degree of pleasure arising from this *social* intercourse is different in the *human* and brute species. Some animals appear to enjoy it in an higher degree than *man*.[71]

Although Rush consistently attributed desire to men, the acknowledgment that such desires started at puberty for both male and female, and the occasional use of "people," "social," and "between the sexes" quietly recognized female desire yet largely skirted the issue. New stereotypes of the passionless woman competed with older ideas of female sexual voracity. Both could be accommodated by aligning the former with the emergent bourgeois respectability and the later with the underclass of working poor and, in America, slaves and freedwomen.[72]

As representations of "Woman," anatomical atlases reduced women to their sex and sexual functions at the very time new ideals of sexual continence for middling and elite women were emerging. In this, they exemplify the attempt to hold contradictory ideas about female sexuality—her erotic and maternal roles—in balance. By including pubic hair, a traditional sign of female erotic capacity, these atlases sensualized the female body, potentially threatening the chastity of respectable, "normal" women. However, because passion became linked to class, the very presence of a sexual marker implicitly linked these images to poor women, which, indeed, they were. Pubic hair forcefully reminded readers that medical illustrations were created from the bodies of poor women whose social invisibility increased the likelihood that their bodies would become the curios of medical collectors.

Furthermore, nudity itself was a marker of rank. Those with means did not expose their bodies, especially their "vulgar and disquieting features, such as the buttocks" to the public eye.[73] The middling and elite women who could afford the fees of men-midwives insisted that all examinations and operations be done without the male doctor actually looking at their naked bodies. Poor women were not afforded the same luxury. At the charitable lying-in hospitals in London, which were largely all-female spaces, the "respectable poor" patients had to agree to physical examinations pre-admittance to weed out the diseased and the "very dirty ragged and others of bad behavior."[74] In Edinburgh, lying-in hospitals were teaching establishments for midwifery professors and their students, and general charity hospitals in America followed British example.[75] Philanthropy was not enough to protect these institutions from being accused with prostituting their poor patients to science.[76] When Smellie, in common with other instructors of midwifery not attached to a lying-in hospital, sought out teaching subjects who could be displayed to throngs of students, he did not seek among his "private" paying patients. He sought among the urban poor— the wives of unskilled laborers, beggar-women, ballad-sellers, and prostitutes. His student Colin MacKenzie, who taught midwifery courses modeled on his preceptor's, hired similar women in all stages of pregnancy to allow his male students to examine them during his lectures.[77] These women, out of need, sacrificed the modesty that was so valued by their society. In exchange for cash or medical care, they allowed any number of men (and women) to physically examine their bodies and to watch them give birth at a time when a saleswoman of any goods might be seen as also offering her body for sale.[78]

Women who exposed their private parts—their pudenda—were supposed to feel shame (*pudor*). The women who exchanged access to their bodies for economic or therapeutic gain seemingly felt no shame. They were immodest and medical men codified in print this seeming lack of modesty. Case histories revealed the intimate details of patients' illnesses and bodies. Although patients were almost always identified by class, their names were usually kept under wraps. Smellie protected the privacy of all his patients, cloaking them in anonymity. However, such courtesy was sometimes not extended to patients

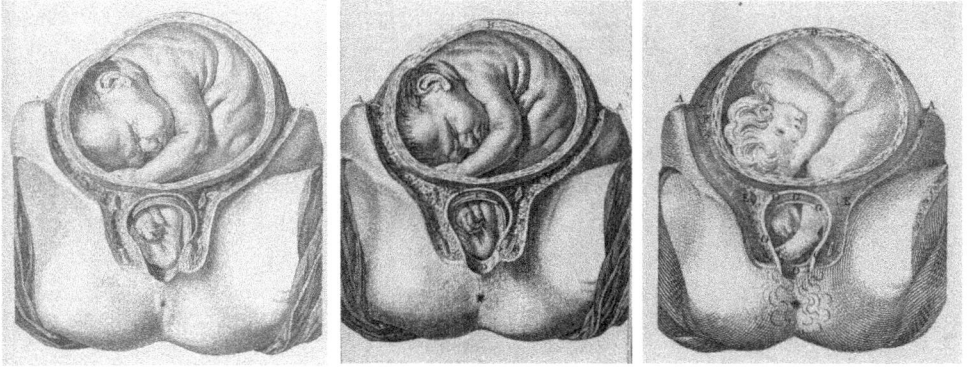

Fig. 2.13 (left): William Smellie, *A Sett of Anatomical Tables* (1754), Table 31. Courtesy of the National Library of Medicine; Fig. 2.14 (center): William Smellie, *Set of Anatomical Tables* (London 1779), Table 31. Courtesy of the Library of the College of Physicians of Philadelphia; Fig. 2.15 (right): William Smellie, *A Set of Anatomical Tables* (Edinburgh 1785), Table 31. Courtesy of the Library of the College of Physicians of Philadelphia.

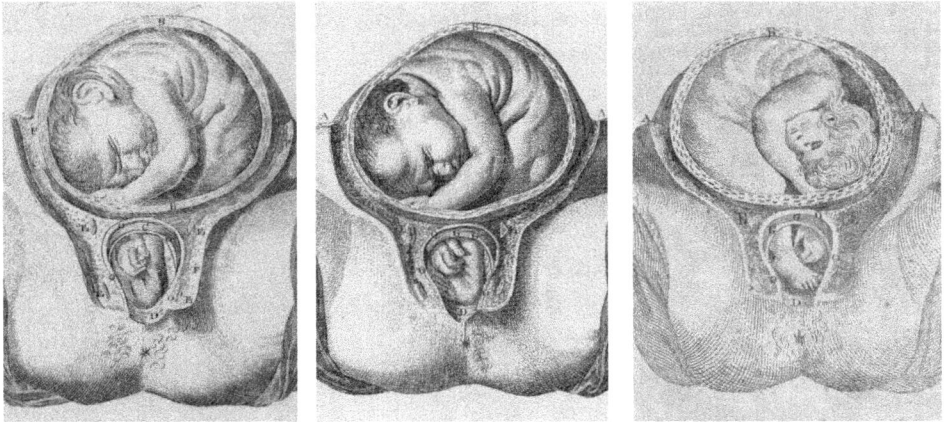

Fig. 2.16 (left): William Smellie, *Abridgement to the Practice of Midwifery, and a set of Anatomical Tables* (Boston 1786), Table 31. The pencil marks on the image are from Dr. Thomas Sewall. Courtesy of the Library of the College of Physicians of Philadelphia; Fig. 2.17 (center): William Smellie, *A Set of Anatomical Tables* (Edinburgh 1790), Table 31. Courtesy of the Library of the College of Physicians of Philadelphia; Fig. 2.18 (right): William Smellie, *A Set of Anatomical Tables* (Worcester 1793), Table 31. Courtesy of the Library of the College of Physicians of Philadelphia.

labeled "poor" by other practitioners. John Leake, who ran the Westminster Lying-in Hospital, followed this pattern in his *Dissertation upon the Lisbon Diet Drink* (1762), a pamphlet hawking his favorite specific for curing a host of diseases, including venereal taints.[79] So did Charles White, who, as was the common practice, dissected poor patients in the Manchester infirmary without the permission of their families. When Betty Riggs died six months pregnant, White seized on this rare opportunity of dissecting a pregnant woman. Working quickly, he managed to examine the contents of her abdomen, including the uterus and fetus before the arrival of "her friends...prevented any further examination."[80] White was not the only accoucheur to take advantage of such opportunities, and these lucky accoucheurs were eager to share the fruits of their efforts. In Volume II, Smellie mentions conversations with William Hunter, Alexander Monro Secundus, and Peter Camper about dissections of pregnant women they had performed and includes a letter from a former student about his own recent opportunity of joining these elite ranks, although like White, his brief examination was ended earlier than he would have preferred. Since even opening a woman with a view to save the child left men-midwives open to accusations of cruelty and butchery, it follows that these hurried, clandestine operations would have been most safely performed upon charity patients. Dissecting the "better" classes without permission would have been social and professional suicide to men whose success largely relied upon word of mouth recommendations from patients and midwives.[81]

Betty's body, and other women like her, was treated as public property.[82] If he had not been interrupted, it is easy to imagine that parts of her body might have found their way into a display case. By including her story in his book, White nonetheless turned Betty into spectacle. The inclusion of the names of poor patients in medical treatises and the inclusion of pubic hair in anatomical drawings both turned subaltern women into public spectacles. Including their names in case histories denied them the veil of modesty and privacy awarded to wealthier women. Adorning their naked bodies with hair drew attention to their sex and sexuality. Obstetric discourse treated them as obscene bodies— spectacular bodies that belonged to the realm of pornography—rather than the spectacle of costume found in the genteel world. In print, poor women became public women, devoid of modesty, whose exposed bodies were available to any comer. Regardless of their actual station in life, in death the pictorial representations of these poor women, in a way, turned them into prostitutes whose bodies were bought by elite men.

## From Folio to Thumbnail: Anglo-Atlantic Circulation of Smellie's *Tables*

Smellie's *Tables* and similar medical illustrations eroticized a classed female body through their adoption of conventions of pornography. The size and cost of medical atlases (Smellie's was on the cheap end at two guineas; Hunter's cost seven guineas) effectively limited their potential impact to the handful of elite men who could afford to include them in their private libraries and to medical students, like those at the Pennsylvania Hospital, who could look through Smellie's and Hunter's non-circulating atlases in the reading room. However, Smellie's atlas did not remain merely in the hands of this limited audience. In addition to the two portfolio editions published in his life time, Smellie's *Tables* was reprinted at least twelve more times; additionally, they were the primary source for the illustrations in the "Midwifery" article in the *Encyclopedia Britannica* and were also included as illustrations in many other midwifery manuals.[83] In this section, I will map out the transatlantic publication history of Smellie's *Tables* and examine ways later engravers and publishers coped with the erotic potential of the images. (See Figures 2.13, 2.14, 2.15, 2.16, 2.17 and 2.18) for images of Table 31 from the original and five of the octavo reprints). The widespread availability of this atlas meant it reached a much larger audience than the medical elite audience for which it was originally intended, greatly increasing its potential impact upon how Anglo-Atlantic society saw and interpreted women's bodies.

Smellie's *Tables* were published in London in 1754 by David Wilson, with William Strahan as a silent partner; in 1761, two years before Smellie's death, Wilson issued another printing of the portfolio.[84] Apparently sometime after this second printing the copper plates made their way to Lanark, Scotland where Smellie had retired and then were lost until the 1780s. After Wilson's death in 1777, the publishing powerhouse syndicate of William Strahan and Thomas Cadell teamed with George Nichol in 1779 to issue "A New Edition" of Smellie's *Treatise on the Theory and Practice of Midwifery*, the three octavo volumes joined by an octavo edition of the *Tables*, which I have found bound with either the first or third volume. This first small-format edition makes almost no changes or additions to the work itself, aside from removing Gringion's name as the engraver in the Preface, but without including the name of the person who supplied his place. A testament to the superiority of London craftsmen, the images themselves are crisp, accurate miniatures of the original *Tables* (Figure 2.14). By and large, any variations are minor and insignificant.

The next year (1780), and again in 1784 and 1785, Edinburgh publisher Charles Elliot, who was establishing himself as the primary medical publisher in that city, issued his own original small edition of Smellie's *Tables*, in duodecimo and octavo, which retailed for five and six shillings respectively. In addition to selling it with Smellie's *Treatise*, Elliot often bound the plates with a work by one of his authors, midwifery professor Alexander Hamilton, whose textbooks conveniently bore names nearly identical to Smellie's.[85] Elliot added two additional plates of obstetrical instruments designed by Drs. Thomas Young and John Evans. Elliot was an ambitious young Edinburgh publisher, "aggressive in purchasing copyrights, especially in the field of medicine, and he used copublishing with London booksellers such as Murray, Robinson, and Cadell as a device for assuring widespread circulation of his books...."[86] In addition to medical publishing, Elliot was an important seller of the second and third editions of the *Encyclopedia Britannica*. At "the time of his death in 1790...Elliot had a book trade network encompassing London, Scotland, the English provinces, Ireland and Europe, and he had shipped large numbers of books to America."[87] He had trade relations with printers and booksellers in New York, Philadelphia, Charleston, South Carolina, and Virginia; moreover, he made use of returning American medical students to bring back trunks of books to sell.[88] Through Elliot's network, Smellie's *Tables* could circulate throughout the Anglo-Atlantic world.

However, what buyers of these three Elliot editions received varied in significant ways from the original. Engraved by Andrew Bell, the plates, while technically elegant, contain many deviations from the original *Tables*. First of all, two of the fetuses (Tables 31 and 32) (Figure 2.15) look like toddlers rather than newborns, and the fetus of Table 16 has strangely feminine features like arched eyebrows and full cupids-bow lips. (Curiously, these mistakes are not readily detectable in the tiny versions Bell engraved for the *Encyclopedia Britannica*). Secondly, Bell greatly reduced the amount of pubic hair on most of the images, and the remaining hair is even more stylized and abstract than in the original drawings. The removal of hair perhaps indicates a level of discomfort with this indelicate detail or simply a lack of skill. In any case, the hair in these plates appears even more decorative or ornamental than in the originals, increasing its power as a framing device. Finally, Bell removed the black line frames that surrounded some of the plates, for instance, the one in Table 4 (Figure 2.9) that I previously argued gave the image an extra level of frisson; this change also seems to speak to a certain discomfort with the design of the originals.

The first American edition of Smellie's *Tables* appeared in 1786 in Boston, engraved and published by John Norman, a prolific if unskilled engraver and recent emigrant from London.[89]  Despite the lack of technical beauty, Norman's edition has the honor to be the work of medical engravings crafted and published in America (Figure 2.16). These images appear to have been copied the Strahan/Cadell/Nichol octavo edition. The engravings themselves are of similar sizes, and the hatchmarks and lines correspond as well. Moreover, none of the fetuses look like toddlers as they do in the Bell/Elliot edition. Like that edition, however, Norman reduced the amount of pubic hair found in many of the images, although the hair is not as stylized and geometric as that of the Edinburgh edition. Norman also did not remove any of the frames from around the Tables. Although he failed to include the circles that indicated the clitoris and *corpus cavernosum clitoridis*, he included their letter keys, perhaps indicating more a lack of skill than anything else.

The next iteration of Smellie's *Tables* appeared again in Edinburgh. In 1787, William Creech published a new royal folio edition of the *Tables*, edited by Alexander Hamilton, reputedly from Grignion's original plates. Apparently the original copper plates had been lost sometime after Smellie's death and eventually were sold as scrap. According to Hamilton, he fortuitously learned of the plates and intervened before the engraver to whom they had been sold could destroy them.[90] The plates appear to be identical to those used in the 1761 printing. Hamilton did remove Grignion's name from Smellie's preface, but perhaps this was because he relied upon one of the small-format editions for the accompanying text rather than one of the original folios. To the explanations of the plates, Hamilton added notes referring the reader to his *Outlines on the Theory and Practice of Midwifery*; he also appended a new plate of Thomas Young's forceps engraved by Daniel Lizars, a former pupil of Bell. Seemingly, the success of this new folio gave provided the impetus to Elliot to bring out a new small-format edition of Smellie's *Tables* edited by Hamilton, only this time engraved by Lizars. Elliot published two runs of the Hamilton/Lizars version, first in 1787 and again in 1790, the year he died of a stroke.[91] The addition of Hamilton's notes justified Elliot's practice of binding the *Tables* with Hamilton's books.

With the newly reprinted folio *Tables* as a model, Lizars' plates are skillfully executed and accurate copies (Figure 2.17). The images in these two octavo editions are nearly identical in all respects to the originals, with one major exception. Lizars significantly altered Table 7. In the original (Figure 2.5), as I previously discussed, the exposed vulva is a secondary focal point in this image of a dissected female torso. Lizars, on the other hand, covered the vulva with a portion of the sheet, hiding the woman's genitals from view. This is a change that cannot be attributed to lack of skill, but a deliberate choice on the part of the engraver or editor to cover what he felt should not be exposed. In the copies that include Bell's engravings, the vulva remained exposed.

We return to Massachusetts for the next printing of Smellie's *Tables*. In 1793, intrepid American printer Isaiah Thomas came out with his own edition. Thomas, one of the most important American printers in the late eighteenth century, controlled the book trade in the greater New England area and he had connections with booksellers outside his region, such as Philadelphians Matthew Carey and Thomas Dobson.[92] He was also not a man afraid to take risks. In addition to respectable medical reprints, Thomas brought out the first American novel *The Power of Sympathy* (1789) that told in its pages the sexual scandals of a founding family, printed an edition of *The Age of Reason* (1794) at the height of Painean controversy, and possibly printed an American version of the notorious *Memoirs of a Woman of Pleasure*.[93] His edition of Smellie's *Tables* were one of many medical reprints that issued from his presses. The lines, crosshatching and size of plates in Thomas's edition of the *Tables* clearly indicate they were copied from Bell's engravings (Figure 2.18). They also repeat Bell's mistakes (the toddlers, the removal of frames, etc) and add new ones through shoddy craftsmanship. By far, the Thomas edition is the least accomplished of any of the various small-format editions. However, eager to provide the most up-to-date text, Thomas paired these plates with explanations taken from the edition edited by Hamilton, with Hamilton's additional notes.[94] Thomas also reprinted both of Hamilton's midwifery guides, although he, nor any other American printer, never issued an American version of Smellie's *Treatise*.

In 1794, London publishers Murray, Kay and Otridge joined together to bring out an abridged version of Smellie's *Treatise* in one volume that included miniature copies of the *Tables* styled after those in the *Encyclopedia Britannica*, with the difference that all of the images are there. Tables 31 and 32 appear to be toddlers, suggesting that whoever engraved these images modeled their versions on the Bell/Elliot edition. For the most part, these images are crude and badly executed. There seems to have been only one printing.

In 1797 and again in 1806, Philadelphia bookseller Thomas Dobson, published new American versions of Smellie's *Tables*, which he often sold bound with Hamilton's midwifery texts in imitation of Elliot. The first page of these editions identifies the plates as having been engraved by J. Norman. The images themselves very closely resemble those printed by Norman a decade earlier, although minor differences in some details suggests that Dobson had the plates re-engraved. However, Dobson had been selling copies of Smellie's

*Tables* (along with copies of the entire *Treatise*) since 1785.[95] He most likely sold copies of the Elliot/Bell editions of the *Tables*. Dobson was Elliot's former clerk whom Elliot intended to be his Philadelphia connection. Elliot had sent Dobson to the newly formed United States with a huge parcel of bookstock, with instructions to set up a bookstore in his own name, keeping Elliot's involvement a secret. Elliot, unfortunately, failed to make this arrangement in writing, providing Dobson with the opportunity to renege on his debts and set up as a major American publisher of British reprints—using, of course, the stock Elliot sent him with as copy from which to work. Apparently, by 1797 Dobson had run out of the Elliot editions, and chose to purchase the Norman plates rather than have his own version engraved. At that point, he was in the midst of underwriting the final two volumes of the American version of the *Encyclopedia Britannica*. The *Encyclopedia* had been an incredibly expensive undertaking, although one that paid off in the end; purchasing ready-made plates was likely more cost effective than paying his *Encyclopedia* engravers to produce both thumbnail and octavo-sized versions of each plate.[96]

Clearly, Smellie's *Tables* were widely available. If each version (counting the folios with the small prints) was printed in a small run of only 100, there would still be 1400 different copies available for the Anglo-Atlantic reading public in the late eighteenth century, exclusive of the *Encyclopedia Britannica* and images borrowed from Smellie to illustrate other books. The Strahan-Cadell publishing syndicate that produced the first small edition was the most powerful British publishing house in the eighteenth century. They had the network and capability of selling their edition of the *Tables* in all parts of Britain and America. Smellie's *Tables* might not have been profitable enough to warrant more than one edition. However, it is just as likely that they worked out a trade arrangement with Elliot, with whom Cadell occasionally collaborated.[97] Elliot himself had a long reach, sending thousands of pounds worth of books to America, many of which were medical titles (including Smellie's *Tables*). The American reprinters of the *Tables*, Thomas and Dobson, were two of the most powerful and important publishers in the early Republic. Between the two, their own bookselling networks blanketed the United States from the northernmost reaches of New England down throughout the Chesapeake and into the western hinterlands.

The reprinting of Smellie's *Tables* was in the hands of some of the most powerful publishers the Anglo-Atlantic world, men who had the capability of seeing their stock marketed across a vast geographical area. Because of the frequent reprinting in small versions, Smellie's *Tables* had a much longer life span than his *Treatise*. New editions of the plates were still being struck as Smellie's students and students' students, who venerated him as a founding father of obstetrics, distanced themselves from his perceived old-fashioned ways. Yet, they had imbibed and embodied Smellie's lesson of heroic man-midwifery, using similar rhetorical stances within the textbooks they themselves penned. They also continued looking toward the images of Woman that Smellie constructed in the *Tables* as normative.

The book's primary audience was medical men. Although Smellie claimed in the Preface that his book was especially meant for "students and young practitioners," as a portfolio, only the very wealthiest among them would have been able to afford their own copies. Most students would have had limited access to copies held by institutions, such as the copy held by the Pennsylvania Hospital. There, it was one of six non-circulating books whose usage limited to within the Library.[98] However, with the transmission into smaller, cheaper formats the numbers of potential buyers proliferated. Nearly every medical student could afford to buy his own copy at six or seven shillings (around $65 today), if he chose to buy the books on the reading lists his professors gave him.[99] For Edinburgh midwifery students of the 1780s and 90s, their main textbook, written by their professor Alexander Hamilton, came ready-bound with Smellie's *Tables*, though the textbook could also be bought separately.

However, circulation of the *Tables* was not limited to medical men. Midwives were an important secondary audience. As medical men claimed authority over female health care, they increasingly argued that midwives be educated about female anatomy. And while some midwives, such as Elizabeth Nihell, resisted anatomical instruction, many midwives, like Sarah Stone, Margaret Mears, or Margaret Stephens, welcomed the access to formal training.[100] Many accoucheurs who taught took female students in addition to male pupils. Hamilton held separate classes for female students and wrote a separate textbook for them which they could buy bound with Smellie's *Tables* for the requisite 6 shillings. The various lying-in hospitals also trained scores of female midwives and anatomy was part of that training. At one British lying-in hospital, a retiring matron bequeathed a folio edition of Smellie's work as her legacy.[101]

Moreover, the inclusion of Smellie's *Tables* into home libraries greatly increased the odds that non-medical individuals—wives, children, or servants—might view the contents of the book. By mid-century, in Britain, 60% of men and 40% of women could sign their names, indicating higher literacy rates since writing was taught separately from reading and was often a skill acquired later in life.[102] Literacy rates were even better in some parts United States. By the turn of the nineteenth century, approximately 80-90 %

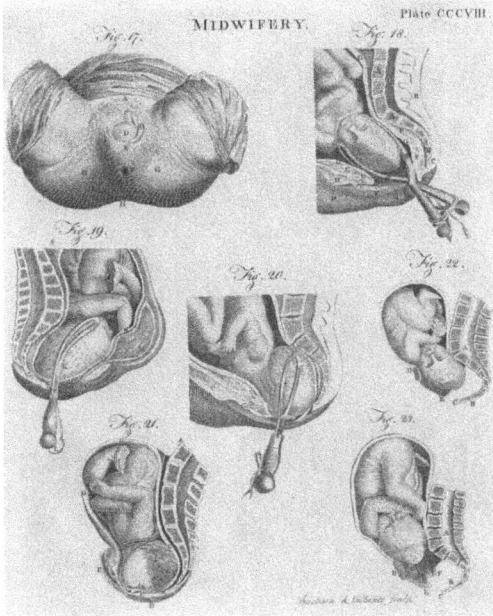

Fig. 2.19: Plate CCCVIII from the "Midwifery" article in Volume 11 of the *Encyclopedia* (Philadelphia 1798). Courtesy of the Library Company of Philadelphia.

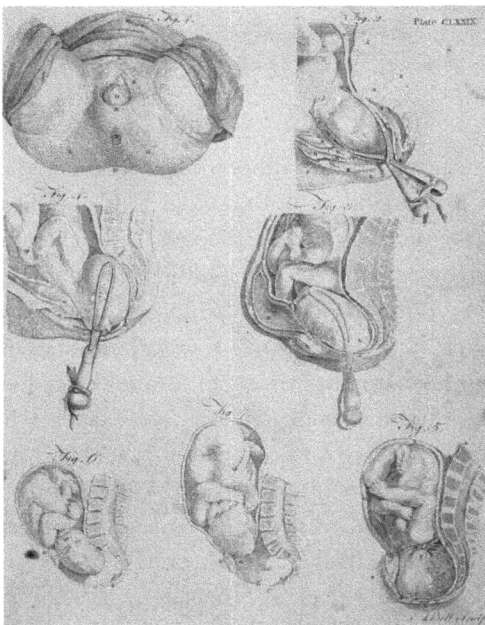

Fig. 2.20: Compare the quality of the engravings between the British and the American productions. Plate CLXXIX of the "Midwifery" article from Volume 7 of the *Encyclopedia Britannica* (Edinburgh 1781). Courtesy of the Library Company of Philadelphia.

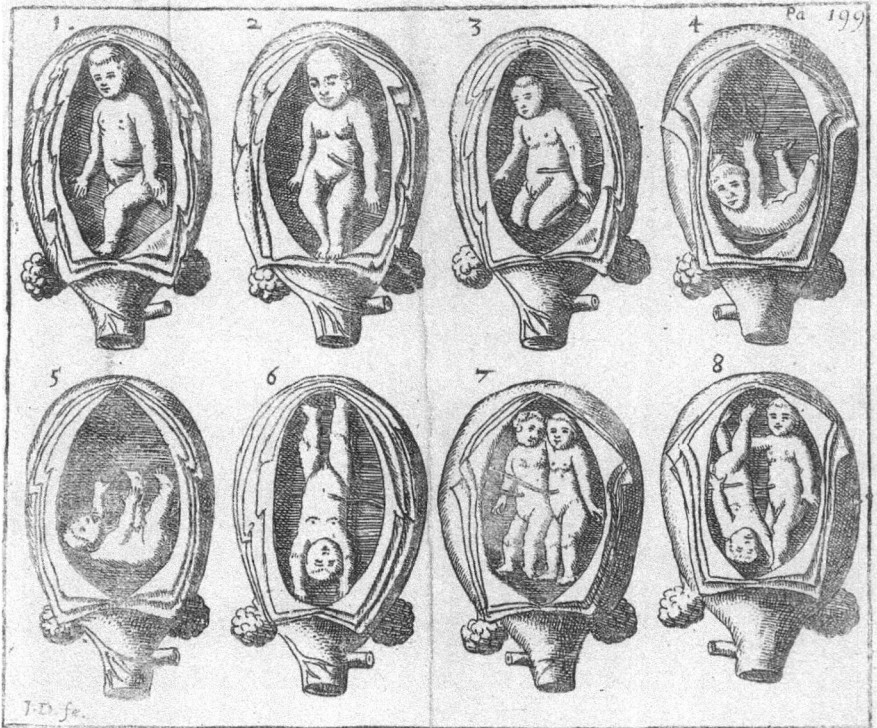

Fig. 2.21: Illustration of fetuses floating in bottle-like wombs. From Jane Sharp's *The Midwives' Book* (London 1671). Courtesy of the Wangensteen Historical Library of Biology and Medicine, University of Minnesota.

of all New England women and nearly half of southern white women could read and write, with men's literacy rates higher in both regions.[103] Nor did one need to be literate merely look at the pictures in the *Tables*. We have evidence of one such family drama in the marginalia of a copy of the Norman edition owned by Dr. Thomas Sewall, the founder of George Washington University's Medical school and infamous graverobber. Dr. Sewall's son got a hold of his father's copy and practiced signing his name in various locations throughout it sometime before his sixteenth year. It is impossible to say exactly what prompted Sewall to sell his copy, which he had owned since at least 1806 when he was a medical apprentice to his brother-in-law, but by 1834, the book was in the hands of a new owner, Charles T. Webb.[104] While this anecdotal incident could be an isolated event, it is much more likely that the young Thomas was not the only unauthorized person to take a peek at Smellie's *Tables*. He was certainly not the only young man known to have looked at a midwifery guide. For example, in 1749, Jonathan Edwards' New England parish was rocked by scandal after several young men had purloined "granny books" (midwifery guides) and then teased girls with the information they found there.[105] The promise of secret knowledge has always lured the curious.

In any event, Smellie's *Tables* were available to non-medical readers in the *Encyclopedia Britannica*, in both its British and American iterations. To be sure, the *Encyclopedia* was an elite text, marketed toward a polite, monied readership who could afford the expensive subscription costs. Thomas Dobson published an American version, based upon the third edition, expanded and revised to represent an American viewpoint. This decade-long undertaking, marketed nationwide to "lovers of science and literature," cost $5.00 per volume. By the time of its completion the cost of an entire set could range from $135 in boards to $207 in Moroccan leather[106]—they would cost $2,680 to $4,120 in today's currency. Those who could afford a set were making a statement about their social and intellectual cachet. Robert Arner argues that "An encyclopedia, and especially the encyclopedia that Dobson chose to reprint, speaks with the voice of unchallenged authority and offers its taxonomy and its version of scientific objectivity as a reassuring metaphor of the underlying order of the universe, the way things really are, despite disturbing appearances to the contrary."[107] What was the worldview that this encyclopedia, in both its American and British forms, presented about the reproductive female body? While this question deserves to be answered in regards to both the text of the "Midwifery" entry and the accompanying images, I am setting the question of the text aside, other than pointing out that it was based primarily upon the writings of William Smellie and Alexander Hamilton.

What readers of the *Encyclopedia* saw were copies of Smellie's *Tables*. However, readers of the *Encyclopedia* did not get an unmediated glimpse at the *Tables*. First of all, the images were reduced to thumbnails, just a few inches wide and long, resulting in a corresponding loss of detail (Figures 2.19 and 2.20). In particular, most of images lack the pubic hair that adorns the larger images.[108] While this change may be due in large part to the change in scale, its end result is to present a female body at once less eroticized and one that corresponds more closely to acceptable conventions of representations of the female form. Nevertheless, people still found the images too shocking and purportedly ripped them out of their *Encyclopedias*.[109] Secondly, not all of the Tables were included in the *Encyclopedia*. Both Scottish and American editions left out Tables 1, 2, 3, 4, 7, 8, 11, 13, 17, 19, 20, 21, 22, 25, 26, 33, 34 and 35. Tables 1-3 are of bare pelvis bones; Table 4 is the close-up of a woman's genitals; 7 is the dissected torso; 8, 13, 20, 21, 22, 25, 33 and 35 depict fetuses in utero; 11 is the gravid uterus; 17, 19, 26, and 34 are the cartoons.

The *Encyclopedia* did include some images of pelvic bones and fetuses in utero, although in greatly reduced numbers. While each exclusion is worthy of analysis, here, I focus on the exclusion of Tables 4 and 7 and the cartoons. Together, these six images are some of the more disconcerting from the *Tables*.

The cartoons are disorienting and unusual. They do not follow the standard conventions of anatomical drawings in that they do not adhere to any sense of realism. They look unfinished and their swirls of black lines force the eye to work to make sense of them. Perhaps they were simply deemed too technical or too alien to be of interest to a general audience. It is easier to speculate on why Tables 4 and 7 were left out, however. Table 7 (Figure 2.5) depicts a dissection *in media res*. It unabashedly shows a cadaver, with her breast and genitals exposed. In this regard it is quite distinct from the images that show fetuses in utero. In many ways, they were merely updated versions of the familiar baby-in-a-bottle images (Figure 2.21) that had graced midwifery guides since the sixteenth century.[110] These images depict disembodied uteri and pelvises, and while their realistic detail might be powerful, their shock value was limited by the exclusion of most of the gore of dissection, such as the exposed intestines in Table 7. Instead, their realism would offer the reassurance of being cutting-edge and sophisticated.

Similarly, Table 4 (Figure 2.9) was simply much too risqué, too pornographic, to include in a polite piece of learning like the *Encyclopedia*. Lay audiences did not share with medical professionals the need for a close-up view of the female genitals, nor could they be trusted to understand that medical professionals might have such a need, especially in an age that still mistrusted men-midwives as potential sexual predators. Moreover, its implicit display of female sexual arousal unmediated by signs of pregnancy would have undermined the claims of disinterested scientific authority claimed by the *Encyclopedia*. As bastion of polite learning, the *Encyclopedia* would need to promote the values of that society. Reproducing what looks like a close-up view of a *scène en flagrante* in an age that put a high premium on female sexual continence would have scandalized "lovers of science and literature" on either side of the Atlantic.

Over the course of the eighteenth century, conventions of medical atlases changed from representing idealized female forms that obeyed the conventions of Western art to hyper-realistic visions of dissection captured *in media res*. In obedience to demands of realism (as opposed to artistic conventions), medical illustrators included pubic hair on images of female bodies as well as close-ups of female genitals, bringing medical illustrations precipitously close to pornographic conventions that praised and eroticized a woman's bush. On one hand, as exemplified by Smellie's *Set of Anatomical Tables*, the presence of pubic hair could act as an orienting device for viewers. On the other, it created an image of universal "Woman" that was largely reduced to her sexual functions. This move, in many ways, was at odds with Anglo-Atlantic expectations that elite and middling women to control the erotic elements of their sexuality by exhibiting signs of sexual continence and restraint. The realism of medical illustrations, however, was at once the cause of this dilemma and its solution. Medical men, the primary audience for anatomical atlases, used the bodies of the poor as the subjects for their scientific inquiries and as models for their illustrations. Because new sexual mores eroticized women of the lower classes and of other races, inclusion of pubic hair (a sign of sexual appetite) could serve as a reminder that these bodies were lower-class.

Nevertheless, this contradictory image of the female body—at once classed yet universal—was disseminated throughout the Anglo-Atlantic world in Smellie's *Tables*. This book was transformed from an elite portfolio to a relatively cheap octavo, available anywhere books were sold in Britain and America. However, later engravers and publishers seem to evince some discomfort with the eroticized character of many of Smellie's images by removing or reducing pubic hair and frames. These types of alterations are most marked in the *Encyclopedia Britannica*, the most widely circulated venue for the *Tables*. In the *Encyclopedia*, almost all pubic hair was removed, and the most shocking of the images were simply not included, bringing them into line with the values of the dominant culture.

In the nineteenth century, pubic hair depicted in midwifery manuals became more realistic. Rather than the hyper-realism that detailed every follicle, giving the appearance of a decorative fringe, new conventions depicted the pubis as covered in a thick furry patch of undifferentiated hair. Yet the normalcy of pubic hair in medical illustrations did not translate into its acceptance in the culture at large. Instead, it became part of the special and taboo knowledge physicians alone were allowed to possess—thereby actually increasing its potential for frisson. Moreover, physicians still exhibited discomfort about female genitals. Midwifery professor Thomas James was remembered by his students for his extreme embarrassment on the days he lectured on female anatomy, while at mid-century, Dr. Charles Meigs, who had approved of his former teacher's shame, "begged" his students to join him in "the disagreeable task" of studying female genitals.[111]

At the same time, although race and class were becoming more securely located within the body, medicine maintained contradictory attitudes toward femininity. The quest for both universal principles and evidence for racial and social superiority within the female body continued. This duality is perhaps best illustrated in the career of Sims, who concealed the fact that his gynecological experiments were perfected upon African-American slaves and poor Irish women, going so far as to lighten his illustrations once he fashioned himself as the gynecologist to New York's elite.[112] The bodies of "respectable" white women, coded as both radically different, yet analogous to the bodies of Other women, were sacrosanct. Anatomical images continued to be made from the bodies of the underclass. Because pubic hair continued to be relegated to the sexual underworld, populated (at least in the "respectable" imagination) by fallen women, its presence in medical illustrations continued to function as a signifier of class; it continued to act as a safety valve for any erotic feelings such images might evoke.

The works of William Smellie continued to influence generations of men-midwives to come. They taught men-midwives how to see and imagine the female body and they taught them to think of themselves as medical heroes destined to save parturient damsels-in-distress. But these future heroes were not picaros or rogues bent on claiming a patrimony. Smellie had done that for them. Rather, as I will argue in the next two chapters, they claimed to be gentlemen, men of feeling, whose good sense and sensibility made them the ideal birth attendants for women, who continued to be, in one way or another, parturient damsels-in-distress.

# Endnotes

1   Portions of this chapter have been presented at the Southern Association for the History of Medicine and Science annual conference, March 2020, in New Orleans, Louisiana, and the American Society for Eighteenth-Century Studies annual conference, March 2011, in Vancouver, BC, and were worked into an essay, Marcia D. Nichols, "Venus Dissected: The Visual Blazon of Mid-18th Century Medical Atlases." In J. Zigarovich (Ed.), *Sex and Death in Eighteenth-Century Literature* (New York, NY: Routledge, 2013), 103-23.

2   Johnstone, *William Smellie*, 87.

3   Jordanova, *Sexual Visions*, 61-62.

4   Andrea K. Henderson, *Romantic Identities* (Cambridge: Cambridge University Press, 1996), 14-16.

5   McGrath, *Seeing Her Sex*, 65-69. See also Sappol, *A Traffic*, 78, 182. That a paradigm shift from generation to reproduction which coincided with the emerging capitalism of the industrial revolution actually occurred has come under criticism for being ahistorical. Allison Muir argues that modern scholars, working with a current definition of "machine" rather than a contemporary one, have misinterpreted what Smellie and other doctors meant when they used such terminology. She also argues that "production" and "generation" were synonymous in the eighteenth century. She suggests that if a shift from "generation" to "reproduction" did occur, it marked a shift in embryological theory rather than changes in society at large. See Muir, "Imagining Reproduction: The Politics of Reproduction, Technology and the Woman Machine," *Journal of Medical History* (2009): 53-67.

6   Lorraine Datson and Peter Galison, *Objectivity* (New York: Zone Books, 2007), 19-26.

7   Michel Foucault, *Discipline & Punish*. Trans. Alan Sheridan (New York: Vintage, 1977), 183-184. See also Julia Epstein, *Altered Conditions* (New York: Routledge, 1995), 9-10.

8   US National Library of Medicine, *Historical Anatomies on the Web*. Last updated August 26, 2016. http://www.nlm.nih.gov/exhibition/historicalanatomies/home.html. Examining actual copies of many of the works found on the website confirmed my impression of a shift in the way the female reproductive body was depicted.

9   Martin Kemp and Marina Wallace, *Spectacular Bodies* (Berkley: University of California Press, 2000), 11-19.

10   Female bodies, into the twentieth century, were typically only depicted to show

how they deviated from male bodies, i.e. the procreative body. McGrath, *See Her Sex*, 1; Laqueur, *Making*, 167; Kemp and Wallace, *Spectacular Bodies*, 67.

11   Lynda Nead, *The Female Nude*. (London: Routledge, 1992), 7. See also Julie Peakman, *Mighty Lewd Books* (London: Palgrave, 2003), 46-47. As Nancy Etcoff points out, "Although greater naturalism has pervaded images of female bodies in both high art and smut, body hair is still, at best, a sometime thing. Playboy models used to have their pubic region hidden or deforested. Botticelli portrayed women without body hair, but centuries later, so did Degas, Matisse, and Picasso" (97). Etcoff, *Survival of the Prettiest* (New York: Anchor Books, 1999). The earliest example of realistic depiction of pubic hair in a work deemed "art" that I could find is Rene Magritte's *Attempting the Impossible* (1928). According to the placard at the Minneapolis Institute of Arts, Gustave Caillebote's *Reclining Nude* (1880), which also depicts naturalistic pubic hair, was neither displayed nor sold during his lifetime because of its "sexual effrontery." Similarly, Gustave Courbet's scandalous *L'origine du Monde* (1866) did pass through a number of private owners in the nineteenth and twentieth centuries. It was not publically displayed until the 1980s. Since then, copies of it, from postcards to Facebook posts, have faced intermittent censorship.

12   Galia Ofek, *Representations of Hair in Victorian Literature and Culture* (Surrey: Ashgate, 2009), 8.

13   See Moscucci, *The Science* ,110.

14   Nead, *Female Nude*, 55.

15   Ofek, *Representations*, 14; Etcoff, *Survival*, 160-61.

16   Nead, *Female Nude*, 2.

17   *Ibid*, 29.

18   Lyle Massey points out that Hunter and Smellie also broke with convention by depicting anatomized cadavers in atlases strictly devoted to the gravid body rather than human anatomy in general. Massey, "Pregnancy and Pathology: Picturing Childbirth in Eighteenth-Century Obstetric Atlases," *Art Bulletin* 87.1 (2005): 75.

19   That men of science searching for nature's secrets through a process of unveiling was an old cliché, often envisioned as a strip tease of sorts, for instance the statue *Nature Unveiling Herself Before Science* (1889) by Louis Barrias, of a bare-breasted woman frozen in the process of undressing. Such imagery was highly sexualized—etymologically "nature" derives from "nascitura" (birth) and "Nature" was used as a euphemism for "a woman's privy parts... because all Men owe their origins to them" (19) Nicolas Venette, *Conjugal Love; or the Pleasures of the Marriage Bed* (1720). Ed. Randolph Trumbach (New York: Garland, 1984). See also Jordanova, *Sexual Visions* 87-88; Schiebinger, *Nature's*

*Body*, 59.

20   For more information on the ambiguous nature of anti-masturbation literature
     see Peter Wagner, *Eros Revived* (London: Paladin, 1988), 8-46; Peakman, *Mighty
     Lewd Books*, 45-48; McGrath, *Seeing Her Sex*, 38-61; Porter, "A Touch of
     Danger" 208.

21   See Guerrini, "Anatomists and Entrepreneurs," 219-34.

22   See Corner, *William Shippen*, 100. Both the original drawings and the images
     in the atlas depict hairless female torsos. Interestingly, while the acquisition of
     the Van Rymsdyck drawings was welcomed and they were immediately put on
     display, the showing of the first nude painting in Philadelphia was an occasion
     for scandal and community outrage. See Beatrice B. Garvan *Federal Philadelphia*
     (Philadelphia: Princeton Polychrome, 1987), 82. Moreover, the Pennsylvania
     Hospital expanded its anatomical attractions after it acquired Abraham Chovet's
     commercial display of skeletons and waxworks in the 1790s. See Knott,
     *Sensibility*, 85-86.

23   See Richard Altick, *The Shows of London* (Cambridge: Harvard University Press,
     1978), 54-55. A handful of similar anatomical displays were shown in America
     in the late eighteenth century; their numbers proliferated over the nineteenth
     century. See Knott, *Sensibility*, 237; Sappol, *A Traffic*, 274-312.

24   See McGrath, *Seeing Her Sex*, 16.

25   "Adollizing, or A Lively Picture of A Doll-Worship" (1748), *Eighteenth-Century
     British Erotica Set II*, Vol. 2, Ed. Deborah Needleman Armintor. (London:
     Pickering and Chatto, 2004), 325-36.

26   See Armintor, Headnote to "Adollizing," *Eighteenth-Century British Erotica Set II*.
     Vol. II, 304; Wagner, *Eros Revived*, 30-31.

27   See McGrath, *Seeing Her Sex*, 16; Kemp and Wallace, *Spectacular Bodies*, 67-
     68; Jordanova, *Sexual Visions*, 44-46; Francesco de Ceglia, "Rotten Corpses,
     a Disembowelled Woman, A Flayed Man. Images of the Body from the End
     of the 17th to the Beginning of the 19th Century. Florentine Wax Models in
     the First-hand Account of Visitors," *Perspectives on Science* 14.4 (2006): 417-56.
     Kemp and Wallace speculate that the ivory miniatures may have been owned by
     midwives or physicians as display pieces advertising their wealth, success and
     expertise.

28   Harvey, *Reading Sex*, 97.

29   See Laqueur, *Making*, 101; Schiebinger, *Nature's Body*, 121-25; Mary Fissell,
     "Hairy Women and Naked Truths: Gender and the Politics of Knowledge in
     'Aristotle's Masterpiece,'" *William and Mary Quarterly* 60.1 (2003): 54. See also
     Venette, *Conjugal Love*, 56-59.

30   "The Discovery," The Cabinet of Love (1739). *Eighteenth-Century British Erotica*

Set II. Vol. 2, 85.

31    Darby Lewes, in *Nudes from Nowhere*, mentions several poems that used the coney-cunny metaphor, including "Black Hare," The Hunt" (1720), and "Bring your Coney Skins Out" (1709). Lewes, 65-75. Our language still abounds in such euphemisms: Think Playboy Bunny, pussy, kitty, beaver, tail, muff, to name but a few.

32    *Little Merlin's Cave* (1737), In *Eighteenth-Century British Erotica Set I*, Vol. 3, Ed. Patrick Spedding. (London: Pickering & Chatto, 2002), 110-112.

33    Benjamin Franklin, "Old Mistress Apologue," *The Papers of Benjamin Franklin*, Vol. 3. Ed. Leonard W. Labaree. (New Haven: Yale University Press, 1961), 31.

34    John Cleland, *Fanny Hill, or Memoirs of a Woman of Pleasure* (1749) (New York: Modern Library, 2001), 90-91.

35    Robert Burns, *The Merry Muses of Caledonia* (New Hyde Park, NY: University Books, 1965), 47; 85.

36    *Ibid*, 112.

37    *Ibid*, 112.

38    *Aristotle's Complete Masterpiece* (1749), 15. See also Harvey, *Reading Sex*, 97. Schiebinger, *Nature's Body*, 165-72.

39    Lucienne Frappier-Mazur, "Truth and the Obscene Word in Eighteenth-Century French Pornography," *Invention of Pornography*, 205-07.

40    See McGrath, *Seeing Her Sex*, 24; Kemp and Wallace, *Spectacular Bodies*, 13-15, 36.

41    Daston and Gallison, *Objectivity*, 42.

42    Jordanova, *Sexual Visions* 46.

43    McGrath argues that the very engraving technique chosen by the author is fundamentally important to understanding the epistemological thrust of individual atlases. See McGrath, *Seeing Her Sex*, 65.

44    Such comparisons were perhaps inevitable: Perhaps the two most influential men-midwives of their day, Smellie had briefly been Hunter's teacher. Although their relationship was often rocky, the two men continued to interact professionally, attending the same rare dissections of pregnant women and using one of the same artists to with very different results. See McGrath, *Seeing Her Sex*, 67-92; Jordanova, *Sexual Visions*, 61-63; Ludamilla Jordanova, "Gender, Generation and Science: William Hunter's Obstetrical Atlas." In *William Hunter and the Eighteenth-Century World*, 385-412; Henderson, *Romantic Identities*, 11-37; Cody, *Birthing the Nation*, 165-67; Johnstone, *William Smellie*, 87.

45    Jordanova suggests this type of detail was added "to make the body as life-like as possible." See *Sexual Visions*, 47.

46    Smellie, *Set of Anatomical Tables*, 2nd ed. (London 1761), n.p. italics in original.

47    See John L. Thornton, *Jan Van Rymsdyk* (Cambridge: Oleander Press, 1982) esp.

pgs 10-21.

48    Dr. Simon Chaplin, personal email, Dec. 14, 2009; Samuel Patterson, *A Catalogue of the Entire and Inestimable Apparatus for Lectures in Midwifery...By the Late Ingenious Dr. William Smellie* (1770).

49    Smellie, *Tables*, n. p., italics in original.

50    Quoted in Johnstone, *William Smellie*, 86-86.

51    Female corpses, especially pregnant ones, were rare and expensive commodities on the anatomy black market. Men-midwives had an advantage, however. They sometimes dissected women who died during labor, ostensibly to try to save the child, and often without permission of her family. William Douglas criticized Smellie for "butchering" women, even to save the child. Don C. Shelton has suggested that the women appearing in these atlases must have been murder victims because it is statistically unlikely that Hunter and Smellie could have successfully had that many bodies of pregnant women randomly exhumed. While this may be a possibility, Shelton fails to take into consideration some important facts. Smellie and Hunter were obstetricians who could and did dissect women who died while in their care. Additionally, as obstetricians, they were called in consultations whenever a pregnant woman fell ill, meaning that they would be aware of such deaths and be able to direct the Ressurectionists to the correct locale. Furthermore, most of Smellie's images are set up using the same cadavers with different fetuses, throwing doubt on Shelton's numbers. Shelton, "The Emperor's New Clothes," *Journal of the Royal Society of Medicine* (2010): 46-50.  Shelton's views are rebutted by A. D. G. Roberts et al, "William Smellie and William Hunter: two great obstetricians and anatomists," *Journal of the Royal Society of Medicine* (2010): 205-06. See also John Glaister, *Dr. William Smellie and His Contemporaries* (Glasgow: James Maclehose & Sons, 1894), 4-45; McGrath, *Seeing Her Sex*, 63.

52    Smellie, *Tables* (London 1761), n. p.

53    Smellie, Vol I, (London 1752), n. p, italics in original.

54    Smellie, *Tables* (London 1761), n. p., italics in original.

55    *Ibid*, n. p.

56    Smellie, Vol. II, 360-79.

57    See Lacqueur, *Making* 43-52 and149-63; Peakman, *Mighty Lewd Books*, 68-70; McLaren, *Reproductive Rituals*, 13-29; Paul-Gabriel Boucé, "Some Sexual Beliefs and Myths in Eighteenth-Century Britain" In *Sexuality in Eighteenth-Century Britain* Ed. Paul-Gabriel Boucé (Manchester: Manchester University Press, 1982), 36-40; Roy Porter and Lesley Hall, *Facts of Life* (New Haven: Yale University Press, 1995), 12-31; McGrath, *Seeing Her Sex*, 49-50; Sharon Bloch, *Rape and Sexual Power in Early America* (Chapel Hill, NC: University of North

Carolina Press, 2006), 39-40.

58    Smellie, Vol. I, 111-17.

59    McGrath, *Seeing Her Sex*, 81.

60    *Ibid*, 52. In Chapter 2 of *Seeing Her Sex*, McGrath analyzes the way a nineteenth-century medical text with images similar to Smellie's transitioned into a pornographic book, one copy of which was confiscated as contraband at Newgate. See 33-62. By the mid-nineteenth century, conventions for depicting pubic hair in medical books had changed, with hair being shown as a fuzzy black mass rather than delineating each individual hair.

61    For Smellie's *Tables* without frames, see editions engraved by Andrew Bell and published by Charles Eliot, Edinburgh, in 1780, 1784 and 1785 and one published by Isaiah Thomas in Worchester, MA in 1793. Samuel Bard, *Compendium of Midwifery* 4th ed. (New York 1817); John Aitken, *Principles of Midwifery* (London 1786).

62    See Roxann Wheeler. *The Complexion of Race* (Philadelphia: University of Pennsylvania Press, 2000), 182-88.

63    See Dierdre Cooper Owens, *Medical Bondage* (Athens, GA: University of Georgia Press, 2017) and Deborah Kuhn McGregor, *From Midwives to Medicine* (New Brunswick, NJ: Rutgers University Press, 1998), 24-28; 105-110.

64    Smellie, Volume II, 9-16. The most baffling of the cases in this section concerns a five year-old whose guardian (Smellie did not clarify the woman's relationship to the girl) had subjected her to two previous operations before Smellie successfully keeps her hymen from regrowing by stuffing her vagina with "a large tent." Smellie does not provide any context for why this surgery needed to be performed on such a young girl; however, the fact that three separate medical practitioners were willing to undertake it, and that Smellie was willing to share it with the world, suggests that nothing considered improper at the time was afoot. Nevertheless, it remains a disturbing read.

65    See Schiebinger, *Nature's Body*, 165-72; Harriet A. Washington, *Medical Apartheid: The Dark History of Medical Experimentation on Black Americans from Colonial times to the Present* (New York: Anchor Books, 2008): 82-85.

66    William Harvey, *On Generation*. In *The Works of William Harvey*. Trans. Robert Willis. (Philadelphia: University of Pennsylvania Press, 1989), 181-82; Sander L. Gilman, *Difference and Pathology: Stereotypes of Sexuality, Race and Madness* (Ithaca, NY: Cornell University Press, 1985): 85-92.

67    See for instances, Thomas Denman, *Introduction* 34. In the past fifty years, medical responses to "abnormal" female genitals have varied from advocating infant genital reconstructive surgery, to, more recently, some medical professionals and advocacy groups arguing for a more conservative response

that would allow patients to make their own decisions in adolescence and adulthood. See Epstein, *Altered Conditions, 79*-120; Anne Fausto-Sterling, *Sexing the Body*, (New York: Basic, 2000), 54-66; Jennifer Yang et al, "Nerve Sparing Ventral Clitoroplasty: Analysis of Clitoral Sensitivity and Viability," *The Journal of Urology* 178.4 (2007); 1598-1601; and Jennifer E. Reifsnyder et al, "Nerve Sparing Clitoroplasty is an Option for Adolescent and Adult Female Patients with Congenital Adrenal Hyperplasia and Clitoral Pain following Prior Clitoral Recession or Incomplete Reduction, *The Journal of Urology* 195.4 (2016): 1270-1274. Advocacy groups like the Intersex Society of North America (isna. org), InterACT (interactadvocates.org), and Human Rights Watch (hwr.org) are fighting to end medically unnecessary genital surgeries on children in the USA. In 2018, the State of California made it illegal to perform genital surgery on children until they are old enough to consent.

68    Katherine N. Kinnick "Pushing the Envelope: The Role of the Mass Media in the Mainstreaming of Pornography," *Pop/Porn*. Eds. Ann C. Hall and Mardia J. Bishop (Westport, CT: Greenwood, 2007), 10; M. Andrikopoulou et al., "The Normal Vulva in Medical Textbooks," *Journal of Obstetrical Gynaecology* 33.7 (2013): 648-50. "Episode 14: Labioplasty," *Hungry Beast*. ABC Australia. Originally aired 3/3/2010. Accessed 5/18/2010 on *Jezebel* http://jezebel. com/5535356/the-labiaplasty-you-never-knew-you-wanted-[nsfw]

69    Schiebinger, *Nature's Body*, 99-106.

70    John Hunter, *Essays and Observations* Vol. I, Ed. Richard Owen, (London: Taylor and Francis, 1861), 194.

71    James Anderson's notes from lectures by Benjamin Rush, 1797-98, Anderson Family Papers, 1797-1913, *HSP*. Emphasis added.

72    See Porter, *Flesh in the Age of Reason*, 258-71; Cody, *Birthing the Nation*, 249-58; Lyons, *Sex Among*, 298-307; Klepp, *Revolutionary Conceptions*, 260-65; John D'Emillo and Estelle Freedman, *Intimate Matters* (Chicago: University of Chicago Press, 1997), 84 and 142; Richard Godbeer, *Sexual Revolution in Early America* (Baltimore: Johns Hopkins University Press, 2002), 306-07. In medical school at Edinburgh, many future medical men pined for the "Ladies" whom they could not marry, while seeking sexual gratification from prostitutes or mistresses. See Lisa Rosner, *Medical Education in the Age of Improvement* (Edinburgh: Edinburgh University Press, 1991), 40-41.

73    Porter, *Flesh in the Age of Reason,* 247. See also Norah Smith, "Sexual Mores and Attitudes in Enlightenment Scotland," *Sexuality in Eighteenth-Century Britain,* 82

74    Qtd. in Lisa Forman Cody, "Living and Dying in Georgian London's Lying-in Hospitals," *Bulletin of the History of Medicine* 78 (2004): 339. Cody speculates that, as the only two lying-in hospitals that advertised male students would have

access to the wards were also the only two that admitted unmarried women, "it was these unmarried women who were exposed to pupils of both sexes, while married women were protected from all 'Persons of the Male-Sex'" (321). Using the poor as guinea pigs continued into twentieth-century hospitals. See Judith Walzer Leavitt, *Lying-In: Childbearing in America, 1750-1950* (Oxford: Oxford University Press, 1986), 73-78; Richardson, *Death*, 40-46; McGregor, *From Midwives*, 33-57; Washington, *Medical Apartheid*, esp. 189-215; and Susan M. Reverby, *Examining Tuskegee* (Chapel Hill, NC: University of North Carolina Press, 2009).

75    See Rosner, *Medical Education* 55.

76    See Lisa Forman Cody, "The Politics of Reproduction: From Midwives' Alternative Public Sphere to the Public Spectacle of Man Midwifery," *Eighteenth-Century Studies* 32.4 (1999): 484.

77    MacKenzie's student William Shippen recorded "examining" seventeen women during MacKenzie's lecture on touching. Shippen would follow his preceptor's example, and hire poor women to act as teaching aids when he began offering midwifery courses upon his return to Philadelphia. See Corner, *William Shippen*, 19.

78    In *Spectator* No. 155, for instance, Richard Steele wrote about the plight of female proprietors of shops and coffeehouses who were regularly sexually harassed by male customers. See *The Commerce of Everyday Life*, ed. Erin Mackie (Boston: Bedford/St. Martin's, 1998), 213-16. On sexual vulnerability of servants see Sharon Bloch, *Rape*, 64-75; Lyons, *Sex*, 280-87; and Bridget Hill, *Women, Work & Sexual Politics in Eighteenth-Century England* (Montreal: McGill-Queen's University Press, 1989), 80-8 and 146-47.

79    John Leake, *Dissertation upon the Lisbon Diet Drink*, 3rd edition (London 1762). By the 1787 edition, Leake was much less reticent about revealing identifying details about well-to-do patients. This could perhaps be accounted for by their deaths in the intervening 25 years.

80    White, *Treatise*, 174-75.

81    Smellie, Vol. II 189-91. See also Wilson, *The Making*, 185-92; Cody, "Living and Dying" 342-48.

82    The 1832 Anatomy Act would indeed turn any poor person "unclaimed" by relatives the property of the hospital and subject to dissection. At the time, "unclaimed" meant that the deceased's relatives were unable to afford burial. See Richardson, *Death*, 195-225.

83    Not included in this count is an abridged version of the *Tables* was published in London in 1837, nor the European translations. Several other midwifery writers borrowed images from Smellie, including John Aiken, *Principles of*

*Midwifery* (London 1786) and Samuel Bard, *Compendium on the Theory and Practice of Midwifery*, 4th ed. (New York 1817), whose work will be discussed in Chapter 4.

84   See Sher, *The Enlightenment and the Book*, 622.

85   See *C. Elliot, T. Kay, and Co's Catalogue of Books, in all the Different Branches of Medicine, Surgery, Anatomy, Natural History, &c. &c. For the Year 1788*. The first edition of Hamilton's textbook intended for his male pupils (although marketed more widely), *Elements of Midwifery,* published in London in 1775, exploded with rage at the degradation of surgeons by their physician brethren. After he was appointed Chair of Midwifery at the University of Edinburgh, he reissued it with a conciliatory preface echoed its new title, *Outlines on the Theory and Practice of Midwifery*, which suggests he perhaps thought of himself as Smellie's intellectual heir. According to Elliot and Kay's London catalog of 1788, either book could be had separately or bound with Smellie's Tables.

86   Sher, *Enlightenment*, 6. See also Warren McDougall, "Charles Elliot's Medical Publications and the International Book Trade," *Science and Medicine in the Scottish Enlightenment* (Glasgow: Tuckwell, 2002), 218-220.

87   McDougall, "Charles Elliot's," 216.

88   *Ibid*, 228-32.

89   F. C. W. "John Norman" *Dictionary of American Biography*, Vol XIII. Ed. Dumas Malone (New York: Charles Scribner's Sons, 1934), 550-51.

90   See Glaister, *Dr. William Smellie*, 289-90.

91   Sher, *Enlightenment, 387.*

92   See James N. Green, "The Rise of Book Publishing," In *History of the Book in America*, Vol. II, Eds. Robert A. Gross and Mary Kelly (Chapel Hill: University of North Carolina Press, 2010), 75-127.

93   See Clifford. K. Shipton, *Isaiah Thomas: Printer, Patriot and Philanthropist.* (Rochester, NY: Leo Hart, 1948), 43-44; 63-68; Cathy Davidson, *Revolution and the Word.* (Oxford: Oxford University Press, 2004), 159-60.

94   I am still struggling to make sense of the hybridity of Thomas's edition. It would appear that he choose the images from the Bell edition rather than using the more accurate ones from Lizars, which is highly suggestive. I do not believe that Elliot ever published an edition of the *Tables* with Bell's plates and Hamilton's notes. In any case, I have never seen such an edition, which, of course, does not mean one does or did not exist.

95   Advertisement, *Pennsylvania Packet and Daily Advertiser.* November 9, 1785. 4.

96   See Sher, *Enlightenment*, 556-61; Robert D. Arner, *Dobson's* Encyclopedia (Philadelphia: University of Pennsylvania Press, 1991), 60-74.

97   See Sher, *Enlightenment, 330-72.*

98    *A Catalogue of the Books Belonging to the Medical Library in the Pennsylvania* Hospital (Philadelphia 1790), 5.

99    These are the prices listed in Elliot's sale catalogue and Dobson's ads, respectively. Lisa Rosner, "Student Culture at the Turn of the Nineteenth Century: Edinburgh and Philadelphia." *Caduceus* 10.2 (1994): 74. Current prices were calculated using the real price index calculator on the website *MeasuringWorth.com* , http://www.measuringworth.com/calculators/. Accessed on 09/08/2018.

100   See Wilson, *The Making,* 202.

101   See Cody, "Living and Dying," 317.

102   See Harvey, *Reading Sex,* 39.

103   See Rosemaire Zagirri, *Revolutionary Backlash* (Philadelphia: University of Pennsylvania Press, 2007), 51.

104   For biographical information on Sewall, see Christopher Beneditto, "A Most Daring and Sacrilegious Robbery." *New England Ancestors* 6.2 (2005): 31-34; the copy owned by Sewall is held at the College of Physicians, Philadelphia, PA. Sewall was also an accomplished engraver, and many of the plates have pencil grids, dated 1806, drawn over them as though Sewall were practicing medical illustration before he entered the Harvard Medical School in 1807.

105   Historian Thomas H. Johnson decided the book in question  must have been one of the *Aristotle* titles based upon the testimony,  because one person mentioned "Aristotle," although another said the title was *The Midwife Rightly Instructed* and was a new book, and another saying it contained pictures of the female body. Most of the *Aristotle* books only contain images of monsters, though some do contain an image of a dissected woman's torso, which could be the image referred to. Johnson decided that the girl mistook the title for a newly reprinted *Aristotle's Experienced Midwife.* Scholars have since accepted his assertion as correct. However, as Ava Chamberlain has pointed out, there were likely two books in circulation, one of the *Aristotle* books and Thomas Dawkes' *The Midwife Rightly Instructed* (1736). Thomas H. Johnson, "Jonathan Edwards and the 'Young Folks' Bible.'" *NEQ* 5.1 (1932): 37-54; Ava Chamberlain, "Bad Books and Bad Boys: The Transformation of Gender in Eighteenth-Century Northampton, Massachuestts," *NEQ* 75.2 (2002): 179-203; Mary E. Fissell, "Making a Masterpiece: The Aristotle Texts in Vernacular Culture." *Right Living: An Anglo-American Tradition of Self-Help Medicine and Hygiene.* Ed. Charles E. Rosenberg (Baltimore: Johns Hopkins University Press, 2003), 59-87.

106   Arner, *Dobsons's,* 28-35; 72-73. Current prices were calculated using the real price index calculator on the website *MeasuringWorth.com* , http://www.measuringworth.com/calculators/. Accessed on 09/8/2018.

107   Arner, *Dobson*'s, 29.

108   This is not true of the Dublin edition, thought to be based upon the third
edition of the *Encyclopedia*.

109   Herman Kogan, *The Great EB: The Story of the Encyclopedia Britannica* (Chicago:
University of Chicago Press, 1958), 13.

110   See Keller, *Generating Bodies,* 136-39.

111   Charles Meigs, *Woman; Her Diseases* 2nd ed. (Philadelphia: Lea and Blanchard,
1851), 61-62. See also Donegan, *Women and Men Midwives*; and Leavitt, *Lying-in.*

112   See Owens, *Medical Bondage*, 111-113.

# Chapter Three

# Domesticating the Man-Midwife: Thomas Denman and the Accoucheur of Feeling

In *The Pioneers* (1823), James Fenimore Cooper satirizes medical education—or the lack thereof—with future "doctor" Elnathan Todd "learning" the art of physic at the "house of the village doctor...sometimes watering a horse, at others watering medicines...[or] lolling under an apple tree, with Ruddiman's Latin Grammar in his hand, and a corner of Denman's Midwifery sticking out of a pocket...."[1] While Elnathan's preceptor's pedagogical choices were beyond questionable and hopelessly outdated, his choice of reading for his pupil was not. Thomas Denman's *An Introduction to the Practice of Midwifery* was cutting edge in the 1790s, when Elnathan was busy learning physic. It remained in print as a standard obstetrics textbook for the first half of the nineteenth century and continued to receive praise well into the twentieth. However, Denman's long-lived work has been comparatively neglected by scholars. Outside of the three fictionalized diaries by Ernest Gray in the 1940s, and the reviews and critiques they've generated, only a children's book and an article by Dr. Peter M. Dunn have focused on Denman exclusively. In most scholarship, Denman's works are used more as a source than as a subject of investigation in themselves. This chapter seeks to remedy scholarly oversight by considering Denman's work in its contemporary medical and literary context.[2]

Denman's obstetric writings, especially the *Introduction*, exerted immense influence over the emerging professional field of obstetrics, and perhaps, British and American medicine as a whole. The *Introduction* reflected the non-interventionist stance most typical of early nineteenth-century man-midwifery. By the early 1800s, men-midwives positioned themselves as the practitioner who relied on the efforts of nature, only intervening in the most dire emergencies, while they positioned female midwives as "meddlesome."

Additionally, the *Introduction* worked as a conduct manual that presented medical men with a heroic self-image, recognizable in the context of domestic fiction, nearly a century before "the doctor" became an apt hero in novels. Working within the paradigms of domesticity and sensibility, Denman's obstetric writings constructed the medical man as the Accoucheur of Feeling, whose self-controlled, manly sensibility made him the best choice for birth attendant and general practitioner. Relying on an essentialist theory of gender, Denman's writings entered the discourse on the domestic—and domesticated—middle-class woman most clearly articulated in domestic fiction. The domestic woman was imperiled by the very sensibility that helped construct the interiority that defined her as desirable; thus, the Accoucheur of Feeling was impelled to rescue the domestic woman from the dangers inherent in her own body.

The sympathetic patience and reliance on nature taught by Denman was perhaps especially appealing in the nineteenth century, as medical men began recognizing the inutility of most of their therapeutics without having any alternatives to offer. Moreover, in contrast the rancorous medical marketplace, Denman's *Introduction* offered a model of fraternity and mutual uplift for the professionalizing medical field. Thus, Denman influenced Anglo-American obstetrics—and the medical profession as a whole—throughout the nineteenth century by offering his readers a means of self-fashioning that allowed medical men not only to distinguish themselves from low-bred apothecary-surgeons, quacks, and female midwives, but most importantly, to conceive of themselves as well-educated, and well-bred, gentlemen.

Denman's efforts to impart advice to young men on how to thrive, especially among a well-heeled clientele, works to "domesticate" the man-midwife. Rather than Smellie's picaresque hero-accoucheur, the *Introduction* creates a hero-accoucheur that mirrors the heroes of domestic fiction—sensible, genteel, and well-bred. Any hint of roguery on the part of this hero would be problematic, though a bit of the rake always threatened to peep behind the skirts of the Accoucheur of Feeling. Moreover, Denman's hero-accoucheur takes on ontological and nationalist significance as Denman separates women from other animals and British from European obstetrics. Because Denman's reputation only continued to rise during the nineteenth century, the Accoucheur of Feeling impacted the profession of medicine by creating a model of a hero whose primary form of action was inaction for the emerging field of obstetrics.

Much has been written about the eighteenth century as a time of great socio-cultural and political change. It has been called the Age of Enlightenment and Revolution, the age that witnessed the beginning of capitalism, nationalism, industrialism, and the modern self. Aspects of these myriad "revolutions" can be located within Thomas Denman's life and works.[3] The second son of a provincial apothecary, Denman rose from his humble beginnings to become one of the leading midwifery instructors in London, inheriting William Hunter's practice and becoming one of the first Licentiates in Midwifery from the Royal College of Physicians.[4] During his early career, he had published a handful of medical pamphlets and numerous contributions to medical journals, and in 1783, he published *Aphorisms on the use of the Forceps and Vectis*. By 1785, he had collected and expanded upon these in the first volume of his *An Introduction to the Practice of Midwifery*. However, the second volume was not published until 1790, causing "Chirurgus jun" to urge Denman to finish it quickly, "prefer[ring] a quarto edition."[5] In 1787, Denman issued an anatomical atlas, the eighteenth-century scientific magnum opus, entitled *A Collection of Engravings Tending to Illustrate the Generation and Parturition of Animals and of the Human Species*, which will be discussed below. Denman continued working on the *Introduction* throughout his life, producing five editions. He was apparently working on a sixth when he died. It was published in 1817.

Denman's impact on man-midwifery did not end with his death. If anything, it only increased with time. The treatise and aphorisms stayed in print in the US and Britain for over 50 years. Three more editions of the *Introduction* were published in London after 1820, with the final edition being published in London in 1839 under the title of *Elements of Practical Obstetricy*. The *Aphorisms* saw five London editions after Denman's death in 1815. Denman's works were widely reprinted in the new United States, with medical editors quick to publish "American" editions of the *Aphorisms* and the *Introduction*. In 1803, aspiring American midwifery teacher Thomas C. James, who had studied under Osborne and Clarke in London, issued an edition of the *Aphorisms*, praising Denman as "one of the most scientific and experienced practitioners."[6] James' edition was quickly reissued by Massachusetts printer Isaiah Thomas in 1807. American editions of the *Aphorisms* were published twice more in the 1820s. *The Introduction* was equally popular. A virtually unchanged version of the third London edition was published in New York in 1802 and Vermont in 1807. Then in the 1820s, New York midwifery teacher John Francis published a revised American edition (to which were added the *Aphorisms*), which went through four editions. Thus, Denman's works were a standard midwifery textbook for over fifty years.

The emerging concept of domesticity is crucial for understanding Denman's work and the emergence of man-midwifery generally. Michael McKeon in his masterful work, *The Secret History of Domesticity*, argues it was the carving out of the domestic as an interior private space that made the articulation of subjectivity possible. McKeon's discussion of the various levels of "domestic"—from the individual home and household interior to the articulation of the national in opposition to the foreign—sheds light on the ideological underpinnings of Denman's *Introduction*. According to McKeon, "the domestic is evidently not only a social, but simultaneously an epistemological practice." [7] In other words, "the domestic" is not only a sociopolitical space, but also a way of knowing, a way of understanding and comparing the family to the state, or even the tame to the wild. Thus, "domestication" makes it possible to articulate the interior space—the lying-in chamber—in which the practice of midwifery occurred as private, as well as the interiority of self, articulated by "the idea of sensibility," which "aim[ed] to articulate the relationship of the outside and the inside, the body and the mind, reason and the passions."[8]

In a similar vein, Nancy Armstrong argues that domestic fiction and conduct manuals for women carved out a space for the modern interiority of self by creating an ideal "domestic woman" who was desirable for her intrinsic qualities rather than fortune or birth. This allowed domestic novels to translate economic and political struggles into the formula of "the sexual contract"; "[t]hus they can pass off the ideological conflict shaping the text as the difference between a man and a woman…. Writing apparently gained a certain authority as it transformed political difference into those rooted in gender." [9] One of the results of this move was "producing a woman whose value resided chiefly in her femaleness rather than in traditional signs of status, a woman who possessed psychological depth rather than a physically attractive surface, on who, in other words, excelled in the qualities that differentiated her from the male."[10]

By providing gender essentialism with a scientific basis, medical writings like Denman's helped create an essentialist distinction between male and female that underpinned the ideology of domestic fiction. For writers like Denman, traditional distinguishing categories like rank or an emerging class consciousness were subsumed by women's common physical nature, which relegated her closer to the animal on the great chain of being. Indeed, the very thing that finally separated woman from animal—her "passions" or sensibility—was the very source of danger that made man-midwifery necessary. Woman's female nature meant that she needed to be protected from herself by the well-educated, right-feeling medical man.

## Sensibility and the Nervous Body

The medical paradigm of the nervous body and the concomitant concept of sensibility created the need for the Accoucheur of Feeling, whose sympathy could comfort and cure, making the dangerous physic and instruments that had come to be associated with man-midwifery no longer necessary. In fact, the rise of the Accoucheur of Feeling allowed male practitioners to project "meddlesome midwifery" onto the shoulders of the traditional female midwife, whose messy, painful profession would have blunted her delicate feminine sensibilities. Sensibility, widely promoted in novels and other belletristic writings, had its foundation in philosophical and medical writings. The late eighteenth-century cult of sensibility was a social attitude that idealized feeling as the best index of a person's self. Properly attuned sensibility dictated an individual's personal responses and tastes, but more importantly, sensibility enabled a person to feel sympathy—the very glue of social relationships. Enlightenment philosopher David Hume described "the human mind" as "very imitative." Thus, the mind's capacity for sympathy "makes us enter deeply into each other's sentiments, and causes like passions and inclinations to run, as it were, by contagion" through a group of people.[11] Sympathy enabled sentiment—feelings—to be shared among friends, neighbors, the nation, doctor and patient. Although sensibility was a human capacity, nevertheless, it was not equally available to everyone. Because sensibility was the bodily conduit of sense impressions to the mind, some people were "naturally" more sensible than others; moreover, education and environment could either blunt or refine one's sensibility. Most medical instructors advised their students to find a *via media*—they mustn't let their education blunt their sensibility, yet overly sensible practitioners would lack the manly firmness necessary to engage in the bloody work of obstetrics.

Paradigms for understanding the body were in flux in the eighteenth century. The old humoral concept of the body was being replaced with a new conception of the body as a nervous, sensitive machine (although the traditional focus on balance, with bleeding and purging to attain it, remained the dominant therapeutics).[12] This nervous body was a network of irritable nerves affected by the senses—touch, sight, taste, hearing, smell. Sensory overload (or underload) from any source could disrupt the balance of the body and cause disease. Thus, violent irritation of the nerves could "not only occasion disorders in particular nerves, but may be a cause of the sympathy so frequently observed among the nerves; which is so necessary to be attentively regarded in many diseases, in order to discover their true state and nature...."[13] In other words, the irritation of one nerve could cause the other sensitive fibers of the body to respond in kind, disrupting and disordering health. Nerves, even when "too small to be traced,"[14] were the source of pain and suffering. According to Karen Halttunen, "The eighteenth-century cult of sensibility redefined pain as unacceptable and indeed eradicable and thus opened the door to a new revulsion from pain, which, though later regarded as 'instinctive' or 'natural', has in fact proved to be distinctly modern."[15] Thus, humanitarian narratives, including medical case studies, often focused on pain in agonizing, yet titillating, detail.

Conceptualizing the body as a sensitive system required medical men to focus on the alleviation of pain in contrast to previous therapeutic models that treated pain as a necessary fact of life. In fact, Denman averred that man-midwifery began because "the passions of men are deeply interested, and there is more than common tenderness mixed with our concern for those who suffer" in childbed.[16] It was crucial for medical men to be able to sympathize with their patients—to be sensible to the pain of their patients. To be, in other words, medical men of feeling, who could listen and empathize. The role of sympathetic listener was especially important for men-midwives, whose assiduities would be necessary if they were to win over the "delicate" women of the middle and upper classes as their clientele. William Hunter counseled his students to exhibit "tenderness, assiduity, and delicacy"[17] toward their patients.

Of course, sensibility could be too acute. One has only to think of Jane Austen's *Sense and Sensibility* (1811). In it, Marianne nearly dies because her nerves are all afire and her constitution delicate because of her novel and poetry reading.[18] Similarly, Henry MacKenzie's titular *Man of Feeling* (1771) Harley meets an untimely demise because of his tender heart.[19] A medical practitioner with sensibility like theirs would quail under the demands of eighteenth-century physic. As John Gregory explained to young practitioners, "a physician of too delicate sensibility is often rendered incapable of doing his duty by anxiety and excess of sympathy." To do his duty, a physician must act "with...steadiness and vigour."[20] The bloody, smelly work of physic required "a cool head" and "a guard over...imagination."[21] A successful, sensible medical man would need to be able to sympathize with the pains and anxieties of his patients, yet subject them to excruciating treatments like surgery without anesthetic. The medical man of feeling would need to be known both for his suave bedside manner as well as his vast collection of anatomical preparations, including skeletons; at least "two preparations of the trunk of a child, the one presenting a fore-view, the other a back-view of the whole viscera; and as many preparations of the organs of sense and generation."[22] In other words, a medical man of feeling would need to be able to tenderly treat an ill child and yet, upon the child's death, be able to dispassionately bisect it and carefully preserve it in wax in order to display it in a curio cabinet.

The medical man's dispassion could bring against him the charge of being an insensible butcher, hacking and slashing away without consideration for the patient or their family. Popular satires of medical men often characterized them as such. For example, William Hogarth's anatomists in his *Fourth Stage of Cruelty* are as insensible as Tom Nero. It appears that the physician overseeing the dissection, though disgusted with the corpse, exhibits no sympathy for it or the other bodies being prepared for anatomical display. The surgeon, on the other hand, with his coarse features and enormous butcher knife, seems to downright relish in his noisome occupation. Surgeons were especially liable to accusations of insensibility because of the nature of their profession. As midwifery was typically classified as a specialty of surgery, men-midwives were not exempt from such charges. *The Petition of Unborn Babes* (1751) describes in lurid detail the surgical interventions of men-midwives from the perspective of the fetus as the "cruelties" of "wicked men" whose "polite and tender Behavior" masks a mercenary thirst for high fees.[23] While some midwifery writers actively and aggressively responded to such charges, others, like Denman, responded more subtly through the construction of the man-midwife as hero.

## Domestic Fiction

Functioning as exemplars of hegemonic masculinity against which men both judge themselves and are judged,[24] fictional heroes help define and promote prescriptive gender roles for the society and culture in which they are created and consumed. Domestic fiction of the late eighteenth and early nineteenth centuries, often defined as female bildungsroman, follows the perils of a young woman as she navigates the dangerous world of courtship to become safely ensconced in the domestic sphere as a wife. Such fiction also functioned as conduct literature, teaching proper manners and etiquette to their middle-class heroines—and heroes. These novels defined the hero as the man of feeling, whose capacity for sympathy, education, and taste (rather than mere rank) qualified him as a well-bred gentleman. To understand the Accoucheur of Feeling, it is useful to compare the ideal of masculinity articulated in domestic fiction and Denman's *Introduction*.

There are two basic types of heroes in domestic novels—the dashing and hot-blooded rake who needs to be reformed, and the affable, but blundering gentleman whose energies need purpose. Bonnie Blackwell argues it is the former to which medicine looked: "Thematically, the medical tracts borrow plots from sensibility stories: the central, animating goal of both genres is the reformation of a rake."[25] According to Blackwell, it is by "imbibing modesty and virtue from a woman whose strict bodily propriety is the chief measure of her value."[26] Blackwell's interpretation is derived primarily from the criticisms and lampoons of man-midwifery. To combat such bad publicity, the self-image of man-midwife projected in male-authored midwifery treatises was quite different. The hero-accoucheur created by male midwifery authors was not the rake in need of reform, but the sensible gentleman in need of direction. Moreover, that transformation comes not from erotically-charged contact with patients, but rather from emulating the ideal practitioner constructed by these authors. Medical students were urged to emulate a "Man of…Goodness and Humanity" and to act with "the greatest Deliberation" and maintain the strictest "Sobriety."[27]

Thus, it was not the rake in need of reform that male-authored midwifery treatises look to, but rather the type of domestic hero whose sensibility is moderated by reason. The heroes are eminently polite, cultured young men, sensitive to the needs and honor of the ladies upon whom they wait. The epitome of sensible manhood, *Evelina*'s (1778) polished Lord Orville, is a fashionable, genteel, yet sensitive and cultured hero. Lord Orville engages in no peccadilos, never exercises his aristocratic imperative tyrannically. He is wealthy and generous without being a spendthrift. This flawless peer treats not only ladies with courtesy but is even outwardly courteous to the prostitutes with whom he is appalled to see Evelina.[28] This is the type of good breeding a man-midwife, whose cases might take him from the stews to most fashionable drawing rooms, needed to emulate.

But not all heroes of domestic fiction could be so accomplished. *Sense and Sensibility*'s (1811) Edward Ferrars is so shy and unassuming that Marianne accuses him of lacking sensibility. He certainly lacks drive. He is so inactive, in fact, that it constantly gets him into trouble. He passively allows Eleanor to fall in love with him. Even when he realizes he shares her feelings, he lacks the will to break up with Lucy in order to pursue Eleanor or to defy his mother for either woman. It is not until his engagement with Lucy is discovered that Edward is forced into action, first by getting a job, and, when finally released from Lucy's clutches, by actively pursuing Eleanor.[29] In contrast, *Belinda*'s Clarence Hervey must learn to be more like Edward and Lord Orville—Hervey struggles to reconcile his native sensibility with the supercilious hegemonic masculinity of the aristocracy he admires. Thus, he half-heartedly engages in the pointless and often cruel gambling (Hervey loses on one occasion because he did not trample playing children) in which his bored, wealthy friends occupy their time, as well as allowing everyone to think he's the lover of Lady Delacour. Edgeworth's novel charts his education in sensible masculinity as much as it does Belinda's entrée into the fashionable world.[30] Hervey must learn not only when not to act, but also the importance of the appearance of propriety.

Similar to such domestic novels, Denman's *Introduction* functions as a sort of conduct manual teaching its young male readers proper conduct to create a stellar reputation that will guarantee entrance to the best bedrooms in town. The two volumes offer a lengthy history of man-midwifery, tracing it to the ancients, interior and exterior anatomy and diseases, menstruation, conception, pregnancy, the different types of labor, and instrument use. Denman described writing the *Introduction* as kind of successful labor, whose fruit made the pain of reading it useful. He hoped that his *"reader will discover that pains have been taken to render it* [his book] *less unworthy of his regard; and the hope of being useful to those who are engaged in studies of this kind has converted the trouble into pleasure."*[31] On the one hand, the instructions in anatomy and obstetrical techniques teach the young practitioner that inaction is often the best course, but when action is required, he must not hesitate. On the other, the treatise provides many hints on the etiquette, carriage, and sympathy a man-midwife needed to display to his female patients. For example, after a "young lady" found herself physically disabled during and after her third, fourth, and fifth pregnancies, Denman accommodated her need to understand her own condition: "At the request of my patient, I explained upon a skeleton the opinion entertained of her complaints...."[32] He took the time to educate this woman on her own anatomy and his theory of her ailment rather than dismissing her curiosity as unimportant.

The tone and style of the treatise make it seem more like a friendly conversation among men who are bonding over a shared interest in "Woman." My thinking is influenced by Eve Sedgwick's analysis of erotic triangles in her masterful *Between Men*, in which she argues that in the traditional erotic triangle of two men vying for the affection of a woman, the relationship between the men is more important than either's relationship with the woman. Both individual women and the concept of "Woman" function much the same way in male-authored midwifery writings.[33] As a type of literary erotic triangle, Denman's *Introduction* creates a Hero-Accoucheur of Feeling—a politely mannered, sympathetic practitioner who is also concerned with his own reputation, the reputation of his friends and fellow practitioners, and of the profession as a whole. The man-midwife must strive for the polish of Lord Orville. Like Edward, he must learn when to act, and like Hervey, he must learn when to refrain from pointless actions as well as the importance of appearances. Appearances were crucial for the young man who hoped to rise socially and professionally in a field against which many still looked askance.

## Domesticated Woman

This lack of focus on the female body as the field of action makes Denman unusual among eighteenth-century medical authors. Early modern scientific endeavors were frequently described as the exploration of a feminine nature's "secrets"—in other words, natural philosophy (including medicine) was imagined as the sexual conquest and subsequent control of a chaotic feminine essence in opposition to "masculine" culture. Indeed, male medical interest in gynecology and women's health had been (and perhaps remains) about controlling and containing the unruly female body. As discussed in Chapter One, for Smellie, the dominant metaphor of this attempt was that of the female body as *terra incognita* to be explored and its borders defined. Hence, the sexual frisson of scientific discovery sizzles from every page as the picaresque accoucheur maps the female body. In contrast, such cupidity would be too dangerous for the reputation of the Accoucheur of Feeling. Thus, Denman employed a different, less sexually charged metaphor for femininity.[34] Rather than chaotic or wild, Woman, for Denman, was a special order of domesticated animal.

Although the comparison between women and animals had existed at least since Aristotle, Denman's focus on comparative anatomy breathed new scientific life into the worn analogy. Denman shared John Hunter's interest in understanding humanity's place in the phylogenic tree of life, though it is doubtful he would have entertained Hunter's proto-evolutionary theories. Denman believed that "The knowledge of the peculiarities of the human species, or of the specific circumstances in which the constitutions of women differ from those of all other female creatures, may therefore be considered as affording the only just and true basis on which both the theory and practice of midwifery ought to be founded."[35] In fact, Denman began his teaching lectures with an extensive review of comparative anatomy rather than the traditional history of midwifery, even briefly discussing plant and mineral propagation before moving to the more relevant viviparous creatures, and his anatomical atlas is a strange collection of comparative anatomy plates.

So what kind of animal was Woman? According to Denman, human women differed from "lower" animals in four basic ways: She walked upright, had a hymen and menstruated, and she was subject to "passions," including that of sexual pleasure. In all other ways, she was essentially like every other animal. Small differences in anatomical structure might exist, but they were largely inconsequential. From the six signs of approaching labor to the state of the uterus after sex, Denman argued that all a man-midwife might need to know could be learned from observing animals as much as humans. Apparent differences were the fault of civilization, and "if a woman was brought up Wild and had no instructions" she would deliver her baby "the same as an animal."[36]

The major difference between women and animals were "The Passions." According to Denman, "Animals are free from [passions]; but Women are not free from them; and it is of great Consequences to Midwives to know the Passions of the Mind; for if a Woman looks at you, & sees that you are afraid, her Pains will leave her."[37] In other words, the sensibility of women made them distinct from other animals. Even Woman's most important physical differences from animals—her hymen and monthly menstruation—were related to her passions. Menstruation itself was not different from the "equivalent discharge" of other animals—the difference lay in its frequency, which indicated women's constant state of readiness for copulation. Animals only discharged "at the time of their being salacious, or in a state fit for the propagation of the species."[38] Women's monthly bleeding meant they were always potentially salacious when not pregnant; in fact, "very chaste women" might have their "menses suppressed" because of their lack of sexual desire,[39] and "a girl that Menstruates late shews her to have kept good Company."[40] However, the hymen indicated that feminine sexuality was naturally "modest" and sex itself was "the peculiar indulgence granted by Providence to mankind."[41] Of course, excessive and dangerous sexual desire could be artificially stimulated by "Luxuriancy of Living, Love Talk, Loose Conversation, [or] Warmth of Weather."[42] Politeness, of course, would forbid love talk and loose conversations, even if the weather was beyond one's control.

Although women were desiring beings, their dominant passions were anxiety and suffering. And while all animals suffered during labor, "Women suffer more than other animals" because of the ill effects of civilization;[43] moreover, and unlike animals, women worry during their entire pregnancy because of the "passions of the minds." "These, in human beings, to a certain degree, in a natural state, and much more when heightened by all the refinements and perversions of society, are found to be capable of producing the most extraordinary effects."[44] Indeed, sensibility was to blame for most of the problems women experienced during pregnancy and labor, and a woman of too exquisite a sensibility could even cause fetal death or miscarriage. Sensibility and a woman's imagination were the biggest obstacles an enterprising hero-accoucheur would face.

Woman was different from other domesticated animals as well in that she would "suffer [men] to assist" her.[45] In fact, according to Denman, the entire field of midwifery, from its earliest prehistory of amulets and charms was developed because women's "supplications for assistance, and the affections of men, would not permit them to remain unconcerned or inactive spectators of the misery of those to whom they were indebted for the chief part of their happiness."[46] Sensible, right-feeling men would exert all their powers to relieve suffering women; the man-midwife, who dedicated his life and career to succoring women, must therefore be the paragon of manly sensibility.

Echoing the advice of other medical writers, Denman instructed readers that the Accoucheur of Feeling would need to be sensible to the fears and pains of his patient, yet temper that sensibility with cool reason and judgement in order to console her without letting "her fears or supplications for relief… prevail upon us to attempt to give assistance when our interposition is not required."[47] The proper action for a man-midwife was primarily inaction— allowing nature to take its course, except in rare emergencies:

> it is the duty of the practitioner to abstain from interfering….It may sometimes be necessary to pretend to assist, with the intention of giving confidence to the patient, or composing her mind. But all artificial interposition contributes to retard the event so impatiently expected…. For these reasons we must be firm, and resolved to withstand the entreaties which the distress of the patient may urge her to make, as we must also the dictates of vehemence and ignorance. Others may be impatient, but we must possess ourselves, and act upon principle. The event will justify our conduct; and, though there may be temporary dislike and blame, if we do what is right there will be permanent favour and reputation.[48]

The Accoucheur of Feeling would need to be calm and unflappable, never letting the emotions of others unduly influence his own. He needed to seem to be assiduous and active in the relief of the patient, or at least to talk soothingly to her and to take her fears seriously, even while attempting to dispel them. But he must never ignore the fears of his patient in the off-chance that they were indicative of a real problem, or if something else unfortunate or fatal occurred that could be blamed on his insensitivity because if "the complaint is not properly considered, but slighted or ridiculed merely as lowness of spirits, the event may prove unfavourable; and on recollection of the circumstances, there may be room to lament that it was misconstrued or disregarded."[49]

Because excessive female emotions posed the greatest threat to both woman and child, emotional caretaking was the main activity for the man-midwife. Fear, for example, could prove fatal to the mother or child by exacerbating the situation, or, earlier in the pregnancy, even causing miscarriage. It could also result in infant death and maternal injury if the man-midwife allowed women's fears to guide him: "Women, impelled by their fears and their sufferings in difficult labours, will very generally implore you to deliver them with instruments," even the crochet for a craniotomy having convinced themselves that the fetus was dead.[50] Men-midwives would need to "advocate" for the child and convince the woman to be patient. Although Denman, like Smellie, thought that "amusing" the patient with palliatives was typically the best course, when mechanical intervention was necessary, Denman, unlike Smellie, thought openness with the woman and her attendants was the best policy, even demonstrating "upon one of my knees, all that I intended to do with the *forceps*."[51] Such candor was the best means to dissipate fear.

The lessons on decorum found in the *Introduction* envisioned the hero-accoucheur as the consummate British gentleman. Denman's sensible, personable Accoucheur of Feeling would not engage in the breathless striving found in Smellie's *Treatise*. Instead, the Accoucheur of Feeling was not only skillful and knowledgeable but also exhibited candor and sympathy. Calm, cool, and collected, his politeness would lead him to treat every lying-in chamber as if it were a respectable drawing-room, and every patient as though she were a domesticated bourgeois lady. There, he would engage in friendly chat, gaining a woman's trust and confidence before attempting to inquire into her ailments or to physically examine her, which he would always do with the utmost delicacy to avoid bruising bodies or feelings.

## Women and other Animals in A Curious *Collection of Engravings*

Like most ambitious medical men of his era, Denman oversaw the production of an expensive anatomical atlas entitled *A Collection of Engravings, Tending to Illustrate the Generation and Parturition of Animals and of the Human Species* (1787). This unusual book visually establishes the equivalency of human and animal.[52] While comparative anatomy of embryos has remained of interest to natural historians and medical men since the days of Harvey, I am aware of no other folio anatomy atlases dedicated to this line of inquiry. *A Collection* is a collection of fourteen plates, ten of which are from humans. The other four contain a nut, a cocoon, and cuttlefish eggs (Plate 1); a frog (Plate 2); a hen's ovary (Plate 3) (Figure 3.1); a cow uterus (Plate 4) and a sheep uterus (Plate 11). Plate 11 disrupts the implied ascending order of the beginning (plant, invertebrate, reptile, bird, mammal, human), coming between the image of an inverted (human) uterus and the image of a uterus of a woman who died while approximately seven weeks pregnant. The disruption of the sheep's uterus conflates Woman with these other domesticated animals, driving home Denman's assertions that women were "the same as an animal." The differences in structure between hen, cow, sheep, and human were merely superficial.

Scientific atlases were published as definitive statements of erudition by the men who claimed authorial control. "They [Atlases] are the guides all practitioners consult time and time again to find out what is worth looking at, how it looks, and perhaps most important of all, how it should be looked at."[53] As discussed in Chapter 2, most anatomical atlases published in the eighteenth century focused exclusively on human anatomy. For Denman, however, much could be learned about reproduction from comparative anatomy. And no generative object was too common or too unworthy of examination—one could learn much about reproduction from the lowly Apricot seed—if one looked at it with the dissecting eye of the learned gentleman. Even more importantly, that gentleman was to look at things "in nature" whenever possible. Denman assured his readers time and again that all these images were "taken from nature." The images were meant to be the exact visual record of what one group of men (the scientists and artists) saw so that other men could diachronically share in the experience. In fact, Denman thought "accurate drawings" could replace Latin as the universal language since publishing in Latin had largely gone out of style.[54]

Atlases were expensive luxury items, items to be collected by men who wanted to display their own taste and learning. Although Denman claimed to be offering his atlas at a "modest price," he also hoped that his book would be "a source of elegant pleasure." In fact, he decided to include "no references, as the beauty of the plates would be thereby injured."[55] These images were meant to be consumed by a genteel male audience for their viewing pleasure. Perhaps the modest price of 10-15 shillings[56] was meant to make this collection affordable to the same ambitious young men to whom Denman's *Introduction* was addressed.

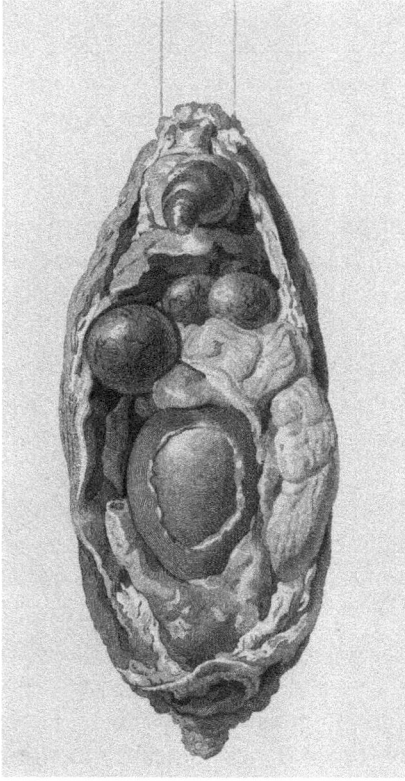

Fig 3.1 (left): Plate 3, a hen's ovary, one of several plates depicting the reproductive organs of various animals; Fig. 3.2 (right): Plate 7, a diseased placenta. The placenta bears a striking resemblance to the hen's ovary. In the era, the embryonic sac with all its contents was often called the "ovum." Courtesy of the Wangensteen Historical Library of Biology and Medicine, University of Minnesota.

Because these images are meant to be consumed primarily as images (the page facing each image does, however, have a brief explanation in English and French), the equation of human and animal becomes even more forceful— if one does not look at the explanation, it becomes difficult to distinguish an animal's uterus from a diseased human one. For example, the globular structures of the hen's ovary (Figure 3.1) look strikingly similar to that of a diseased placenta (Figure 3.2). The emerging hen's egg is just as difficult to distinguish as the blighted bean of an embryo near the bottom of the "human ovum."

Several of the plates (like Figure 3.2) are images of what Denman claimed were spontaneous "abortions"—what we would call miscarriages today. Physician collection of the matter expelled from the uterus during

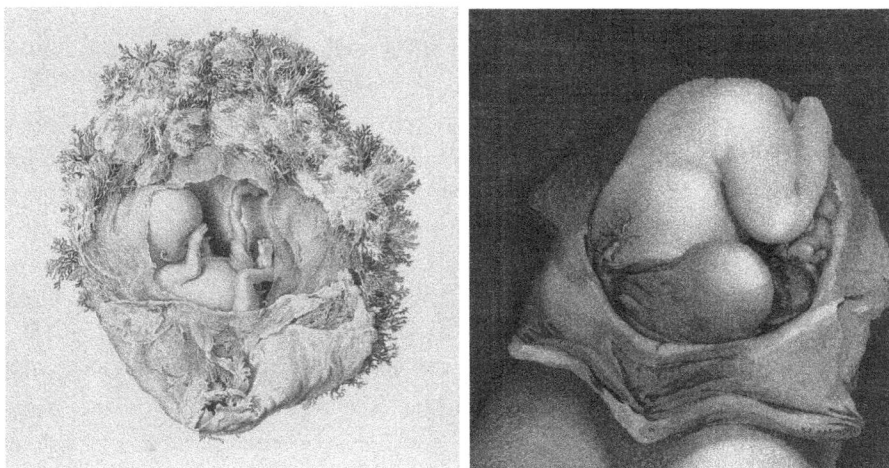

Fig. 3.3 (left): Plate 6 depicts what Denman believed to be a fetus at three months gestation (probably closer to eighteen weeks); Fig. 3.4 (right) Plate 10 depicts the aftermath of a ruptured uterus "painted from life." Note that despite the deep chiaroscuro, pubic hair is still visible. Courtesy of the Wangensteen Historical Library of Biology and Medicine, University of Minnesota.

miscarriage or failed birth was long-standing. For example, in the seventeenth century, Frederik Ruysch used tiny fetal remains extracted from miscarriage to create macabre dioramas, and physicians continued collecting fetal remains into the twentieth century as they sought to understand the development of life.[57] However, Denman was a promoter of what is now called "partial-birth abortion," mostly to save the life of the mother, averring that when it was "not possible that the lives of both the mother and child should be preserved" then to "secure the life of the parent," the man-midwife should treat "the child as if it were already dead."[58] Because of the perfection of the specimens depicted, we may wonder exactly how he obtained them. Indeed, the hyperrealism of one of the images, which Denman claims he got from a German named Nall, strains the imagination to believe that the embryonic sac with decidua still attached survived a vaginal miscarriage onto bedsheets or close stool before being retrieved and handed over to the anatomist who washed it several times in preparation for drawing it.

While the "beauty of the preparation"[59] is undeniable, it is also highly disturbing. At first glance, it could appear to show a small boy asleep inside of cave overgrown with brush or shrubs. Perhaps he is troubled, his hand pressed to his brow in distress. Perhaps he is Merlin, trapped in the tree by Nimue, aged backwards back to fetushood. In any case, the floral decidua—the endometrium lining during pregnancy—appear to be engulfing, suffocating the little homunculus. This maternal nature is chthonic, chaotic, and since we know this is an "abortion," deadly.

Plate 6 (Figure 3.3) stands in stark contrast to Plate 9 (Figure 3.4). Plate 9 (Figure 3.4) depicts the thighs and opened abdomen of a woman, a large fetus sprawling into her guts, her uterus contracted around its head. It is as though the baby from Plate 6 grew until it burst the maternal cave. The explanation informs the viewer that Denman was called to the woman, but she "died suddenly" after her uterus ruptured.[60] Although we cannot tell if this fetus was male or female, the presumption of maleness makes this image seem like a fatal triumph over the maternal body. Denman assures us, however, that ruptured uteri are not always fatal, and includes an image of a bestial-looking calcified fetus that had remained in its mother's abdomen for thirty-two years (Plate 14, not included here).

The images in Denman's *Collection of Engravings* visually work to equate women with "other animals" and to present the female body as diseased. The focus is not so much on the fetus as on the uterus and its monstrous productions. This is a female body that needs the superintendence of the man-midwife, without whom, a woman's body becomes her own worst enemy.

## Reforming the Rake

As discussed in the first chapter, much of the criticism leveled at man-midwifery accused practitioners of being sexual predators. Critics of male practitioners throughout the century charged that men, especially young men, could not be in such close physical proximity to women without lust being aroused. In fact, it was assumed only a "young man…[of a] lascivious disposition" would seek to enter the field of obstetrics in order to have easy access to women's bodies.[61] One had to look no further than men-midwives' own writings for evidence of such prurience; anti-man-midwifery tracts are filled with lengthy quotations that supposedly reveal the sexual impropriety of their authors. For their critics, men-midwives were nothing but rakes and libertines, out to prey on unwitting and incautious women.

Denman's focus on decorum is an implicit answer to such charges. The student reader he seemed to envision was not at risk for committing sexual impropriety but rather at risk for *accusations* of sexual impropriety, if his manners were not polished and his language delicate. In the Georgian medical marketplace, reputation was crucial for success. While publishing was one way of establishing one's chops—Denman reminisced that his 1768 essay on puerperal fever (a type of staphylococcus infection we now realize was often transferred by physicians' unwashed hands and instruments), "procured him some business" and his "letter to Doct Huck on the construction & use of the Vapour Bath" helped him "become more generally known"[62] – word of mouth would convey information about one's skill and behavior at the bedside much further, and not merely among current and potential patients. Several of the examples Denman mentioned are presented as events he "knew" about or had been "informed" about. Since Denman carefully attributed cases, opportunities, and information to their sources throughout the *Introduction,* these instances of non-attribution suggest that practitioners gossiped among themselves about the relative skillfulness of their fellows. Obtaining the good opinion of successful, older practitioners would be crucial for the young man who might need to call in a discreet consulting physician who could shield him from blame in unfortunate cases.

Proper decorum and skillful practice were equally crucial for a young practitioner to establish himself; thus, the *Introduction* scrupulously pointed out what behaviors and actions would help or harm the reputation of an Accouchuer of Feeling. For example, "Touching," or the manual examination of the cervix or vagina was, on the one hand, one of the most controversial activities of the man-midwife. Critics were scandalized that men touched the genitals of respectable women, seemingly with the permission of husbands! Philip Thicknesse bewailed such complacence, exhorting the husband who "loves his wife, or regards his own honor, seriously to figure to himself a smart Man-midwife, locked into his wife's apartment, lubricating his fingers with pomatum, in order to introduce them into his wife's *Vagina,* or into the *Rectum!*"[63] The gynecological examination becomes a pornographic fantasy in which the cuckolded husband imagines the doctor arousing his wife to a "Furor" with cantharides (Spanish fly) laced lubricant.[64] For Thicknesse, the detachment and dispassion of the medical gaze—or touch—was unfathomable.

On the other, the manual examination was an important diagnostic technique—one that, according to Denman, was crucial for the reputation of the accoucheur. Because touching was so controversial, Denman advised his students and readers to be cautious about their own reputation. The "examination *per vaginam,*" as Denman preferred to call it, must "be performed with the utmost care and tenderness, and the strictest regard to decency; for… an opinion is formed of the skill and humanity of the practitioner, and of the propriety of his conduct, by his manner of doing it."[65] Performed incorrectly, it could label the young practitioner clod or cad rather than a genteel (and successful) Accoucheur of Feeling. Unlike the intimate tête-à-tête, imagined by Thicknesse, Denman advised students to "never examine a Woman without a third person being in the Room."[66] Accusations of sexual impropriety could be avoided by the presence of a witness, including the husband, who could vouchsafe for the conduct of both parties. Thus, Denman implied, the best way to reform a rake was never to have been one in the first place.

Perhaps in response to the outrage at Smellie's explicitness, Denman's written account is vague about the process of touching, focusing on "first, the manner in which patients are to be examined; and, secondly, the information to be gained by the examination."[67] The use of passive voice continues throughout the entire section, mimicking the detachment the medical practitioner would need to assume during the consultation. However, in the homosocial privacy of the lecture hall, Denman was more forthcoming about the particulars of what to feel for under the covers. He advised students to engage in small talk before proceeding with the examination, to perform the examination carefully to avoid hurting the patient and one's own reputation, and "never let the People see you look at your Fingers":

> You must do it Tenderly, & Effectually, for if you Hurt her, she will be afraid of you, & they will judge of your abilities by it. He advises not to Examine a Woman immediately, when you are sent for to her, when she is in Labor, but sit down by the Bed Side & ask her several Questions; as how long she has been Ill, How many Pains she has had, & wether [sic] she bears down. After you have been in ye Room some time then Examine, the reason why he delays it as long as Possible is, they'll be Plaguing you to know what Part presents, how long it will be before she is delivered &c. After you have Examined he advises us to be carefull wth [sic] regard to our Prognostic, How long she will be before she is delivered, & rather wave it by telling her you don't mind the time as long as she goes on well, she must bear it with Patience; but if there is any danger you'll let them know. For if you should make a Prognostic that she'll be delivered in so many Hours & she goes longer, they'll loose [sic] their opinion of you, & very likely call in another Practitioner.[68]

Rather than a steamy scene of romance, patient consultation and the procedure of touching was an embarrassing ordeal for all parties involved, with young practitioners more gauche bungler than debonair rake.

The rakish image Denman sought to overcome was due in large part to critics' reading of Smellie, discussed in Chapter One. Smellie's *Treatise* was frequently quoted for evidence of men-midwives' inherent lasciviousness and sexual impropriety. The explicit description of the female body and the act of "coition" shocked lay readers unaccustomed to such frank descriptions appearing in what purported to be a polite work. Denman silently responds to these critics by practicing a genteel reticence. Compared to many contemporary works, the anatomical descriptions in the *Introduction* lack detail nor does it rehearse the controversies over conception that would have required a discussion of the many theories on how sperm meets egg.

Moreover, Smellie's numerous case studies provided critics with unlimited ammunition. Each of the case studies is a small drama filled with riveting details. The literary quality of the case studies[69] has is a factor in the long-term success of the book, according to both contemporaries and historians. In contrast, Denman's *Introduction* is remarkable for the near absence of similar narrative. In two volumes and over 1,000 pages, it includes just over twenty case studies, including his own and those of his contemporaries. In many ways, the paucity of case histories keeps the domestic private because the lying-in chamber is spoken of in the abstract without the narrative detail. Denman's reticence draws a veil over the lying-in chamber that protects female modesty. The generic interchangeableness of each patient takes the focus of the action off of the female body. The woman at the center of each case is most typically identified as simply, "the patient" or as a "young woman." None are very young or very old. Only three patients are identified as "ladies," with three more who were hospital patients, one a servant, one a soldier's wife, and one the "wife of an eminent tradesman." Thus, the majority of the women were seemingly unmarked by a particular class or station—or, rather, the middle-class woman becomes the unmarked default object of medical attention—just as she had become the default subject of conduct literature and novels.[70] Moreover, Denman seemed to have accepted wholeheartedly the dictums ensconcing woman in the private realm away from public (and male) prying eyes. The few case studies that are included in the *Introduction* are brief and focused almost entirely on the actions of the accoucheur rather than on his field of action, the female body. Thus, while the case histories, like domestic novels, should give a glimpse into the private world of the boudoir, instead they use anonymity and generalization to practice the politesse that the novels preach.

## The Domesticated Man-Midwife

Denman's *Introduction* not only domesticates Woman but also works to domestic man-midwifery as a thoroughly British enterprise, beginning with the requisite history of the field in the preface of the first volume. Most such prefaces focus primarily on the ancients, but include discussions of the contributions of important figures across Europe. In contrast, Denman's preface quickly summarizes the ancients, merely mentioning Hippocrates, Avicenna, Galen, and other classic writers to bring the story up to the Roman conquest of Britain, a seemingly odd discussion for a history of midwifery. In fact, the preface recounts a history of England, highlighting invasions by the Saxons, Danes, and Normans, until it arrives at the "beginning" of the English medical tradition with Roger Bacon in the thirteenth century. From that point, important medical and midwifery treatises published in English through the centuries fall under more detailed discussion. In the 1788 first edition, continentals Herman Boerhaave and Ambrose Paré both deserve "digressions," but in subsequent editions, Denman deletes Paré, pointedly ignoring French contributions to midwifery, a politically inflected silence during yet another British war with France. Rather, the lengthy preface works to affirm British identity by tracing the history of British medical writing or translations, in particular those which focused on reproduction and obstetrics, until 1740. Interestingly, by ending his history at 1740, Denman entirely left out William Smellie, considered by contemporaries as one of the most important writers and practitioners of the time. Nevertheless, the names of the greats— William Harvey, Thomas Sydenham, Francis Bacon—mingle with the obscure and largely forgotten—a John Arden of Newarke in Nottinghamshire, a Sir Ulrich Hutton who translated a book on syphilis, a Scottish surgeon named Peter Lowe. Man-midwifery is introduced as a private British affair.

This domestication of man-midwifery continues in the treatise proper. British practitioners are central to the text, while continental contributors are pushed to the margins. Of the fifty-six medical men mentioned by name in the text of the treatise, thirty-eight of those are British. In contrast, of the forty-two names that show up exclusively in the footnotes, only nineteen are British. (Seven British names and two continental European names are in both footnotes and the text). Of the eighteen continental names mentioned in the text, half of those are found solely in the history of the vectis, the instrument Denman preferred to use.[71] By confining continental European practitioners to the paratext, Denman literally marginalizes their contributions to the practice of midwifery. Man-midwifery, practiced by and invested in by medical men across the isles, from Scotland to Ireland, from London to Manchester, is consummately British. Similarly, Denman borrowed no case studies from eminent continental writers so the domestic scenes are all British. In fact, all but two of the twenty-six case histories come from English or Scottish practitioners working in London, including fifteen of Denman's own.

Thus, London became the epicenter of man-midwifery with Denman and his colleagues positioned as the *sine qua non* of man-midwifery.

In Denman's hands, man-midwifery became another way to consolidate a British identity in the face of American betrayal and the fears caused by the tumultuous early years of the French Revolution. Moreover, by constructing a British identity that included the Irish and the Scottish, Denman perhaps sought to ease ongoing anxieties about the provinces. By turning man-midwifery into a stolidly British affair, Denman perhaps sought to preserve the field from any taint of republicanism or regicide. Man-midwifery might be revolutionizing the medical establishment, but it had no intention of disturbing the social milieu.

This emerging nationalist identity enabled Denman to imaginatively link together upwardly mobile medical practitioners before class-consciousness had fully emerged. As Britain's social order shifted from landed aristocratic to bourgeois capitalist, new possibilities emerged for the aspiring sons of the middling ranks.[72] The successful London physician, with his chariot and cane, must have appealed to the ambitions of the provincial young men, like Denman himself, who came to the metropole either to further their education (at a private school like Denman's or with clinical experience at a hospital), or to pass the surgeons' exam to meet the military's capacious needs. The Oxbridge-educated elite might have looked askance at these motley upstarts fresh from apprenticeships, but the medical marketplace was open to those with the right skill, address, or connections. Denman's *Introduction* modeled how to acquire and utilize all three.

Rather than lingering on the interesting suffering of a worthy fair, the few case histories and the multitude of intertextual references in Denman's *Introduction* capture a coterie of male professionals, both surgeons and physicians, collegially working together toward a common end of professional uplift. Unlike Smellie's works, in which the subject position blurs to create a collective man-midwife, Denman carefully attributed his colleagues. Denman made it clear that most of the individuals he names were personally known to him, not merely authors he had read. He introduced many of them as "my friend" and many of the cases described as having been shared with him through personal correspondence. For instance, the first hospital case is introduced as being "so well described in a case sent to me by my very ingenious friend Mr. Everard Home."[73] Other practitioners are introduced as being personal acquaintances to Denman. He was able to participate in an autopsy "by favour of Mr. Cline"[74] and consulted with a "Mr. Watson, a surgeon of great experience and ability."[75] Denman was equally complimentary to all of the men-midwives and surgeons he mentioned by names. The only breath of animosity in Denman's commentary comes in a case history of Caesarean section originally printed in *Medical Observations and Inquiries*. In a footnote, Denman sniped, "It is remarkable that the oldest physician or surgeon in London, could not recollect a case of this operation, or had heard it spoken of by their predecessors; yet that two cases, in the same street, should have occurred to one gentleman, within a very short space of time."[76] Denman clearly disapproved of Mr. Thomson's alacrity with the knife and would seem to be hinting that the surgeon's unwonted experiments approached murder, as Denman averred that victims of the "Cesarean operation…will probably die, and should anyone survive, her recovery might rather be considered an escape than as a recovery to be expected."[77]

Denman's collegial tone is surprising in an era famous for its medical animadversion. Medical writers frequently spewed vitriol, often quite personal, as they attacked, criticized, and lampooned one another's medical techniques and practices. Few physicians, no matter how respectable, were above hurling accusations of quackery at their competitors[78] and some, like William Buchan, dared the wrath of the whole profession with his sweeping criticisms of "the Faculty."[79] Even the polished William Hunter publically engaged in a bitter conflict with Edinburgh professor Alexander Monro secundus over precedence in anatomical discoveries,[80] and privately, the elder Hunter alienated his brother John so thoroughly that they were never reconciled. In fact, Denman's own *Introduction* resulted in a public break with his long-time collaborator William Osborne, who announced in his own subsequent midwifery publication he was "astonished and mortified" by Denman's praise of the vectis and found himself compelled to "disavow" such pernicious practice.[81] Denman, on the other hand, modeled the polite collegiality and suavity needed by the young practitioner who wanted to aspire to Denman's London-based fraternity, even if only in imagination.

Within the printed pages of the *Introduction*, Denman's coterie becomes a virtual or imagined community available to a public shaped, at least in part, by the truth-claims of epistolary novels and newspaper and magazine correspondence. The letter, despite its careful crafting, was frequently understood as offering a glimpse into an authentic self and therefore became the vehicle for apparent truth-telling in a variety of genres.[82] It is perhaps unsurprising, then, that early case histories in medical journals were commonly presented as letters to the editors, or that authors like Denman, preserved the form of the letter in their own works. For example, some of the cases are introduced as letters, such as one "sent to me by my very ingenious friend Mr.

*Everard Home,* now one of the surgeons of *St. George's* hospital" or another communicated to me by Dr. *Maclaurin*."[83] The letter-writing coterie presented by Denman promised to reveal the authentic actions and interactions of established medical practitioners, to give insight into the actions and sentiments of men esteemed by the most eminent man-midwife of the day

The collegial tone of the treatise itself borrows the authenticity and authority of the personal letter. Denman's work becomes that ubiquitous letter of advice from elder to novice, like Chesterfield's letters to his son or the fictional Augustus Tyrold's oft-reprinted letter of advice to Camilla.[84] The inclusion of Denman's memoirs—which recounted his childhood, military service, and the beginnings of his London practice—in many of the nineteenth-century editions of the *Introduction* reinforces the apparent intimacy of the work. This was not merely a textbook, but the earnest advice of a man who once stood in the reader's shoes—those of a young man, with spotty training and little money but boundless ambition. Following Denman's advice and example would put the reader on the path toward success and honor.

## From Heroic Medicine to Medical Heroes

For much of the nineteenth century, British and American medicine was in a remarkable state of flux, yet a stable professional identity was also emerging. The unsettled catch-as-catch-can state of medical education at the beginning of the century settled down by the end into medical schools with recognizable academic and clinical programs and the establishment of licensure procedures.[85] New medical technologies like the stethoscope (and by the end of the century, the X-ray), new theories about the spread of disease with the discovery of "germs," new surgical techniques, and the use of anesthesia all transformed the practice of medicine. Interestingly, one thing that remained stable, however, was praise for Thomas Denman. While the first edition of the *Introduction* only merited "a favourable reception among" readers of midwifery books,[86] Denman's reputation grew with each successive edition. By the 1820s, a reviewer of an American edition averred that Denman's work was "absolutely, and by many degrees, the very best book upon the subject."[87] Falling out of print did not cause the tarnish of time to dull Denman's reputation. In 1850, another American doctor praised his works as "the best in the English language."[88] At the turn of the twentieth century, an English doctor agreed, calling *The Introduction* "perhaps the most splendid work on Midwifery in the English language."[89] On the one hand, Denman's largely non-interventionist stance surely appealed to the standards of practice in the nineteenth century, although, the equal popularity of the *Aphorisms* with the *Introduction* highlights the tension between non-intervention as the ideal and with the frequent use of instruments in actual practice. On the other, Denman's techniques and insights cannot account for the lavish praise heaped upon his works. Rather, Denman's Accoucheur of Feeling appealed to nineteenth-century medical men's heroic sense of self.

Nineteenth-century Anglo-American medicine was a hodgepodge of competing theories and practices. Because there was little state regulation, almost anyone could set up a shingle and practice the healing arts, and because, for most of the century, there were few effective therapeutics, irregulars appeared to have as much claim to practice as formally-trained doctors. Successful challenges to allopathic medicine like homeopathy, hydrotherapy, or Thomsonian medicine abounded. Traditional practitioners who obtained at least some formal medical training at American, British, or Continental medical schools were at pains to distinguish their practice as more qualified and professional than that of lay healers and quacks. Medical societies and journals were one way of doing so, as was the claim to anatomical knowledge and dissection experience.[90]

Man-midwifery was in a similar state as the profession as a whole. Almost anyone could claim to be a midwife or accoucheur, from the out-of-work hatter or illiterate milkmaid caught at a labor to the highly-trained men and women who had attended midwifery courses with respected teachers like the Hamiltons in Edinburgh or Thomas James in Philadelphia.[91] Most probably fell somewhere in between. In fact, just because a practitioner had attended midwifery courses did not mean he had had much clinical experience. One nineteenth-century physician recounted that at his first obstetrical case, he recalled "every circumstance that I had learned from books....But whether it was head or breech, hand or food, man or monkey, that was defended from my uninstructed finger by the distended membranes, I was uncomfortably ignorant, with all my learning, as the foetus...."[92] Nevertheless, by the early nineteenth-century, midwifery was considered a necessity for new medical men. Attending women during pregnancy and labor were often the first patients a new medical practitioner would have, and it was widely believed that the gratitude a woman toward her birth attendant would lead her to call in the same practitioner to treat additional family illnesses.[93] Moreover, midwifery courses, as inadequate as they often were, offered some of the only opportunities for real clinical practice for most medical students, making many students eager to take them, and by the early decades of the nineteenth century, many medical programs, including the medical school at Edinburgh, began making midwifery mandatory. However, midwifery was still considered a lower occupation, a calumny which its practitioners steadily fought against. As more and more hospitals and clinics that specialized in "women's diseases" were established and the development of specialty medical societies like the Obstetric Society of London in 1825, gynecology and obstetrics were gradually legitimized as lucrative and honorable male medical professions.[94]

In fact, medicine as a whole was professionalizing. Slowly, medical theory, practices, and practitioners were becoming recognizable by today's medical standards. Much of the work of this professionalization was done rhetorically through medical publication. Both medical journals and medical books helped create a fraternity of readers. The doctor-centered case history was an important part of this. Lisa Rosner argues that "In its presentation of the physician as hero, the romantic case history was part of the process of collective self-fashioning that we call professionalization....the case history as exemplary act of the well-educated physician had a part to play."[95] By envisioning themselves as heroes, medical practitioners could justify their actions to themselves and their colleagues. The language used in case histories presented the physicians' actions as the mythic striving for the life and health of the patient against Disease and Death. If the patient succumbed, it was the tragic defeat of the hero by disease. For example, in a case history of American obstetrician Charles Meigs, he describes the woman as "persecuted" with abdominal pain and pressure because of a prolapsed uterus, which he healed by pushing the uterus back into place, an operation which took "long perseverance" on his part.[96] In a second, the physician succeeded because he "watched for and seized the favorable moment" to replace an inverted uterus.[97] In a case published in *The Lancet*, the surgeon found his "fine-grown, well-looking woman, [who was] a little above the ordinary in height, freckled, [with] a profusion of dark-brown hair" in danger from a hemorrhage. He quickly acted, "introduced [his] hand into the uterus" and "withdrew" what of the placenta he could before he "ordered the child to the breast" and gave the woman ether, camphor, and an opiate.[98] The eroticized patient was the victim of her body and disease against which the hero-physician the hero actively strived to save her.

This idea is presented in Ivo Saliger's piece *The Physician Struggling Against Death for Life* (1920) (Figure 3.5), in which a broad-shouldered physician supports a supine, naked woman with one arm while pushing away a skeleton that is grasping at the woman's knees and breast. Here Death, the physician, and the patient exemplified as woman form an erotic triangle, with the heroic physician and a masculinized Death competing over a sexually objectified

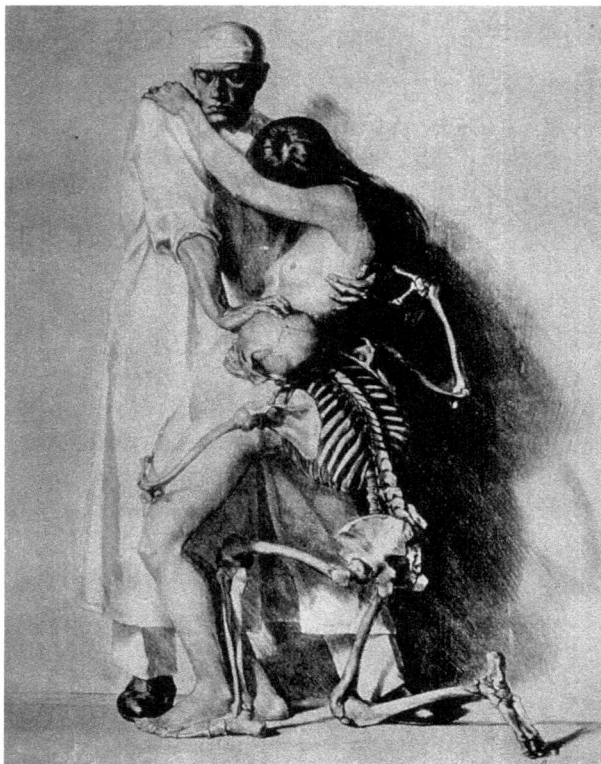

Fig. 3.5: This image presents the heroic physician rescuing the helpless female patient from death. Only his strong arms and wisdom can save her from death's icy grasp. Ivo Saliger, *The Physician Struggling Against Death for Life*. 1920 US NLM Digital collections.

woman. The woman in the image is completely passive, at the mercy of whichever of her suitors is successful. Of course, the confident, erect posture of the physician assures viewers that he, not Death, will claim the woman. Yet the woman is merely the object through which Death and the Physician battle—the doctor and Death gaze at one another, not the faceless woman who represents "Life," and we know that the object of the titular struggle matters less than the struggle itself.

Woman was the ideal medical object. "Woman was, by definition, disease or disorder, a deviation from the standard of health represented by the male."[99] As such, she demanded the attentions of medicine, inviting a medical gaze that, according to Foucault, "penetrates the body, as it advances into its bulk, as it circumvents or lifts, its masses, as it descends into its depths."[100] The erotic possibilities of this penetrative masculine gaze were most safely contained when its object was already female; however, feminized objects such as the corpse could function as this homosocial glue and object of exchange as well. On the one hand, obstetrics was ideally situated to model the professionalization of medicine through its bonding over and exchange of real and textualized female bodies. On the other, obstetrics was suspect because it was a traditionally female profession in which women still worked. It was still being criticized as a "dishonorable vocation" in the mid-nineteenth century[101] with its practitioners accused of being lecherous or too feminized, even potentially sodomites.

Moreover, obstetrics could complicate the heroic self-presentation of medical men. Obstetrics required patience and passivity on the birth attendant's part. In the nineteenth century, the ideal midwife—male or female—patiently awaited the outcome of nature. As one doctor explained, "The best treatment, and that which ought always to be first administered, and which likewise should accompany all other remedies, is, patience and sympathy, with cheerful and encouraging conversation."[102] In fact, as another doctor explained if "an accoucheur, on all occasions, puts the lever in his pocket when he goes to attend a labour, proves that he is an officious, meddlesome, and therefore…a bad accoucheur."[103] The unnecessary interference of practitioners often seemed to stem as much from the desire to be actively engaged in heroic activity as it did from ignorance.[104] Thus, Denman's Accoucheur of Feeling offered a heroic model in line with the nineteenth-century ideal standards of practice that held "patience and *bon-hommie*" as the most important "obstetrical instruments."[105] Denman's hero-accoucheur's inactivity was counterbalanced by the good-breeding and manly sensibility that many novels held up as ideal for the domestic hero. The hero-accoucheur might seldom engage in activity that could borrow military language, as writers in other medical fields did,[106] but then neither did heroes of domestic fiction like Jane Austen's Mr. Darcy or Charlotte Brontë's Mr. Rochester need to engage in physical struggle to be recognizable as heroes. Rather, Darcy struggles to master himself, much as a man-midwife might need to master his own impatience.[107] Rochester's primary struggle is against social conventions, something he must learn to submit to.[108] When he does engage in "heroic" activity, it is in (a futile) attempt to save a diseased woman from herself. Rochester's inaction except in the face of exigency made him, in many ways, the precise sort of hero for the nineteenth-century man-midwife. Like Rochester, the hero-accoucheur needed to ignore the importunities or "hysteria" of the women under his care unless her life was in imminent danger. If that danger existed, the hero-accoucheur would need to fly into action, willing to employ lever or forceps or the new medical technologies of ergot or ether.

Denman's downplaying of female sexuality would also have appealed to nineteenth-century mores. The erotic potential of obstetrics and gynecology was an ever-present threat to the respectability of these fields. Denman's reticence about intercourse and conception would have made him a more palatable forefather than Smellie, whose explicit and matter-of-fact descriptions of "coition," the clitoris, and even female ejaculation would no doubt have made Victorians swoon since even lecturing on midwifery was enough to cause at least one professor to blush: the subject "frequently sent the mantling blood over his cheeks and brow to testify that he had the deepest sense of the delicacy of the task assigned to him...."[109] Thus, Denman's description of the clitoris as "*supposed* to be the principle seat of pleasure" (emphasis added) would have rung true with the men who nodded in agreement with Krafft-Ebing's assertion that "if [a woman] is normally developed mentally, and well-bred, her sexual desire is small."[110] When nineteenth-century physicians did describe female genitals like the clitoris, they felt compelled to apologize. In answer to the hypothetical question of why Meigs included illustrations of dissected female genitals, "which seem fit to make the cheek tingle with shame," he excused himself for violating "decency" by explaining that these parts are sometimes subject to fatal disease.[111]

Additionally, Denman's comparative anatomy became enshrined as high science in the nineteenth century. As Europeans expanded their domination into all corners of the world, natural historians and scientists rushed to categorize and classify flora and fauna, including the human variety. Craniometery and pelvimetry were utilized not only to distinguish the sexes from one another, but also to provide "scientific" justification for racial ideologies that invariably exalted the "European type" as superior to other races.[112] Many people in Britain and the United States would have further specified that the English were the highest type; Anglo-American physicians could have turned to the nationalist preface of Denman's *Introduction* for evidence of English scientific precociousness.

The nineteenth-century anthropologizing bent led, on the one hand, to the sinister theory of polygenesis; on the other, the fad for classifying undoubtedly influenced Darwin's theories of evolution and sexual selection. Although Denman understood comparative anatomy as evidence for the hierarchy of Creation, his admirers in the late nineteenth and early twentieth centuries might have seen Denman's efforts as evidence of his early understanding of the descent of (wo)man. All would have agreed that Woman, domesticated or wild, was closer to nature and therefore inferior to man. The domesticated woman especially needed and deserved male guidance and protection—a role the accoucher-turned-obstetrician was ideally suited to play.

Denman's *Introduction* and other works constructed the Accoucheur of Feeling as the paradigmatic midwifery practitioner. This was a practitioner who exhibited a manly sensibility, who could listen and empathize with the fears and sufferings of his patients, but who would remain in control of his own emotions. This practitioner would seek to relieve pain and suffering, but would also consult his own reason and knowledge in order to try to preserve life. He would not let suffering importune his better judgment. Moreover, this man was friendly with his fellow colleagues and endeavored to protect and elevate his profession. He would seek to remain on good terms with all, preferring mutual uplift over-indulging individual injury. He would seek to know his fellows, cultivating the friendship and esteem of both his peers and his elders. Generations of obstetricians read his works in preparation for their careers. Even after his textbook was finally superseded, his influence was felt as his admirers continued to hold him and his works up as models to emulate well into the twentieth century. Thus, the ideal practitioner as envisioned by Denman wielded immense influence over the emerging profession of obstetrics. One of those individuals he greatly influenced, American physician and author Samuel Bard, is the subject of the next chapter.

# Endnotes

1    James Fenimore Cooper, *The Pioneers* (New York: Penguin, 1988), 72.

2    See Ernest Gray, *The Diary of a Surgeon, 1751-1752*. (New York, London: Appleton-Century, 1937); Ernest Gray, *Surgeon's Mate: The Diary of John Knyveton, Surgeon in the British Fleet during the Seven Years War, 1756-1762*. (London, R. Hale Ltd., 1942); Ernest Gray, *Man Midwife; the Further Experiences of John Knyveton, M.D., late surgeon in the British fleet, during the years 1763-1809*. (London: Hale, 1946); Martin H. Evans and Geoffrey Hooper, "Three misleading diaries: John Knyveton MD—from naval surgeon's mate to man-midwife." *The International Journal of Maritime History* 26.4 (2014): 762-88; P. M. Dunn, "Dr. Thomas Denman of London (1733-1815): rupture of the membranes and management of the cord." *Archives of Diseases of Childhood* 67 (1992): 882-84; and Colin McCall, *Naval Warfare to Natal Care: A Brief Look at the Life and Work of Thomas Denman (1733-1815), a Founder and Contributor to Male Midwifery and Modern Medical Practice*. (Matlock: SOLCOL, 2010).

3    Most of the details of Denman's biography are taken from Thomas Denman (1733-1815, physician and obstetrician collection, 1833-1849, MS 6014 and the Biography of Thomas Denman, 1818, MS 5620, both held at the Wellome Library (WL).

4    It has been frequently reported, at least since Denman's obituary in *The Gentleman's Magazine*, that Denman took Smellie's midwifery classes. This seems highly unlikely, since Denman, serving in the Seven Years War, did not return to British shores until 1763, the year Smellie died, and four years after Smellie had retired from teaching and returned to Scotland. See *Gentleman's Magazine* (London: Nichols, Son and Bentley, 1815), 566. See for instance, The Royal College of Physicians' biographical entry on Thomas Denman. http://munksroll.rcplondon.ac.uk/Biography/Details/1235

5    *Gentleman's Magazine*, (London: John Nichols, 1788), 1186.

6    Thomas Denman, *Aphorisms on the Application and Use of the Forceps and Vectis; on Preternatural Labours, on Labours Attended with Hemorrhage, and with Convulsions. The First American Edition*. Ed. Thomas C. James. (Philadelphia: Benjamin Johnson, 1803), np. Unless otherwise noted, all quotations will come from this edition.

7    Michael McKeon, *The Secret History of Domesticity: Public, Private, and the Division of Knowledge*. (Baltimore: Johns Hopkins University Press, 2005), 327.

8    *Ibid*, 674.

9    Armstrong, *Desire and Domestic Fiction*, 30.

10    *Ibid*, 20.

11   David Hume, "Essay XXI: Of National Characters" *Essays Moral, Political, and Literary.* Ed. Eugene F. Miller. (Indianapolis: Literary Fund, 1985), 202.

12   See, for instance, J. Worth Estes, "Patterns of Drug Use in Colonial America." *New York State Journal of Medicine* 87 (1987): 37-45.

13   *Anatomical Lectures; or, The Anatomy of the Human Bones, Nerves, and Lacteal Sac and Duct.* By a Society of Gentlemen. (London, 1775): 137.

14   *Ibid,* 12.

15   Karen Halttunen, "Humanitarianism and the pornography of pain in Anglo-American culture." *The American Historical Review* 100.2 (1995): 304.

16   Thomas Denman, *An Introduction to the Practice of Midwifery, Volume II.* (London: J. Johnson, 1794), 464. Unless otherwise noted, all quotations from the *Introduction* come from the 1794 second edition, the first time both volumes came out simultaneously.

17   Quoted in Wilson, *The Making,* 176. See also Cody, *Birthing,* 190.

18   Jane Austen, *Sense and Sensibility.* Ed. Claudia L. Johnson. (New York: Norton, 2001).

19   Henry MacKenzie, *The Man of Feeling.* Ed. Brian Vickers. (Oxford: Oxford University Press, 2009).

20   John Gregory, *Observations on the duties and offices of a physician; and on the methods of prosecuting enquries in philosophy* (London: Strahan and Cadell, 1770): 8-9.

21   William Hunter, *Two Introductory Lectures, Delivered by William Hunter, to his last course of anatomical lectures at his theatre in Windmill-Street: As they were left corrected for the press by himself.* (London: J. Johnson, 1784): 94.

22   *Ibid,* 220.

23   [Nicholls], *Petition,* esp. 8-10.

24   I am drawing on the concept of hegemonic masculinity as developed by R. W. Connell. Briefly defined, hegemonic masculinity is the most honored way of being a man within a given culture or social group. See R. W. Connell and James W. Messerschmidt. See Connell and Messerschmidt, "Hegemonic Masculinity: Rethinking the Concept." *Gender & Society* (2005): 829-59.

25   Blackwell, *"Tristram Shandy,"* 85.

26   *Ibid,* 86.

27   Benjamin Pugh, *A Treatise of Midwifery, chiefly with Regards the Operation. With Several Improvements of the Art.* (London: J. Buckland, 1754): 240-1.

28   Frances Burney, *Evelina.* Ed. Edward A. Bloom. (Oxford: Oxford University Press, 2008.)

29   Austen, *Sense and Sensibility.*

30   Maria Edgeworth, *Belinda.* Ed. Katherine J. Kirkpatrick. (Oxford: Oxford University Press, 2009).

31   Denman, *Introduction Vol.* I, iii. Italics in original.

32   *Ibid*, 23.

33   Eve Kosofsky Sedgewick, *Between Men: English Literature and Male Homosocial Desire.* (New York: Columbia University Press, 1985).

34   Doyle has recently argued that the reduction of the maternal body to its reproductive organs was a rhetorical strategy that eighteenth-century medical writers employed to de-sexualize the medical encounter. See Doyle, *Maternal Bodies,* esp. 14-50.

35   Denman, *Introduction Vol. II,* 3.

36   Notes Abstracted from several Courses of Lectures on Midwifery, given by Dr. Denman, & Dr. Osborn. Taken down By Frans. Kingston In 2 Books. Book ye 1$^{st}$ Began attending them June 1777, and finished June '78. MS 2099. *WL.* Hereafter referred to as Denman and Osborne Lectures.

37   *Ibid.*

38   Denman, *Introduction Vol.* I, 174.

39   *Ibid*, 181-82.

40   Denman and Osborne Lectures, WL.

41   Denman, *Introduction Vol. I,* 176.

42   Denman and Osborne Lectures, WL.

43   *Ibid.*

44   Denman, *Introduction, Vol. II.* 12.

45   Denman and Osborne Lectures, WL.

46   Denman, *Introduction, Vol. II.* 117.

47   Denman, *Introduction, Vol. I,* 353.

48   *Ibid*, 375-76.

49   *Ibid*, 304-05.

50   Denman, *Aphorisms*, 15.

51   *Ibid*, 15.

52   See also Cody, *Birthing the Nation*, 245-47. Embryology as a science wasn't established until the late nineteenth century. See Shannon Withycombe, *Lost* (New Brunswick, NJ: Rutgers University Press, 2019), 125-60.

53   Datson and Gallison, *Objectivity*, 23.

54   *Engravings,* 1.

55   *Ibid*, 2.

56   This would be around £55-83 or $70-107 today, making it comparable to the cost of an average university textbook. Current prices were calculated using the retail price index calculator on the website *MeasuringWorth.com*, http://www.measuringworth.com/calculators/. Accessed on 09/17/2018.

57   See Withycombe, *Lost*, 126-58.

58    Denman, *Introduction*, Vol. II, 172-73. See McClaren, *Reproductive Rituals*, 126-28.

59    Denman, *Engravings,* np.

60    *Ibid*, np.

61    John Blunt [S. W. Fores]. *Man-Midwifery dissected; or, the obstetric family-instructor.* (London: 1793), 66.

62    Biographical Sketch of Dr Denman. MS 6014. *WL*.

63    Thicknesse, *Man-Midwifery*, 42.

64    *Ibid*, 12.

65    Denman, *Introduction*, Volume I, 340-1.

66    *Ibid*, 341.

67    Denman, *Introduction*, Volume I, 340.

68    Denman and Osborne Lectures, WL.

69    See Erickson, "The Books of Generation."

70    Armstrong argues that eighteenth-century conduct manuals actually carved out the space for the middle class by articulating the ideal woman. See esp. 59-95.

71    See Wilson, *The Making*, 135-44.

72    Nationalist identities began emerging in the Western world in the late eighteenth century. See Benedict Anderson, *Imagined Communities: Reflections on the Origin and Spread of Nationalism* (London: Verso, 1983/2006); Michael Warner, *The Letters of the Republic: Publication and the Public Sphere in Eighteenth-Century America* (Cambridge, MA: Harvard University Press, 1990); Ernest Gellner, *Nations and Nationalism*, 2nd edition (Ithaca, NY: Blackwell, 2008); Thomas Neville Bonner, *Becoming a Physician: Medical Education in Britain, France, Germany, and the United States, 1750-1945* (Baltimore: Johns Hopkins University Press, 1995); Armstrong, esp. pgs. 59-95; and Nelson, *National Manhood*.

73    Denman, *Introduction*, *Vol.* I, 130.

74    *Ibid*, 30.

75    *Ibid*, 156.

76    Denman, *Introduction*, Vol. II, 245.

77    *Ibid*, 244.

78    Roy Porter, *Quacks: Fakers and Charlatans in Medicine.* (Stroud: Tempus, 2003).

79    See Buchan's preface to *Domestic Medicine*.

80    William Hunter, *Medical Commentaries Part I. Containing a Plain and Direct Answer to Professor Monro Jun. Interspersed with Marks on the Structure, Functions, and Diseases of Several Parts of the Human Body.* (London: A. Hamilton, 1762); Alexander Munro, Jun., *An Expostulatory Epistle to William Hunter, M.D.* (Edinburgh: G. Hamilton and J. Balfour, 1762).

81    William Osborne, *Essays on the Practice of Midwifery, in Natural and Difficult Labours.* (London: T. Cadell and J. Johnson, 1790), vi-viii.

82    See Julia Epstein, *The Iron Pen: Frances Burney and the Politics of Women's Writing* (Bristol: Bristol Classical, 1989), esp. pp. 47-51.

83    Denman, *Introduction*, Vol. I, 130; 158. Italics in original.

84    See *Ibid*, 127-130. See also George Lamoine, "Lord Chesterfield's Letters as Conduct-Books." In *The Crisis of Courtesey: Studies in the Conduct-Book in Britain, 1600-1900*. Ed. Jacques Carré. (Leiden: E. J. Brill, 1994), 105-117; and Armstrong, 62-81

85    See Bonner for more information about the transitions of medical education in the nineteenth century.

86    "Article VIII," *The English Review; or an Abstract of English and Foreign Literature for the Year M,DCC,LXXXIV* (London: J. Murray, 1789), 120.

87    "Article XVII," *The American Medical Recorder, of Original Papers and Intelligence in Medicine and Surgery* (Philadelphia: James Webster, 1822), 528.

88    Wooster Beach, *An Improved System of Midwifery, Adapted to the Reformed Practice of Medicine; Illustrated by Numerous Plates. To which is added, a Compendium of the Treatment of Female and Infantile Diseases, with Remarks on Physiological and Moral Elevation* (New York: Baker & Scribner, 1850), 13.

89    Quoted in Palmer Findley, *Priests of Lucina: The Story of Obstetrics*. (Boston: Little, Brown & Co. 1939), 192.

90    See Sappol, *A Traffic*, esp. pp. 80-90.

91    See Donnison, *Midwives*, 52-55.

92    Qtd. in Wertz and Wertz, *Lying-in*, 50.

93    See Donegan, *Women and Men Midwives*,142.

94    For more information about the change in attitude toward obstetrics, see Donnison and Moscucci.

95    Lisa Rosner (1999), *The Most Beautiful Man in Existence: The Scandalous Life of Alexander Lesassier*. Philadelphia: University of Pennsylvania Press, 192.

96    Charles D. Meigs, *Obstetrics; the Science and the Art. Fifth Edition, Revised*. (Philadelphia: Henry C. Lea, 1867), 265-66.

97    *Ibid*, 613.

98    W. H. Borham, "A Case of Hour-Glass Contraction of the Uterus." *Lancet* 61: 1531 (1853): 19.

99    Moscucci, *Science of Women*, 102.

100   Foucault, The *Birth of a Clinic*, 136. See also Sappol, *A Traffic*, 225-27.

101   Donnison, *Women and Men Midwives*, 57.

102   Beech, *A Improved System*, 137.

103   James Blundell, *The Principles and Practice of Obstetricy*. (London: E. Cox, 1834), 213.

104   See Donegan, *Women and Men Midwives*,142-45.

105   Blundell, *The Principles*, 215.

106   See also Michael Brown, "'Like a Devoted Army': Medicine, Heroic Masculinity, and the Military Paradigm in Victorian Britain." *Journal of British Studies* 49.3 (2010): 592-622.

107   Jane Austen, *Pride and Prejudice* (1813), Ed. Robert P. Irvine (Ontario: Broadview, 2002).

108   Charlotte Brontë, *Jane Eyre* (1847), Ed. Deborah Lutz (New York: Norton, 2016).

109   Meigs speaking about James. Qtd in Donegan, 150.

110   Richard von Kraff-Ebing, *Psychopathia Sexualis with Especial Reference to the Antipathetic Sexual Instinct. A Medico-Forensic Study.* Trans. F. J. Rebman. (New York: Rebman, nd), 13.

111   Meigs, *Obstetrics*, 105.

112   For more information on craniotomy and pelvimetry, see Schiebinger, *Nature's Body*, 115-80; Moscucci, *Science of Women*, 7-40; and Ann Fabian, *The Skull Collectors: Race, Science, and America's Unburied Dead* (Chicago: University of Chicago Press, 2010).

# Chapter Four

# The American Hero-Accoucheur and Medical Education: Samuel Bard's *A Compendium of Midwifery*

Samuel Bard was not the first American to publish on midwifery. Valentine Seaman's prospectus (1800) for classes predates Bard's work by a decade, William Dewees and others were editing American reprints of important British and French works, and many American medical journals printed obstetric cases. However, Bard did pen the first original, full-length midwifery treatise in the United States. An important rhetorical strain within all this ink spilled on child-bearing and pregnancy demonstrates that Early American medical men were invested in professionalizing and masculinizing the practice of midwifery. Lack of regulation and licensing meant that anyone could practice medicine in the free-wheeling medial marketplace of the early Republic. Claiming mastery over obstetrics gave the regulars pecuniary and symbolic clout. First, it was widely believed that guiding a woman through a successful labor nearly guaranteed that she would then rely on that man as her family physician, thus becoming a regular source of income. Moreover, because men-midwives generally charged higher fees than their female counterparts, paying midwifery patients were generally well-heeled and were seen as offering an entrée into wealthier social circles. Second, claiming mastery over obstetrics allowed medical men to claim mastery over *the* "secrets of Nature"—the womb and birth—and by extension, women and all the "mysteries" of the "fairer sex." In an era when many women were agitating to be included within the freedom and agency promised by the "self-evident truth" that "all men are created equal" and should be guaranteed the right "to life, liberty, and the pursuit of happiness," the ability to claim superior knowledge over the truth of feminine nature and the female body was an invaluable tool to put women back in their place. Medicine sought to prove that women were biologically unfit to engage in the demands of citizenship by constructing dimorphic, incommensurable biological sexes that focused almost entirely on women's reproductive capacity.

Originally published in 1808, Bard's *A Compendium of the Theory and Practice of Midwifery* is an especially important window into this construction of dimorphic, essentialist gender roles because of the way the book transformed, through five editions, from an instruction manual for midwives into a textbook for male medical students. Attention to the revision processes offers a snapshot of changing attitudes toward female midwives, ideas about the female body, and the development of a masculine, heroic identity for medical men during the 1810s in New York. It is crucial to contrast an early edition with a later edition of the *Compendium* because attention to the differences among editions has the potential to alter the narratives that we tell about the intersection of gender and medical professionalism. Therefore, throughout this chapter I will contrast the midwife editions with the student editions, primarily using the second and fifth editions. The former offers a glimpse at how Bard desired to be seen shortly after he had taken on his role as President of the College of Physicians and Surgeons of New York and the latter was the final published revision before he died. In these pages, Bard constructs an American hero-accoucheur that not only consolidated a white national manhood, to use Dana D. Nelson's phrase, but also envisioned himself as an important contributor to an international fraternity of medical men.

Unlike the physicians focused on in the preceding chapters, Bard was not an influential teacher of midwifery. However, Bard's book synthesizes Thomas Denman's and William Smellie's works (as well as many others), and like his two British predecessors and sources, the *Compendium* constructs a heroic identity for male readers that is opposed to both the inept midwife of either gender as well as the abjected, mastered female body. Bard greatly admired Thomas Denman, and seems to have modeled his American hero-accoucheur on Denman's Accoucheur of Feeling. Formally trained in Scotland and conversant with important medical writers of his day, Bard would have been well-versed in the medical and social ideas of sensibility. Indeed, Bard was famous in his own day for his exquisite sensibility, and according to his son-in-law, he was an avid reader of "every new publication of merit" be it a "work...of taste [i.e. novel] or of science."[1] One of Bard's favorite books was the sentimental novel *The Vicar of Wakefield* (1766) by Oliver Goldsmith.[2] Thus, sensibility and sympathy are crucial qualities for the American hero-accoucheur. Moreover, as his book transformed from an intended female readership to an exclusively male medical student one, the increasing number

Fig. 4.1: Copies of Samuel Bard's *Compendium,* arranged in ascending chronology from 1808 first edition (far left) to the 1819 fifth edition (far right). Against conventional wisdom about book sizes, Bard's book actually gets larger in later editions. Courtesy of the Library Company of Philadelphia.

of case studies made the novelistic elements of this "humanitarian narrative" more pronounced.[3] However, increasingly explicit anatomical descriptions amplify the frisson of women's sexual secrets and constantly threatened the decorum of the text. This chapter will trace the history of Bard's *A Compendium* and his career before placing it in the larger context of changing attitudes toward female midwives and the professionalizing obstetric medicine. Finally, this chapter will explore in more detail Bard's relationship with his predecessors Denman and Smellie as well as his role in the creation of the personages of the American hero-accoucheur and his patient, the American Fair.

## The History of a Book

Just looking at the five editions of *A Compendium* shelved next to one another raises a red flag that this book bucks traditional book history trends (See Figure 4.1). Typically, each successive edition of a book became smaller and cheaper, as the market became saturated and booksellers sought new buyers—much as hardback first editions are reissued in paperback today. Bard's midwifery textbook, however, is at odds with that trend—over the five editions this book became larger and more expensive. The changing size and price clues us in that the history of this textbook requires careful scholarly attention— the changing physical characteristics are due to the significant changes in the content of, and desired audience for, this book. In this section, I will sketch some of the significant differences among the five editions of the *Compendium* before delving briefly into Bard's biography and the changing medical scene to seek explanations for why this book changed dramatically over the course of a decade.

Digitization has made it increasingly easier to compare different editions of a work. In the past, scholars have had to rely on whatever edition of a text was available on microfilm or the rare book libraries to which they had access. As a result, this limitation has resulted in conflicting views of Bard's place in and contribution to Early National obstetrics. For example, two classic histories of American obstetrics, Jane B. Donegan's *Women & Men Midwives* and Richard D. Wertz and Dorothy C. Wertz's *Lying-In*, both refer to Bard's *Compendium* for evidence of how midwifery was practiced in the Early National Period. While Donegan notes that the editions changed focus, gradually becoming more geared toward students, only the fifth edition is cited in the endnotes. Bard is indexed under "meddlesome midwifery," and the analysis is focused on his views on obstetrical instruments. As only men were permitted to use obstetrical instruments, "the meddling midwives" would have been male. Indeed, the fifth edition has little to say about female midwives. Wertz and Wertz, on the other hand, refer to the third edition, and their Bard comes across as still in favor of female birth attendants and completely anti-instrument because the third edition is still addressed to a mixed audience and Bard animadverts on his "reluctance" to discuss the use of instruments. Both of these offer an incomplete view of Bard's changing attitude toward male and female midwifery practitioners or how he understood his own role in shaping medical education and practice.

The tone of the midwife editions created a provincial voice from the periphery of the British cultural empire about the grand doings of the metropole. These editions of the *Compendium* were presented as a vector of British knowledge to the ill-trained American bumpkins of both sexes who had not the wherewithal to finish their education in the British medical schools. The first edition, *A Compendium of the Theory and Practice of Midwifery, Containing Practical Instructions for the Management of Women During Pregnancy, in Labour, and in Child-Bed; Calculated to Correct the Errors, and to Improve the Practice of Midwives; As Well as to Serve as Introduction to the Study of this Art, for Students and Young Practitioners* (1808),[4] was a relatively inexpensive ($1.25) duodecimo. Changes to the second edition (1812) were minor. The most important change was Bard's justification not to acquiesce to "friends" who "solicited" him to add a chapter on obstetric instruments; by the third edition, he had conceded and added chapters on touching (manual examination of the vagina) and obstetrical instruments, beginning the shift toward a student audience.

The shift to a male medical student audience was complete by the fourth edition (1817), a more expensive octavo ($3.50); in fact, the fourth and fifth editions were, in many respects, brand-new books, retitled *A Compendium of the Theory and Practice of Midwifery, containing Practical Instructions for the Management of Women during Pregnancy, in Labour, and in Child-bed; Illustrated by Many Cases, and Particularly Adapted to the Use of Students.* This change in size and cost is reflective of Bard's change in purpose—he began by wanting to reform female midwives, but gradually altered the book into a textbook for male medical students. As the audience shifted from midwives to medical students, the tone shifted as well, from scolding condescension to collegial guidance. Rather than the paternalist condescension toward "ignorant" women, Bard introduced male students to a world of masculine homosociality constituted through the recounting of heroic endeavors on female bodies in the "Many Cases." The student editions of the *Compendium* present midwifery as a cosmopolitan, international affair. Most of the references are still to British practitioners and publications; however, Bard also included many continental Europeans, including not only the standard French references like Jean Louis Baudeloque and Laurent Charles Pierre Leroux, but also other European notables like Albrecht von Haller and Lazzaro Spallanzani. He even included Russian and Italian cases that had been published in London medical journals. Moreover, the inclusion of American practitioners provided homespun heroes for readers. In the pages of the *Compendium*, American accoucheurs join as equals these European medical men and scientists. Readers are introduced to a cosmopolitan profession that could bring international fame for those intrepid enough to dare new innovations or at least publish their cases. The student editions of the *Compendium* created a medical republic of letters, one that is constituted through the exchange of textualized female bodies.

## The Making of an American Midwifery Author

The changing face of American medical education and Bard's place in it go a long way towards explaining the changes Bard made to the *Compendium*. Before the late eighteenth century, few medical practitioners in the North American British colonies were university trained. Most "doctors," if they had any formal training at all, were apothecaries or surgeons brought up in the apprentice system, with many having gone through the crucible of British military medical service–a school of hard knocks, perhaps, but not one of high standards. However, this situation began to change in the decade preceding the Revolutionary War, as an increasing number of colonials sought medical training in premier European hospitals and universities, most especially the University of Edinburgh. At the center of the Scottish Enlightenment, the

University of Edinburgh offered one of Europe's best medical educations. It offered better quality teaching than that offered at Oxford and Cambridge, and it admitted non-jurors whose religious scruples would have barred them from the English schools.

Among the students thronging to the University of Edinburgh's medical school and the private and hospital schools of London were numerous Americans. Some attended for only a season or two, while some stayed to earn medical degrees. These young men, including William Shippen, John Morgan, Benjamin Rush, and Samuel Bard, were sent by their fathers, who were often apothecary-surgeons, to receive formal training and polish after their apprenticeships. For example, Bard's father, John was a successful apothecary-surgeon, and Samuel's early medical training had been under his father as an apprentice.[5] In 1761, John sent Samuel to Britain to further his education. Sailing was a dangerous proposition during the Seven Years' War, and the ship Samuel was in was captured by the French. Samuel did not allow his brief stint in France as a prisoner of war to deter his studies. After being ransomed, Samuel first went to London where he became a hospital student at St. Thomas's and studied midwifery under Colin MacKenzie, one of Smellie's lead students. He then attended to the University of Edinburgh from which he obtained an M.D. in 1765. Letters between father and son show Samuel in close consultation with his father about the trajectory of his studies—as well as frequently asking for money, which John regularly sent, either in cash or in the form of goods, such as Virginia snakeroot, for Samuel to sell. John was also solicitous for his son to buy good books, live in fashionable lodgings, attend the occasional concert and assembly, and "Cultivate an acquaintance with some Sensible and agreeable Young Ladies"—so that his son would obtain the polish and social graces to ensure his eminence in the profession.[6] In total, John spent over £1000 on Samuel's British education, a handsome sum that would have been the envy of most medical students.

After returning to New York, Samuel joined his father's practice and was instrumental in founding King's College medical school (later Columbia University), where he was the professor of Natural History. Samuel bought out his father's practice in 1772. However, the Revolutionary War stymied Bard's career for a while. For the most part, the Bard family were Tories and remained loyal to the British during the conflict, causing many of Bard's patients to desert him. Even after the war, Bard's Toryism continued to shadow his career until President George Washington sought Bard's services when Washington became ill with anthrax in 1789. Credited with saving the president's life, Samuel's reputation rebounded and he became the most fashionable physician in New York City. His reputation as a man of feeling who grew faint at the bloody business of surgery likely helped both his general popularity as well as his popularity as the leading accoucheur of the city. Bard retired from active practice in 1798, rusticating at his estate in Hyde Park, where he experimented raising merino sheep, on which he also wrote a treatise in 1811.

However, the work Bard is now best known for is his *Compendium on the Theory and Practice of Midwifery*. Unlike most midwifery authors, Bard never taught midwifery courses. Rather, he chose to write on this subject from a civic-minded interest because he had not approved of the general practice he had witnessed during his attendance on midwifery cases. According to Bard's early biographers, the first edition was commercially successful, selling out in only four years. The book may indeed have been popular in New York where Bard was known as a co-founder of Kings (Columbia) College medical school and as the Washingtons' family doctor. Outside of the region, however, the first edition proved a harder sale. Mason Weems reported to Matthew Carey that Bard's *Compendium* "stuck to me like wax, but I called it, in my MSS catalogue, 'The Grand American Aristotle' and it sold like green peas in spring."[7] This bit of snake oil was intended to give the book a titillating aura borrowed from the popular sex manual *Aristotle's Masterpiece*. Weems attempted to palm off this medical textbook onto unsuspecting customers, knowing he would be long gone by the time the buyers remembered *caveat emptor*.

Bard's biographers claimed that demand prompted the 1812 second edition; however, a larger factor was probably his 1811 appointment as President of the College of Physicians and Surgeons of New York, founded in 1807, a position he held the remainder of his life. Although the second edition still addressed midwives, it made more sense for the "President of the College of Physicians and Surgeons in the University of the State of New York" to address his book to the ready market of better-heeled medical students. Bard's publisher, Collins & Perkins, attempted to corner this market by advertising that they were the official "printers and importers of Medical Books" to the College of Physicians and Surgeons of New York and the New York Hospital.[8] The prestige of Bard's position provided the symbolic capital to legitimize their standing as the main medical publishers in New York. Collins & Perkins published three more editions (and Bard was working on another when he died) at their own cost, investing more capital with each edition grew as it in length (and size) and included more woodcuts, and paying the author—for the fifth edition alone, Bard was to receive stationers' goods and books to the value of more than $500.

Bard's changing position among the medical elite in New York City likely prompted many of the alterations to Bard's *Compendium*. Bard's position within New York medical society also changed when he entered into the tempestuous arena of university politics in the 1810s. Competition between medical schools caused rancorous divisions to emerge among New York physicians and surgeons that were not completely quelled when the College of Physicians and Surgeons cannibalized the failing medical school at Columbia College.[9] Certainly personal and political considerations played a role in the revisions and references Bard made. In the 1812, edition, Bard refers to a recently appointed professor of the College of Physicians and Surgeons in New York, but the reference is removed from the 1817 edition after that professorship had been revoked four years earlier. Moreover, there are several references in the 1812 edition to "my friend David Hosack." Hosack was Bard's partner for a time and largely inherited his practice. Bard's grandson Francis U. Johnson was apprenticed to Hosack in 1817. Thereafter, however, Hosack and Bard's relationship declined because of political differences over the New York medical schools and Johnson's unsuccessful courtship of Hosack's daughter. Thus, the references in the 1819 edition were reduced to one, and Hosack was no longer introduced as "my friend."

The *Compendium* was intended as a useful, comprehensive textbook for the beginner, replete with small woodblock illustrations. Bard disavowed "all claims to originality" and confessed that he had "not hesitated occasionally to use the language of others, where I have found it sufficiently clear and familiar for my purpose...."[10] In the earliest editions, Bard briefly mentioned his primary sources—the works of Denman, Charles White, Robert Bland, John Burns, Baudeloque, and Smellie. He also had occasion to mention a few American practitioners—such as Hosack and by the second edition, William Dewees of Philadelphia. The first edition referenced ten other male midwifery authors and included four case histories. The number of cases remains the same in the second edition, but the number of references increased to sixteen. By the 1817 fourth edition, sixty-nine individual names are cited, plus several medical journals, and the number of cases had increased to 131. The fifth edition increased the references to 91 individuals and 152 case histories. Undoubtedly, the sixth edition would have been even more erudite. Shortly before his death, Bard entreated Johnson, who was still a student in the city, to send him "Burns' Gravid Uterus, Burn's Midwifery, & anything new they may have on the subject" because he needs them "to prepare the next Edition of my Compendium."[11] Unfortunately, his grandson never sent the books.

Although Bard's changing position within New York's medical elite accounts for many of the changes to the *Compendium*, to fully understand why the book completely changed focus from a female readership to an exclusively male one requires exploring the medical profession's increasing animosity toward female midwives.

## Midwives and Medical Men

At first, Bard had likely chosen to write for a female audience because, a practical man, he realized that most births in the far-flung settlements would be attended by women, often with little-to-no formal training. Moreover, Bard had originally learned midwifery in the Smellie school of thought, which tended to view female midwives as necessary helpers to male practitioners. American doctors often held similar views. According to Sylvia Hoffert, "there is some evidence to suggest that doctors sought to relegate" female midwives to the role of assistant and nurse. For example, "In a eulogy of William Potts Dewees, an early nineteenth-century physician, Hugh L. Hodge described the way in which Dewees sought to reduce the position of the midwives who called him in to consult in difficult obstetrics cases."[12]

However, beginning in the early nineteenth century, male practitioners on both sides of the pond increasingly dismissed female midwives as ignorant bunglers. As Nelson has argued, "Gynecological practice becomes another way for white men in the United States to extend the purview of professional male authority over culture...and another arena in which they can 'consolidate partnerships with authoritative males' over the bodies of their 'others'..."[13] These men defined their own "enlightened" practice and masculine, professional identity against, on the one hand, female competitors they characterized as incompetent and old-fashioned, and, on the other, against female patients defined as weak and imperiled. Moreover, midwifery was increasingly seen as crucial for the success of the proliferating number of young doctors emerging from medical schools: although it was low-paid, treating a woman through a successful delivery was believed to be the key to setting up a teeming general practice. If a physician gained a parturient woman's trust, she would be likely to consult him for medical advice for her entire family and she would recommend him to her friends, who would do the same, gradually building the doctor's patient list, his reputation, and his wealth.

Pecuniary and professional interests caused male authors to celebrate the rescue of midwifery from the clutches of ignorant women. For instance, medical popularizer William Buchan celebrated the male take-over of midwifery as a "happy revolution."[14] Other British physicians like William Osborne argued that pregnancy *was* a diseased state, childbirth was necessarily dangerous and painful, and therefore parturition invariably needed to be under the supervision of male doctors.[15] Charles White, considered by his contemporaries to be the leading expert on puerperal fever, blamed this fatal disease on nurses who undermined and thwarted the improvements of men-midwives.[16] In Maine, Dr. Daniel Cony's professional conflict with long-time midwife Martha Ballard was merely part of a larger trend to separate "scientific" medicine from traditional practice perceived as feminine.[17] For the American men involved, that consolidation was imagined as universal, the partnerships not relegated to white Americans, or even with the British, but with all of Europe.

Perhaps the best example of this anti-midwife attitude can be found in an anonymous pamphlet, *Remarks on the Employment of Females as Practitioners in Midwifery by a Physician* (1820), believed to have been written either by Dr. Walter Channing or Dr. John Ware. The occasion of the pamphlet was the arrival of Mrs. Janet Alexander, an Edinburgh-trained midwife, who was invited to Boston by Drs. John Collins Warren and James Jackson to take over their obstetrical practices. The choice to bequeath their patients to a woman practitioner rather than one of the many young doctors trying to establish themselves in Boston alarmed the author of the pamphlet as a regressive move. In a sort of double-speak, the pamphlet condemned "introducing [women] into the practice of midwifery" at the same time it celebrated their recent removal from it.[18] It included a variety of objections to female practitioners, ranging from the assertion women "have not that power of action, or that active power of mind, which is essential to the practice of the surgeon."[19] A woman who did receive the requisite anatomical and physiological training of a surgeon would "destroy[] those moral qualities of character, which are essential"[20] to the practice of midwifery. Moreover, even a trained woman midwife, "as a female would be find herself totally inadequate to manage"[21] in any emergency, but she would "too confident to imagine herself wrong" and too ignorant "to determine danger,"[22] resulting in maternal and fetal deaths. Additionally, if employing female midwives became fashionable again, then women of all ranks would employ them, depriving young accoucheurs of the opportunity to gain "practical midwifery"[23] experience by treating poor women for free, so the entire medical science would decline. Thus, a right-feeling man should never "entrust his wife or his daughter into [a midwife's] hands"[24] if a male practitioner was available. The author even argued that "Hamilton of Edinburgh reprobate[s] in the strongest terms the introduction of females into the practice"[25] —a bizarre assertion considering James Hamilton taught Mrs. Alexander as well as countless other female midwives, a fact that William

Channing, if he was the author, should have known, since he, too, trained under Hamilton.

Amid the overblown objections, the author's true complaint against female midwives is readily discernable. Young physicians were afraid of the competition: "Heretofore, where midwifery has been in the hands of women, they have only practiced among the poorer and lower classes of people; the richer and better informed preferring to employ physicians… but if be again introduced among the rich and influential, it will become fashionable; it will be considered as indelicate and vulgar to employ a physician, and the custom will become general."[26] The author feared that Warren's and Jackson's well-to-do patients would find they preferred being delivered by another woman rather than by a male doctor and that their preference would influence their friends to follow suit. Wealthy clients hiring female birth attendants threatened the livelihood—and the social and professional mobility—of aspiring physicians because the "practice of midwifery becomes desirable to physicians [because] [i]t is this which ensures to them the permanency and security of all their other business."[27] As Bard advised his grandson that same year: "attend them [poor patients] (particularly the midwifery patients) for nothing, or for such very moderate compensation as they can afford, leave your card of Direction with them, then they may know where to find you when they or any of their friends may need you…."[28] Midwifery had become the first rung on the ladder of professional success.

Nevertheless, not all medical men were antagonistic toward female midwives. Clearly, the Boston physicians who contracted with Janet Alexander to take over their practices had faith in the ability of trained female midwives. To cite another example, the early twentieth-century editors of the case book a midwife, Susanna Müller, who practiced in rural Pennsylvania in the early nineteenth century, recounted an anecdote that, upon an occasion that called for the assistance of a physician during a difficult case, the physician reportedly responded, "[u]pon hearing that Susanna Müller was in attendance…at once replied, 'Then it is all right, she knows as much about the case as I do."[29] Nor were men-midwives universally trusted. And, in 1848, the Boston Female Medical College was founded to train female midwives largely because of continued objections to the impropriety and sexual danger posed by men-midwives.[30] Most births in the United States were continued to be conducted by female midwives until the move to hospital births in the early twentieth century. Currently, the popularity of midwives seems to be on the rise again, despite some lingering professional animosity.[31]

## Triangulating the Old and the New: Bard, Denman, and Smellie

Unlike most authors on obstetrical matters, Bard never pretended to any originality or exclusive insight into midwifery or the female body. He candidly confessed to "borrowing" material and was, in fact, fairly scrupulous for his time in citing his sources. In many ways, all five editions of the *Compendium*—but especially the two student editions—function primarily as a synthesis or triangulation of the works of William Smellie and Thomas Denman. Because Bard preferred Denman, I'll first examine that writer's influence on Bard's book before turning to Smellie and William Perfect, a relatively obscure practitioner whom Bard cast as the epitome of bad man-midwifery.

The name that shows up most frequently in every edition of the *Compendium* is Thomas Denman. Denman's *Introduction* was Bard's primary source, and Denman was consistently praised as a "high authority" on midwifery, who could be read without endangering the minds of accoucheurs-in-training and presumably female midwives as well. Denman's non-interventionist practice aligned with Bard's opinion on the proper activities for both female and male birth attendants. Bard was lavish in his praise for Denman and seemed unable to bear criticism against him. Bard presented a case from William Osborne, Denman's one-time partner, as an example of a justifiable use of the crochet. However, he also felt compelled to animadvert against Osborne's "irritation against Denman...which continually betrays him into a vehemence of expression..." that could prove dangerous to young practitioners.[32]

The *Compendium* adopted Denman's domesticated hero-accoucheur of feeling, whose primary role was to be a source of quiet strength and comfort to the laboring woman. The American hero-accoucheur should "leav[e]... nature to her own unassisted efforts" and instead "encourage his patient by appearing perfectly calm and easy himself, without hurry or assumed importance; by assuring her that as far as now can be discovered, all matters are perfectly natural; by entering into easy conversation with her himself, and by encouraging her to do so with her friends."[33] This could almost be a drawing room scene of a gentleman entertaining a group of ladies with comfortable chat and perhaps a game of cards. Indeed, "by an easy, familiar, and cheerful behavior, the accoucheur should give to his presence, as much as possible, the appearance of an ordinary visit."[34] Calm non-interference should be the accoucheur's course of actions, even in lingering dangerous cases. At those times, he would need the strength of character to "hear[ ] and resist[ ] the distressing complaints and apprehensions of his suffering patient, and the solicitude, and sometimes the reproaches, of her friends."[35] However, on those rare occasions when interference was justified—hemorrhage or too-narrow pelvis, for instance—the hero-accoucheur must act decisively. "A hesitating, vacillating conduct, governed neither by principle nor experience, is equally dangerous, whilst it blunders on between timidity and rashness."[36] He should "never refuse, or hesitate to make the attempt" even if "the probability of saving her life" was "very slight indeed."[37]

Bard seems to have been converted to Denman's noninterventionist practice sometime before the first edition of the *Compendium* in 1808; however, Bard had practiced midwifery for over twenty years before Denman's *Introduction* would have been available, and one assumes that his practice probably resembled that taught by Smellie. Bard had learned midwifery under Colin MacKenzie, Smellie's lead pupil. In fact, because MacKenzie's lectures were so similar to Smellie's teaching, Bard wrote to his father that he read Smellie's *Treatise* in conjunction with the course. The *Compendium* is vague on whether reading or practice, or a combination of both, convinced Bard that Smellie's style of practice was more dangerous than useful. Regardless, by 1808, Bard was highly critical of "ignorant" midwifery practitioners of both sexes who read Smellie without the guidance of a preceptor to help them distinguish what was good in Smellie from what encouraged meddlesome violence. Rather, Bard joined the ranks of numerous other medical men who recommended Denman as the best available author on midwifery.

In the earliest editions, Bard excused himself from "not mention[ing] *Smellie*"[38] since he has no occasion to discuss instrumental deliveries, which was what Smellie had become known for, despite his greater focus on non-instrumental births, as discussed in Chapter One. However, as the *Compendium* changed focus from "ignorant midwives" to students, Smellie became a larger presence. Although the too-easy access of Smellie's *Treatise* was still lamented because of the danger it posed for the ill-trained and over-confident, it was also one of the primary sources for case histories and examples. More case studies come from Smellie than any other individual (28 cases in the 1817 edition, 25 in the 1819), and most of these were used as positive examples of practice. This use of Smellie would seem to cut across the edge of the condemnation of Smellie as dangerous. Bard might lament that Smellie was too frequently read; however, Smellie's *Treatise* apparently remained the best source of examples for the students Bard imagined reading his own book. Perhaps Bard felt that Smellie was best presented to the novice in a pre-digested form in order to remove the dangerous appeal of the picaro-accoucheur, whose meddling heroics might seduce these young men, trained to see women as damsels-in-distress, away from the patient inaction held up by Denman (and Bard) as the *beau ideal.*

The best illustration of the differing attitudes toward these two accoucheurs appears in the commentary on both authors' discussions of their own error-ridden early practices. One of Smellie's early cases, in which Smellie freely admits to his own ignorance and mistakes, was quoted at length. Though acknowledging that Smellie "confesses" to not knowing the best treatment for uterine hemorrhage,  Bard used the case as an example of what not to do, criticizing Smellie for not only his ignorance but also for his caution in using laudanum "in too small doses."[39] In contrast, Bard presented Denman's confession of error as a mantra for the student reader:

> Upon this subject [difficult labors], one of the most eminent and respectable practitioners, and the best writers, of London, (Doctor Denman) with great candour, says, "…*I am fully convinced, that the far greater part of really difficult labours, to which I have been called, and I must not conceal the truth on this occasion, many of those which have been under my care originally, were not of that description from unavoidable necessity; but were rendered such by improper management in the commencement or course of the labour.*" Such a confession from a man of Doctor Denman's great experience and unquestionable knowledge, is of inestimable value; and if duly reflected on, and constantly recollected by the young and inexperienced, will preserve the lives of very many women and children, save themselves many painful recollections; and do more to improve their knowledge and usefulness, than years of careless and inattentive practice.[40]

According to Bard, Denman's admission of fault was more useful to the student than any amount of practice, whereas Smellie's was just another example of outdated practice. More is at work here than merely Bard's preference for Denman. Bard seemed to understand himself as a lesser Denman, and Denman's admission became Bard's tacit confession of "painful recollections" of his own mistakes. Bard only "confess[ed], not without severe regret, that towards the end of thirty years practice, I found much less occasion for the use of instruments, than I did in the beginning…"[41] There are few specific references to Bards' own practice (however, three cases that are present in all five editions of the *Compendium* appear to from Bard's own practice).

Rather, it is Bard's contemporary and fellow MacKenzie alumnus William Perfect who is the foil for the hero-accoucheur. Better known to history as a mad doctor,[42] William Perfect also published a volume of midwifery cases from which Bard heavily borrowed—Perfect's cases are the second most cited after Smellie. Perfect was made to represent what was problematic in man-midwifery. Although not all the negative examples Bard gave came from Perfect, and not all of Perfect's cases are used as negative examples (only about half), Bard frequently and roundly criticized Perfect. Since Bard and Perfect both learned midwifery from Colin MacKenzie, it seems likely that their practice would have been similar. Thus, it is likely that Bard projected his regrets and reservations about his own thirty years practice onto Perfect, criticizing those cases in which Perfect "meddled" instead of waiting patiently or for not acting when decisive action was required. For example, in a case in which several medical men could not agree on a course of action in a hemorrhage, in which "the patient died undelivered, and without any effort to save the child," Bard accused Perfect of "want[ing] that firmness which should always induce an honest man to risk his own reputation, rather than his patients safety...."[43] Bard thought the cowardly accoucheur should have acted against the opinion of the first physician and immediately delivered the woman, with instruments if necessary, or at least have attempted a post-mortem C-section to try to save the fetus. According to Bard, the hero-accoucheur should always try to save the woman and/or infant, even if that meant raising the ire of more established medical men. However, one wonders how Bard the young practitioner would have handled this case? If he, so deferential to his father, would have dared to defy John Bard or others of his father's experience? Or if he, too, would have, like Perfect, rather hazard his patient's life rather than the good opinion of established medical men?

If Perfect, too deferential to authority and too concerned with his reputation, represented the faulty man-midwife, how then should the American hero-accoucheur act? For Bard, the answer was clear—American medical men should emulate Denman's Accoucheur of Feeling.

## The American Hero-Accoucheur

Although Bard drew heavily upon Smellie, Denman, and other eminent practitioners, he also included references and quotations from dozens of other contemporaries, both those of increasing fame and prominence as well as obscure, rural practitioners, from New York and Pennsylvania, to Scotland, England, Ireland, France, and elsewhere. The multivocality and numerous case studies of the student editions of the *Compendium* constructed a medical republic of letters in which American practitioners rubbed shoulders with the European elite, both current and historical. The inclusion of well-known colleagues in the United States like Drs. William Dewees and David Hosack as well as more obscure graduates from American universities created a sense of a thriving American obstetric profession, demonstrating to the "students and young practitioners" that publishing in medical journals was the first stop on the way to establishing professional clout. Famous practitioners and men of science like Sir Everard Home, Dr. John Clarke, Dr. Thomas Denman, and Dr. William Dewees engaged in these periodical conversations before and after they published weightier treatises like the one the "students and young practitioners" were reading. The *Compendium* was an entrée into this ongoing conversation, and a challenge to its readers to enter it by raising their own pens and sharing their experiences with their current and future colleagues, whose white, masculine, professional identity was in part created through the exchange of stories about investigations of the female body.

The aspiring young medical man needed to soften his dispassionate reason with feeling and sympathy. Sensibility was influential in early America, impacting medical, moral, and political ideologies. As a medical theory, sensibility bridged the body-mind divide through the theory of the nervous body (as opposed to a humoral one) that was equally sensitive to physical and mental/emotional stimuli. Indeed, emotional stimuli could have physical effects and vice versa. This sympathy of the parts led to an understanding of sympathy as fellow-feeling among individuals (real or fictional), simultaneously giving a biomedical explanation for a moral faculty and providing a biomedical theory with a moral dimension. In turn, sympathy and fellow-feeling undergirded the development of an American national identity. As Knott explains, for example, soldiers during and after the Revolutionary War, "imagined themselves as a community of sensibility and sympathy and served as a prototype for the patriot cause and nation formation."[44]

Sensibility continued to permeate popular discourse into the early decades of the nineteenth century and was key in defining gender roles for the new nation. Although women were considered to have too much sensibility to enable them to pursue political or professional paths, ideally, men who pursued these paths would exhibit the proper degree of sympathy and fellow-feeling that would enable them to navigate with morality and justice the demands of being a citizen of a republic. Early American fiction interrogated and defined gender and citizenship in the new nation, often through character types—the fallen woman and the rakish seducer, the republican wife and the benign patriarch, and, of importance here, the virtuous damsel-in-distress and her heroic rescuer.[45]

The contours of this ideal masculine hero can be traced by comparing the hero of the first American-authored play performed in the United States,

*The Contrast* (1787) by Royall Tyler, with the hero of one of America's earliest and most popular historical novels, *The Last of the Mohicans* (1826) by James Fenimore Cooper.[46] *The Contrast*, modelled after Richard Sheridan's *The School for Scandal* (1777), depicts the intrigues of New York society youth to condemn the aping of aristocratic British fashion in favor of Republican simplicity and sensibility. Published almost forty years later, *The Last of the Mohicans* recounts the captivity and rescue of the beautiful Monroe sisters during the Seven Years' War. The heroes of both texts, *The Contrast*'s Col. Henry Manly and *The Last of the Mohican*'s Maj. Duncan Heyward have much in common, despite being created decades apart. Mostly obviously, both Manly and Heyward are military men called upon to defend their nation by taking up arms. Both are officers, signaling that, although engaged with violence, they not only can command their own violent actions but also can control those of other men. This ability to control their violent potential implies that they are also able to control their sexual desires because of their innate reason and restraint. At the same time, these are men who allow themselves to be affected by sensibility.[47] Manly is expressly described by his sister as a "pensoroso" with "a heart replete with the noblest sentiments."[48] The narrator of *The Last of the Mohicans* frequently comments upon Heyward's "handsome, open, and manly brow" and his outpourings of sympathy and tenderness are lavished not only upon the Monro sisters and their father, but he is also moved to "admiration and pity" for his Native American ally, Uncas. Both Manly and Heyward, in fact, consider protecting "female virtue" their first duty.[49] Heyward treks, even into the heart of the enemy camp, through two long volumes, in his quest to protect the Monro sisters, both the frail, tottering blonde Alice and the brave quadroon Cora, from that fate worse than death—capture by hostile Native Americans. Manly only draws his sword once—to protect his sister from sexual assault; however, his attempts to "rectify [the] foibles"[50] of his sister through lectures and sermons are preventative measures that he hoped would have kept her out of that sitting room with her would-be seducer/rapist Dimple.

Through this brief outline, the contours of the manly hero in both works can be summed up as "brave and the generous," willing to raise his "arm… for our [i.e. virtuous women] protection, when nerv'd by virtue and directed by honour!"[51] This also describes the ideal American hero-accoucheur as envisioned in Bard's midwifery textbook, written in the intervening years between *The Contrast* and *The Last of the Mohicans*. The American hero-accoucheur needed manly fortitude and sympathy as he sat with laboring women, doing little but attempting to comfort, coach, and cheer them through birth. He needed to be sympathetic, yet in command of his emotions to protect women from their own emotional excess. Bard condemned equally men-midwives who were "timid and ignorant" and "rash and impatient."[52] Nothing was more dangerous than a "hesitating, vacillating conduct"[53] because the American hero-accoucheur needed to be willing to act with boldness and risk his reputation to try to save the American fair and her "pledges of love." In fact, "in extreme cases, extreme remedies may be called for, and not with due caution must be hazarded, rather than suffer a patient to perish without an effort to save her."[54]

This creation of a heroic persona for the doctor was part of the process of professionalization that medicine underwent in the eighteenth and nineteenth centuries. Like other obstetrical authors, Bard employed a rhetorical strategy that encouraged the male reader to identify with this heroic identity through pronoun choices, especially first-person plural and the inclusion of case studies from other practitioners. Bard's prose was written in first-person—Bard referred to himself as "I," and, while he did discuss the accoucheur in third-person, he also often addressed his readers as "we" (a pronoun not used in the midwife editions). The use of "I" and "we" created a feeling of collegiality: Bard was the mentor, guiding and welcoming the rising generation. He creates what Foucault describes as "A group…formed …of the master and his pupils, in which the act of recognition and the effort to know find fulfillment in a single movement….medical experience now has a collective subject; it is no longer divided between those who know and those who do not; it is made up, as one entity, of those who unmask and those before whom one unmasks."[55]

Case studies permitted medical men to self-create as heroes of their own stories, battling Nature in the guise of the Body and Death. "Medical authority" becomes linked to "a mode of masculine identity."[56] This linkage helped university-educated medical men in the Early National era align themselves with scientific progress against superstitious folk practices that included traditional midwifery. Through the narrative act, physicians could revision their practices into valorous battles while minimizing the consequences of their actions for patients. The case studies depicted men valiantly working to rescue women and children from the clutches of death. Their successes and failures showed heroes-in-training how to conduct themselves in similar situations. Cases taught students to put forth every effort, no matter how fatiguing, messy, or disgusting, necessary to defend against the deadly debility inhering in civilized female bodies.

Unlike in Smellie' *Treatise*, cases in the *Compendium* were almost always carefully signaled, so the change in tense is not abrupt, and almost all cases are carefully attributed. Thus, there isn't the same blurring of identity as discussed in Chapter One. Further, because most of the cases tended to be short, with little description, Bard avoided the picaresque qualities present in Smellie. However, the frequent use of third-person and passive voice created more of a clinical gaze with the veneer of objectivity and mastery. At the same time, many of the case studies feature an "I" acting heroically upon the bloody and exposed female body. This oscillation of style of the case studies--between detached observation and heroic first-person accounts—is mediated by the presence of the narrator, whose frequent addresses to "the reader" function as guideposts to know with whom to identify and who to condemn.

Most of the cases included in the fifth edition of the *Compendium* are from British sources; however, seventeen are clearly American in origin. Thirteen are from named sources, three seem to be from Bard's own practice, and one is from an anonymous "gentlemen" in personal correspondence with Bard.[57] Slightly more than half of these are presented in a clinical, passive voice, while the rest are in active voice (either first- or third-person). In all of these cases, labor had gone awry, resulting in a medical emergency that put the life of the female patient and her unborn child at risk.

The emergencies include convulsions and burst or prolapsed uteri, and, even though not all of the women or children are saved, the American hero-accoucheurs valiantly struggle to save them—like Bard's father John or Dr. Mcknight of Philadelphia who both "operated boldly,"[58] performing risky abdominal surgery to extract a fetus, without anesthesia or an understanding of sepsis, in attempts to save women whose uteri had burst. Four of the cases are William Dewees', who advocated massive bleeding in dangerous obstetric cases like convulsions, draining "quarts" of blood to "tranquilize" women.[59] The three cases that are likely from Bard's own practice are all of women who suffered prolapsus after labor. Bard reported, "It is not easy to express my feelings at this moment; still however, I commanded so much presence of mind, as neither to lose my time nor alarm my patient."[60] He here exemplifies the hero-accoucheur—emotionally affected, but in command of his feelings; bold to act, but careful and deliberate in his actions.

Five of these American cases recount experiments with ergot—a fungus that grows on rye that produces strong uterine contractions when ingested. Though American medical men began experimenting with it in 1808, Bard disapproved wholeheartedly of this innovation, preferring the traditional use of forceps or lever as safer for mother and child. The effects of ergot might be astonishing, but for Bard, its use proved the practitioner to be a rash and impatient man who did not properly value the life of the child—the child was stillborn in four of the five cases. He also feared that if ergot was publicized, it would "be employed to cover and conceal licentiousness."[61] Perhaps to discourage its use as an abortifacient, Bard included one case study in which a woman "took ergot" during a tedious labor, the result of which was a vaginal injury that "in spite of all our endeavours to the contrary...healed with so firm a stricture...as entirely to preclude all satisfactory connubial intercourse."[62] This, however, didn't keep her from becoming pregnant within two years, and although that birth proceeded naturally and the child lived, "the stricture... returned in as great degree as ever."[63]

The woman in this case, rather than the attending physician, was held responsible for taking the drug that condemned her to a lifetime of painful sexual intercourse, which she could not refuse if her husband demanded—as he clearly had. Although this case was ostensibly meant as a warning against the use of ergot, its focus on the woman's bodily pain held erotic potential. Halttunen argues that, as sensibility redefined pain as "unacceptable, taboo," the focus on pain in novels and humanitarian narratives, such as the medical case study, eroticized pain to the point that "The spectacle of suffering... became the dominant convention of sexual pornography by the early nineteenth century." Further, "the pornography of pain... represented pain as obscenely titillating precisely because the humanitarian sensibility deemed it unacceptable, taboo."[64] The spectacle of pain intended to stir up sympathetic action could simultaneously stimulate pleasure and even sexual arousal. Thus, the intended male student reader, encouraged to identify with the heroic medical men of the case history, might imagine himself the one probing the woman's injured vagina with pessary or penis.

Although the *Compendium* attempted to maintain a disinterested, decorous tone, ultimately the repression of the erotic subtext inherent in medical discussions of women's genitals was not entirely successful. Indeed, sexual frisson snakes through the text. For example, the *Compendium* asserted that a "deformed woman" either shouldn't marry or should submit to a manual vaginal examination before marriage to determine if her pelvic capacity was sufficient to ensure a live birth.[65] However, because deformed pelvises did not always manifest external symptoms like a limp, the only real way to determine deformity was through an internal pelvic examination. The implication seems to be that many, if not most, unmarried, presumably virginal, young women should undergo a manual examination by a male physician who would "carry [his fingers] up till we get them to the Fossa Magna then let them slip gradually into the Vagina"[66]—likely using the clitoris as a guidepost while feeling for the vulval vestibule in order to locate the vaginal opening. It's no wonder that

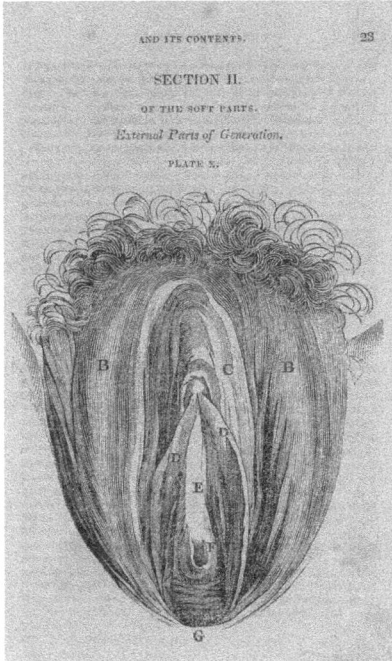

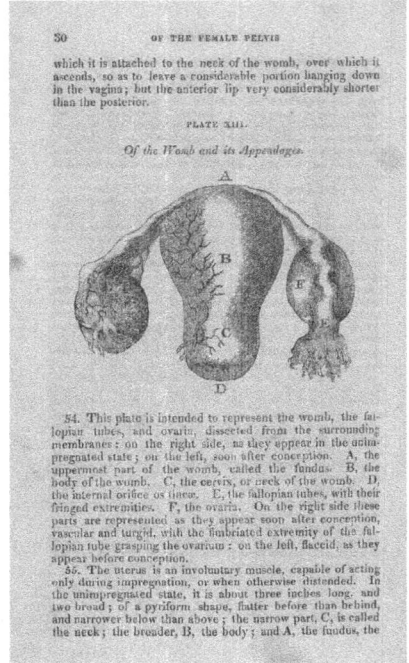

Figs. 4.2 and 4.3: On the left, a highly detailed drawing of the vulva found in only the student editions of *A Compendium*. Note the corona of pubic hair. On the right, a drawing of a uterus found in all five editions of *A Compendium*. *Courtesy of the Wangensteen Historical Library of Biology and Medicine, University of Minnesota.*

charges of sexual impropriety lingered about the profession.

An illustration that appeared solely in the student editions of *A Compendium*, the image of a finely detailed, free-floating vulva, would seem to cement midwifery's salacious underbelly. (Figure 4.2) As explored in detail in Chapter Two, midwifery books had long been used for pornographic purposes. In fact, when Mason Weems called the first edition of Bard's book "the American Aristotle," he was betting on the prurience of his customers for sales rather than their need for medical advice. Although plenty of "secrets" were revealed in the text, the only illustrations were of pelvic bones and simplified torso bisections. The visual arcana of women's genitals was reserved for the medical elite.

This close-up of a vulva completely fragments the female body by completely disassociating it from the torso or pelvis of the woman. This *l'orgine du monde* could be purchased for a few dollars when displaying artistic nudes in American museums was still considered a scandalous affair. The fine detailing of this image also stands in contrast to the more simplified, cartoonish images of the uterus (Figure 4.3) or the fetus inside the body.

Although the image of the vulva is still idealized, it is at the same time a realistic, sexually charged image. The female sex was not only on display, it could also function as a possessed secret that young medical students could bond over. Their masculine, professional identity was constructed through the perceived sharing of a fetishized, textualized female sexuality—although actual women were the private property of a single man, the secrets and "truth" of *all* women could be shared by those men privileged enough to attend medical school.

Much like the similarly idealized images of female genitals still found in anatomy books today,[67] the vulva illustration and the accompanying explanations were insidiously normalizing. The image reaffirms the verbal description that "in their natural situation" the nymphaea (labia minora) "are completely covered by the labia, but are apt, particularly in warm countries, to project beyond them; and in that state, to be inflamed and ulcerated, become callous, and grow so large and troublesome, as to require extirpation."[68] This not only pathologized healthy and "normal" labia minora that extend beyond the labia majora (a common occurrence); it also potentially racialized what was perceived as an undesirable trait, thus further pathologizing black bodies. As another midwifery writer explained, "It not very uncommonly happens that the nymphaea enlarge; in the Hottentot women, more especially…nor are our own females of the Caucasian variety of mankind altogether free from this defect."[69] As discussed in Chapter Two, this perceived racial difference, used to confirm that Africans were less human than Europeans, was fetishized.

The climate theory used by Bard and other writers to account for differences in puberty, menarche, and menstruation cast the socio-racial hierarchy as natural.[70] According to this theory, menarche happened too early to girls (at eight to twelve) in tropical regions, while in frigid regions, girls did not reach menarche until after their beauty began to fade—that is after twenty. However, in temperate climates, like Britain and France (and the United States, according to Bard), menarche occurred in girls at the ideal time of mid-adolescence, unless their systems were disrupted by luxury or hard labor. The bourgeois white woman becomes the scientific norm. However, the racial taxonomizing of women's anatomy undoubtedly hurt women of all races. It dehumanized women of color and justified their sexual exploitation. It also pathologized white women whose bodies fell outside "the norm." For example, most obstetric writers recommended excision of enlarged labia minora and clitorises, sometimes for seemingly medically necessary reasons, sometimes because "a woman is anxious to have this defect of the genitals remedied."[71] How many women underwent unnecessary genital surgery because they believed they were "defective?"

The man-midwife held the secrets of both Woman and the actual women he had as patients. He not only examined their bodies but also would engage in the medical confession, asking women about what, in any other context, would be unspeakable. For example, the leading medical opinions of the day held that every illness a woman might have could be traced back to (or at least impacted) uterine health. The primary indicator of female health and fertility for non-pregnant women was menstruation.[72] Menstruation was a taboo topic in polite mixed company. However, the physician was expected to broach it. To fully understand his female patients, he must violate social taboo and explicitly discuss the details of a woman's menstrual cycle. As one instructor explained,

> When Women labor under Diseases and the regular appearance of the Menses does not take place, they always attribute their Want of Health to this Circumstance... and if a practitioner happen to commit any Errour in conversing on the Subject they constantly look on him as an ignorant Man who knows nothing of his profession. Hence in every disease in which we see a Woman we should make Enquiries concerning Menstruation, not indeed because it is absolutely necessary but because the patient always expects such Enquiries to be made.[73]

Female patients expected physicians to discuss menstruation with them; failure to do so on the part of the physician could stymie an otherwise promising career. But how could a physician discuss the unspeakable with his patient? More broadly, how could a man discuss the unspeakable with any woman without violating the modesty of both? The medical student who took the above notes, who would go on to become a midwifery professor at the University of Pennsylvania, was reported to find the topic so embarrassing as to be almost unspeakable before his all-male classes. What must his embarrassment have been with his patients? Perhaps delicate euphemism and a darkened chamber were offered as a solution in the consulting chamber.

Masculine reason and self-control were supposed to enable the hero-accoucheur to repress the erotic potentialities of obstetrics and gynecology and to sublimate sexual desire into the professional desire to rescue the woman in distress. However, such precautions were not always enough to stave off accusations of sexual impropriety. According to one anti-man-midwifery author, "the submission of women, to the unnecessary examinations of physicians, exposing the secrets of nature...is a violent attack against chastity" that would lead to adultery.[74] The decorous sensibility taught by Bard and others only served to mask the danger, sometimes even from the accoucheur himself: "Many of these modest looking doctors, inflamed with thoughts of the well-shaped bodies of the women they have delivered, handled, hung over for hours, secretly glorying in the privilege, have to their patients, as priests to their penitents, pressed for accommodation, and driven to adultery and madness, where they thought most innocently occupied."[75] For opponents of man-midwifery, the hero-accoucheur only aided damsels-in-distress beset by the dangers inherent in their own bodies in order to gain sexual access to those bodies. Beneath the guise of the hero lurked the rake, whose uncontrolled desires, as seduction novels repeatedly depicted, imperiled the American fair.[76]

## The American Fair

The nature of women was hotly debated at the turn of the nineteenth century. Novelists, educators, politicians, and medical men argued about the proper role of women in the family and in society. Many educated white women, like Abigail Adams in her now-famous "remember the ladies" letter to her husband argued that they too should have political rights. Early American novels like *The Coquette* (1797) seem to explore if (white) women too, had an inalienable right to life, liberty, and the pursuit of happiness.[77] However, by the first decades of the nineteenth century, as Rosemarie Zagarri documents, there was a backlash against women who demanded political rights and public presence, and the biological sciences were used to justify the exclusion of women from politics: "In practice, biological essentialism meant that women's biological nature would prevent them from ever claiming the political rights and privileges that men enjoyed....If sex roles were inscribed in nature, then no human being could alter them."[78] Bard's *Compendium* is grounded in this incommensurability of the sexes. Woman, for Bard, was a monolithic creature, subject to the vagaries of her uterus—which produced the nervous sensibilities that made her timorous, emotional, and impressionable—and weakened by her broad pelvic bones—or incapacitated if they were narrowed by disease. Weak, delicate, even imperiled, Woman was unfit for physical or "public" exertions. *A Compendium*, with its scads of reference, would seem to offer incontrovertible proof that women's biology barred them from the public sphere.

However, as Pauline Schloesser has argued, the presence of free and enslaved African-American women, and to a lesser degree, the numerous white working poor, had to be ignored for these configurations of biological essentialism to work. Schloesser argues that by focusing on the "fair sex," popular discourses created a "sense of subjectivity" for propertied white women. In fact, "strategic deployment and ordinary usage of the term 'fair sex' produced white women as a special category: a racialized sex group that lost consciousness of itself as bounded by race and class, retaining the memory of its identity as one based on gender alone."[79] In other words, by coming to mean universal Woman, "the fair sex" erased or subsumed class and race differences. Bard's *Compendium* was one of the pieces of discourse that worked to establish the middle-class domestic white woman as Woman— the norm by which all members of the sex should be judged. Bard carefully identified women of color by their race and women of the upper and lower classes as ladies or poor women, thereby normalizing white women of the middling classes as Woman. The bodily, societal, and medical experiences of bourgeois white women subsumed and masked the markedly different realities of marginalized women upon whose bodies medical progress was made.[80] This rhetorical sleight of hand naturalizes the bourgeois domestic Woman as the medico-scientific ideal by which all other women were to be measured. The normalizing and naturalizing domestic Woman was another page taken from Denman. However, unlike Denman, Bard seemed less concerned with protecting the privacy and secrets of the domestic woman. The explicit descriptions of her body, from her bones to her genitals, frequent mention of sexual intercourse, as well as the inclusion of case studies, eroticized the bourgeois domestic Woman, a trait Bard's *Compendium* shared with the novels of the day.

The disdain Bard and his contemporaries tended to express toward female midwives was a by-product of biological essentialist thinking that defined "real" women as weak and dependent. A successful female midwife would require both bodily and mental strength, qualities that Bard thought women innately lacked. For example, the opening of Chapter One in the second edition (1812) reads:

> Of the skeleton, the knowledge of the bones of the pelvis or basin only is necessary to the practice of midwifery; but of these the more accurate *her* knowledge, the better will the *midwife* understand the causes of most of the difficulties which occur in tedious and dangerous labours; and will thereby be taught to avoid many errors in practice. *She* will therefore do well not only to study their form and connections, from plates and descriptions, but, whenever *she* has an opportunity, to correct and improve *her* knowledge, by examining them on the skeleton.[81]

The dangers and difficulties of labors seem to be the fault of the midwife's "errors," and women needed the knowledge contained within the pages of the book to avoid committing them, although the paternalistic tone and clear preference for men-midwives in the rest of the book would seem to belie Bard's belief in the female midwife's capacity to learn. In fact, he went on to apologize to any male readers for not going into specific detail because Bard wanted to avoid "burthening the memory" of female readers with inappropriate details.[82]

In the midwife editions of Bard's *Compendium*, the female midwife was positioned as the source of problems that the male practitioner would need to remedy. She was the foil against whom the hero-accoucheur's enlightened practice and identity was defined. However, as the *Compendium* switched focus to the growing numbers of male medical students, the female midwife slipped from focus. Women were still the source of problems for the man-midwife, but in the student editions, it was the frail female body that was the source of problems during pregnancy and labor. It is worth comparing this same passage from the student editions:

> Of the skeleton of the adult, the knowledge of the bones of the pelvis or basin is all that is necessary to the practice of midwifery; but of these the more accurate *his* knowledge, the better will the *accoucheur* understand the shape and dimensions of the cavity through which the foetus must pass; and the causes of most of the difficulties which occur in tedious and dangerous labours. *He* will do well, therefore, not only to study their form and connections, from plates and descriptions, but, whenever *he* has an opportunity, to correct and improve *his* knowledge, by carefully examining them on the skeleton: which is the more necessary, as the complex and irregular shape of these bones is very difficult to be expressed in words or represented in drawings.[83]

The man-midwife does not need to be "taught to avoid errors." Rather, the source of difficulties appear to arise from the female body itself and not the male practitioner, whose knowledge enabled him to assist the fetus as it navigated this dangerous terrain. The accompanying anatomical images drove home this message: the midwife edition was illustrated with several views of the "well-formed pelvis" (Figure 4.4) visually affirming that complications stem from the midwife's actions, not the laboring woman's body. In contrast, the student edition contains a new subsection not found in the earlier editions on "Deformed Pelvises," complete with four plates of misshapen pelvises

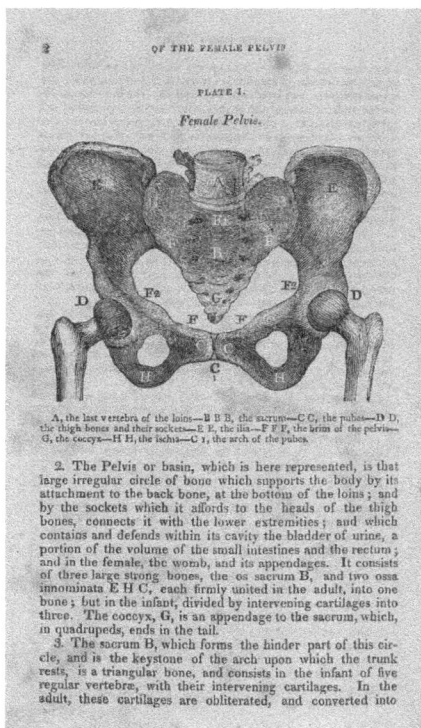

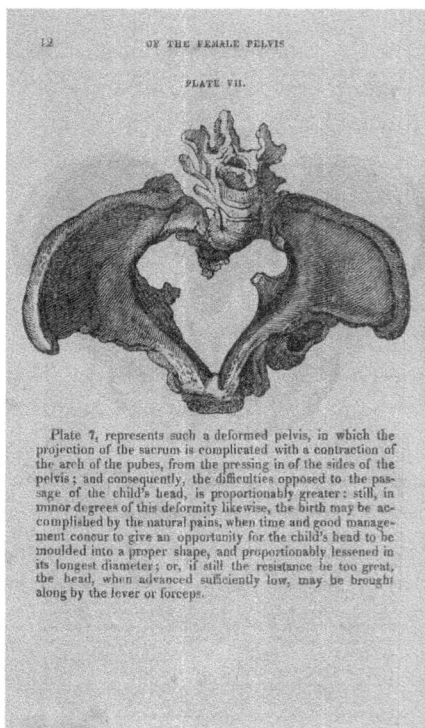

Figs. 4.4 and 4.5: On the left, the "well-formed" pelvis that appeared first in the 1812 (and subsequent) edition of *A Compendium*. On the right, one of several deformed pelvises that appeared only in the student editions. The inclusion of deformed pelvises subtly shifted blame for complicated births onto hidden dangers lurking in the female body itself. Courtesy of the Wangensteen Historical Library of Biology and Medicine, University of Minnesota.

and several case studies of women tortured by their faulty bodies. (Figure 4.5)

On the one hand, because man-midwifery was still typically an emergency surgical practice, the inclusion of deformed pelvises was a necessary learning tool. On the other, this focus on broken, deformed pelvises would seem to construct women as fragile, diseased creatures. Although the attentive accoucheur could usually tell the "deformed" woman from her outward appearance, sometimes the infirmity hidden from view, requiring the hero-accoucheur to train his eyes to see the skeleton beneath the flesh. Additionally, the *Compendium* asserts that even the healthy woman was incapacitated by her "light, shallow, and capacious" pelvis, preventing her from having the "firm step" and strength of a man.[84] Woman's perceived weakness and delicacy lay in her very bones. This also perhaps offers an explanation as to why so many sentimental heroines "tottered" through the pages of novels—even without being overcome by sensibility, a "real" woman, according to medical thinking, might have trouble walking! Moreover, a woman's pelvic health was always imperiled by her lifestyle. Women who had to engage in hard labor or work in factories risked deforming their pelvises—suggesting that the home and domestic employments were optimal for women's health. In fact, pelvic-deforming hard work was not the only lifestyle risk. The wealthy and indolent, with their delicate sensibilities, were at great risk for equally-fatal hysterical convulsions. The safest mode of life for women was the bourgeois domesticity that employed women in various household tasks without straining their delicate skeletons too strenuously. The domesticated woman was the ideal down to her bones.

However properly a woman lived, her health was always at risk because of the connection between her uterus and her mind. The uterine nerves "accounts for its [the uterus] extensive and various sympathies, which reach to the whole system of the female, and seems to draw under its control all the functions and every action of women; and on its healthy or diseased state, [depends] the delicacy of her frame, the liveliness of her passions, and the calmness or irritability of her temper."[85] Thus, every mental upset or swell of emotion had dire consequences for the pregnant womb. Not only could fear or depression—or even extreme joy or passion—retard the progress of labor by halting contractions, but these emotions could also kill the fetus and cause miscarriage. And these emotions and their tragic results were contagious among pregnant women, which is why Bard thought they should "restrain a dangerous propensity they too frequently have of visiting their friends, in dangerous labours, and under symptoms of miscarriage" because it made the visitors prone to miscarriage or dangerous labors themselves.[86]

Medical opinions like this sought to discourage "caudle and cake" visits[87] and have been blamed by historians for disrupting female care networks.[88] However, while the apparent sensitivity of the uterus called for the isolation of mothers, the opposite was true for unmarried adolescents at the time of menarche—at least if they were "feeble." "Feeble young women" needed to travel to "watering places of pubic resort," dance, ride, and generally socialize for their health. ("Robust" girls, on the other hand, needed to be kept home and bled to "lower" their systems).[89] Women's ill-health was eroticized. Thus, for the young woman who wanted to enjoy balls and outings—and to make herself as attractive as possible on the marriage market—it would behoove her to be as "languorous," "weak," and pale as any sentimental heroine.

Menarche was considered a crucial time in a girl's life, setting the tone of her future health and happiness. At the same time, menstruation placed women on a chain of being. It both distinguished women from animals and made them more animal-like. Although only human females menstruated, "something of the nature of menstruation takes place in most animals which in them is termed heat...."[90] Unlike males, who were (ideally) always fertile and ready for copulation, females were controlled by sexual cycles like estrous. Their fertility and sexual-readiness were manifested through distinct somatic signals—menstrual blood in human females, the "law of [her] constitution." The periodic and involuntary shedding of menstrual blood, like the periodic and involuntary return of "heat" in other animals, symbolized women's lack of control over her sexuality, indeed, her subservience to it.

In the eighteenth century, the communication between the uterus and brain that made women more "exquisitely sensible" was also understood as evidence of their sexual libido. For instance, because ovulation was believed to occur because of orgasm, the corpus lutea—the scars of ovulation left on the ovary—were often cited as evidence of masturbation. However, because it was also increasingly recognized that women conceived without apparently enjoying sex, orgasm was often defined as an involuntary paroxysm that could occur without pleasure or even conscious awareness.[91] In fact, by the turn of the nineteenth century, women were typically believed to be less susceptible to sexual appetites than men and therefore became sexual gatekeepers. Wollstonecraft argued that it was only false education and an overvaluation of sensibility that made women "systemically voluptuous."[92] One of the "rights of woman" Wollstonecraft advocated for was the right for women to be seen as something other than a sexual object. At the same time, beliefs about moral or Republican motherhood envisioned women as rational, domestic beings. As Knott explains, "Neither mode had much role for sex. Republican womanhood depended on a femininity marked by reason and control of the passions, and plotted against autonomous female sexuality. The typical flavor of revolutionary radicalism, meanwhile, was idealistic moralism...."[93] This de-emphasis of female sexuality eventually led to the Victorian ideal of passionlessness and the cult of true womanhood's valuation of sexual purity. Nancy Cott has argued that "the view that women (although still primarily identified by their female gender) were less carnal and lustful than men"[94] was a way for women to exert power over their own bodies: "women might hail passionlessness as a way to assert control in the sexual arena—even if that 'control' consisted in denial....More essentially, passionlessness served women's larger interest by downplaying altogether their sexual characterization, which was the cause of their exclusion from significant 'human' (i.e., male) pursuits."[95]

Cott argues that medicine didn't embrace the idea of female passionlessness until the mid-nineteenth century, at which point, many women rebelled at being asked to take passionlessness "literally" as a somatic condition.[96] However, the factuality of women's ability to enjoy sexual intercourse began to be debated a full century earlier. Moreover, the view of women as completely lacking in sexual desire never fully took hold among the medical profession. Nevertheless, most male midwifery writers tended to deemphasize the importance, or even the existence, of female sexual desire, as a way of legitimizing their own profession. The primary charge against the man-midwife—in 1750 or 1850—was sexual impropriety. As Samuel Gregory expostulated, man-midwifery "breaks down all barriers, and affords the most unbounded liberties and temptations to the unprincipled and licentious."[97] Such dangers were somewhat mitigated if women were seen as less susceptible to sexual arousal than men. Thus the importance of the figure of the hero-accoucheur in midwifery textbooks—medical men needed to be trained to see themselves as the heroes and defenders of women's health, reputations, and lives.

An exchange of letters between Drs. William Dewess and Peachy Harrison in the *Philadelphia Medical Museum* highlight the contradictory and convoluted ideas about conception and the role of female sexual desire to it. The controversy was spurred by Dewees' essay on the occurrence of superfoetation (essentially becoming pregnant while already pregnant) in humans. Harrison took issue with Dewees' claims because "venereal sensibility resides in the os tincae [cervix]" and "venereal orgasm," necessary for conception, was only caused by "irritation [of the cervix] from the soft and velvet-like head of the penis."[98] Therefore superfoetation couldn't occur because the obliteration of the cervix during pregnancy would make orgasm and therefore conception impossible. In the next issue, Dewees countered that not only was the cervix "insensible," but that pleasurable "venereal orgasm" was "absolutely unnecessary to impregnation" because "many women are perfectly indifferent to the venereal congress, some affirm they never felt anything like pleasure, and others that it is not only disgusting, but extremely painful" yet these women were often "prolific."[99] Harrison did not back down from his position, and even took issue with what he read as Dewees' claim that "the majority" of women "feel no pleasure from the venereal congress."[100] However, the editor, John Redman Cox, gave his friend Dewees the last word, although the argument might have continued via private letter, as proposed by Dewees, because…*every* thing we know on this subject may not be fit for a discussion like the present, which is to meet the public eye…."[101]

After such an explicit exchange, one wonders what information was deemed too indecorous for even a medical public. Much of the exchange must have raised eyebrows. For instance, both men ground their arguments in proofs gained either through "the testimony"[102] of female patients or through the "testimony of experiments"[103] on female patients. Seemingly, doctors were interrogating their female patients on their experiences of pleasure during sexual intercourse and possibly even attempting to stimulate sexual arousal (out of scientific curiosity). Revelations like these fanned the fire of anti-man-midwife authors. Thus it is significant that Dewees, part of the Philadelphia medical elite and professor of midwifery at the University of Pennsylvania medical school, already claimed that "very many women" were passionless—repulsed by sex even—by the early nineteenth century. As these women were the "most prolific," they would presumably have the most contact with men-midwives. Perhaps because they supposedly lacked the ability to feel "venereal" pleasures, their virtues, and the accoucheur's reputation, would be secure.

The *Compendium* was nowhere so explicit about sexual pleasure; however, the student editions seem more frank and detailed about female anatomy and theories of conception than the midwife ones. The *Compendium* seemed to share Harrison's belief that ovulation was "stimulated by the semen masculinum,"[104] but it avoided discussing orgasm or pleasure as factors. By the early nineteenth century, most medical writings demoted the clitoris to a lump of unimportant erectile tissue that, if too large, needed to be extirpated. Nearly a century before Freud, female sexual desire, if it existed, had already been relegated to the vagina, the sensibility of which was debated.

Medical men constructed a professional, heroic identity and imagined community through the exchange of textualized female bodies, but they had to do so without threatening individual men's property rights in actual female bodies. Female passionlessness—or at least the elision of female sexual pleasure—was the lubrication that made that possible. Denying women's sexual agency enabled medical men to discount accusations of impropriety—if women largely lacked sexual passion, and what little they had was only stimulated through male ejaculate, private consultations and manual physical examinations posed no threat to husbands' property rights in their wives' sex. The heroic persona taught by midwifery textbooks encouraged men-midwives to display a dispassionate empathy that would comfort both patient and her spouse.

Midwifery textbooks and case studies enabled men-midwives to understand themselves as possessing the "secrets of women," and imagine themselves as hero-accoucheurs saving women in distress. Bard's *A Compendium of the*

*Theory and Practice of Midwifery* offers an important snapshot into American man-midwifery during the 1810s. As the texts' stated audience changed from women to male medical students, it became more cosmopolitan, more committed to seeing American physicians and surgeons as members of a transatlantic medical community. The American hero-accoucheur constructed by Bard's text was no backwater bumpkin, but an educated man of reason and feeling committed to saving women and children from the dangers of the maternal body and Death itself.

# Endnotes

1    John M'Vickar, *A Domestic Narrative of the Life of Samuel Bard, M.D. LL.D.* (New York 1822), 148. Moreover, as Sari Altschuler as recently demonstrated, literary endeavors and the active cultivation of the imagination were crucial elements of medical training. See Altshuler, *The Medical Imagination: Literature and Health in the Early United States* (Philadelphia: University of Pennsylvania Press, 2018).

2    Oliver Goldsmith, *The Vicar of Wakefield* (1766) Ed. Arthur Friedman (Oxford: Oxford University Press, 2008).

3    See Laqueur, "Bodies Details, and the Humanitarian Narrative."

4    Some of the first editions bear 1807 as the publication date.

5    Biographical information on Samuel Bard is derived from manuscript collections of his family's letters and from early biographers. Henry William Ducachet, *A Biographical Memoir of Samuel Bard, M.D. LL.D. Late President of the College of Physicians and Surgeons of the University of the State of New-York, &c. With a Critique Upon His Writings. Read Before the New-York Historical Society, August 14th 1821* (Philadelphia 1821); John Brett Langstaff, *Doctor Bard of Hyde Park.* (Dutton & Co: New York, 1942); M'Vickar, *A Domestic Narrative*; Bard Family Papers. *BC*, Annandale-on-Hudson, New York; Bard Collection, *NYAM* New York; Bard Family Papers. *NYHS*, New York; Bard Family Papers, 1658-1898. Hudson River Valley & Dutchess County Manuscript Collection. *FDRPL*, Hyde Park, New York.

6    John Bard to Samuel Bard, April 9, 1763, Bard Collection, Box 1. *NYAM*.

7    See James N. Green, "'The Cowl knows best what will suit in Virginia': Parson Weems on Southern Readers." *Printing History* 17 (1995): 34.

8    See Advertisement for medical books at the back of *A Compendium* (New York 1808). Rosner, "Thistle on the Delaware," 28-29.

9    See "Proposed Union of the Medical Schools in New York." *The American Medical and Philosophical Register,* (July 1810). *American Periodical Series Online;* Samuel Bard and John W. Francis, "University of the State of New York— College of Physicians and Surgeons." *New York Medical and Philosophical Journal and Review* (January 1811). *American Periodical Series Online;* Idem., "Domestic Intelligence." *The American Medical and Philosophical Register* (July 1813). *American Periodical Series Online;* David Hosack, "Original Communications: Sketch of the Origin and Progress of the Medical Schools of New York and Philadelphia." *The American Medical and Philosophical Register* (July 1811). *American Periodical Series Online.*

10   Bard, *A Compendium* (1808) 3.

11   Samuel Bard to Francis U. Johnson. March 21, 1821. Bard Family Papers, Box 3. *BC.*

12   Sylvia D. Hoffert, *Private Matters: American Attitudes toward Childbearing and Infant Nurture in the Urban North, 1800-1860.* (Urbana, IL: University of Illinois Press, 1989), 122.

13   Nelson, *National Manhood,* 173.

14   Buchan, *Advice to Mothers* (Boston, 1809): 26.

15   Osborne and Denman taught, among other Americans, Dr. Samuel P. Griffitts and Thomas C. James, the first professor of midwifery at the University of Pennsylvania. See Osborne, *Essays on the Practice of Midwifery* (London, 1792). See also Sayer Walker, *Observations on The Constitutions of Women, and on Some of the Diseases to which they are more especially liable* (London, 1803); Lyle Massey, "Pregnancy and Pathology: Picturing Childbirth in Eighteenth-Century Obstetric Atlases," *Art Bulletin* 87.1 (2005): 73-74; Ornella Moscucci, *The Science of Woman,* (Cambridge: Cambridge University Press, 1990), 50-52.

16   White *Treatise on the Management of Pregnant and Lying-in Women* (Worcester, MA, 1793).

17   See Ulrich, Laurel Thatcher. *A Midwife's Tale: The Life of Martha Ballard, Based on her Diary, 1785-1812.* (New York: Vintage, 1990): 251-61.

18   Anonymous, *Remarks on the Employment of Females as Practitioners in Midwifery by a Physician* (Boston, 1820). See also Amalie M. Kass, "The Obstetrical Casebook of Walter Channing, 1811-1822," *Bulletin of the History of Medicine* 67 (1993): 494-523 and Amalie M. Kass, *Midwifery and Medicine in Boston:* Walter Channing, M.D. 1786 to 1876 (Boston: Northwestern University Press, 2002).

19   Anonymous, *Remarks,* 4.

20   *Ibid,* 7.

21   *Ibid,* 9.

22   *Ibid,* 15.

23   *Ibid,* 13.

24   *Ibid,* 12.

25   *Ibid,* 21. See also Rosner, *The Most Beautiful Man.*

26   Anonymous, *Remarks,* 12.

27   *Ibid.,* 19.

28   Bard to Francis U. Johnson c. 1820, Bard family papers, ca. 16th cent – 1892, Box 1, *CUBL.*

29   M. D. Learned and C. F. Brede, eds. "An Old German Midwife's Record (Kept by Susanna Müller, of Providence Township, Lancaster County, Pennsylvania, during the years 1791-1815)," *German American Annals* (1903): 3.

30   See Kass, *Midwifery in Medicine.*

31    For instance, the documentary *The Business of Being Born* (2008, Dir. Abby Epstein) pointed out that many insurance policies will not cover the cost of hiring a midwife rather than an obstetrician, even though the former is much less expensive. However, many hospitals, including the Mayo Clinic, now include midwives on their obstetric staffs.

32    Bard, *A Compendium* (1819), 312.

33    *Ibid.*, 190

34    *Ibid.*, 220

35    *Ibid.*, 215.

36    *Ibid.*, 293.

37    *Ibid.*, 162.

38    Bard, *A Compendium* (1808), 8. Italics in original.

39    Bard, *A Compendium* (1819), 170.

40    *Ibid.*, 212-13. Italics in original.

41    *Ibid.*, viii.

42    See Shirley Burgoyne Black, *An Eighteenth-Century Mad Doctor: William Perfect of West Malling* (Sevenoaks, Kent, UK: Darenth Valley, 1995).

43    Bard, *A Compendium* (1819), 171.

44    Knott, *Sensibility in the American Revolution*, 18.

45    See, for instance, Gareth Evans, "Rakes, Coquettes and Republican Patriarchs: Class, Gender and Nation in Early American Sentimental Fiction," *Canadian Review of American Studies* 25.3 (1995): 41-63.

46    Although it has been argued that Cooper is actually mocking Duncan throughout the novel, Duncan's survival and fate to help found and populate the future United States—seemingly with his sensibility intact—suggests that it's his immaturity and not his character that Cooper might have been satirizing. See, for instance, Robert Milder, "*The Last of the Mohicans* and the New World Fall," *American Literature* 52.3 (1980): 407-49; Lora Romero, "Vanishing Americans: Gender, Empire, and New Historicism," *American Literature* 63.3 (1991): 385-404; Nina Baym, "Putting Women in their Place: *The Last of the Mohicans* and other Indian Stories," *Feminism and American Literary History* (New Brunswick, NJ: Rutgers University Press, 1992): 19-35; Ian Dennis, "The Worthlessness of Duncan Heyward: A Waverly Hero in America," *Studies in the Novel* 29.1 (1997): 1-16; and Stephanie Wardrop, "Last of the Red Hot Mohicans: Miscegenation in the Popular American Romance," *MELUS* 22.2 (1997): 61-74.

47    Patricia Myers Spacks argues convincingly that a key difference between masculine and feminine sensibility was that women had no choice but to be sensible, whereas the man of feeling chose to engage his sensibilities. See

Spacks, "Oscillations of Sensibility," *New Literary History* 25.3 (1994): 505-520.

48   Royall Tyler, The Contrast: *Manners, Morals, and Authority in the Early American Republic,* Ed. Cynthia A. Kierner (New York: New York University Press, 2007): 50, 54.

49   James Fenimore Cooper, *The Last of the Mohicans*. Ed. Paul C. Gutahr (Ontario: Broadview, 2009): 58, 284.

50   Tyler, *The Contrast*, 54.

51   *Ibid.*, 47-48.

52   Bard, *A Compendium* (1819), 307.

53   *Ibid.*, 292.

54   *Ibid.*, 108.

55   Foucault, *The Birth of the Clinic,* 110.

56   Keller, *Generating Bodies* 182.

57   Several more cases are anonymous and unsourced, so they could also be from American practices.

58   Bard, *A Compendium* (1819), 52.

59   *Ibid,* 240.

60   *Ibid.*, 330.

61   *Ibid.*, 233.

62   *Ibid.*, 297.

63   *Ibid.*, 298.

64   Halttunen, "The Pornography of Pain," 304, 317.

65   Bard, *A Compendium* (1819), 9-10.

66   Denman and Osborne Lectures, WL

67   See, for instance, M. Andrikopoulou et al., "The Normal Vulva"

68   Bard, *A Compendium* (1819), 25.

69   James Blundell, *Observations on Some of the More Important Diseases of Women* (London: E. Cox, 1837), 283.

70   For a compelling recent study of climate theory, race, and sex, see Greta LaFleur, *The Natural History of Sexuality in Early America*, (Baltimore: Johns Hopkins University Press, 2018), esp. Chapter One.

71   James Blundell, "Lectures on the Diseases of Women and Children Delivered at Guy's Hospital," *The Lancet* (1828-9), 707.

72   See also Alexandra Lord, "'The Great *Arcana* of the Diety': Menstruation and Menstrual Disorders in Eighteenth-Century British Medical Thought," *Bulletin of the History of Medicine* 73.1 (1999): 38-63 and Helen King, *The Diseases of Virgins: Greensickness, Chlorosis and the Problems of Puberty* (London: Routledge, 2004).

73   Mss Notes from Drs. Osborne's and Clarke's lectures on midwifery, taken by

Thomas James 1790-91, *COP*

74    Thomas Ewell, *The Ladies Medical Companion* (Philadelphia: William Brown, 1818): 25.

75    *Ibid.*, 26.

76    Much has been written about the seduction novel in early American literature. For a classic analysis, see Cathy N. Davidson, *Revolution and the Word* (Oxford: Oxford University Press, 2004).

77    See, for instance, Davidson, *Revolution*, 221-32; Gillian Brown, "Consent, Coquetry, and Consequences," *American Literary History* 9.1 (1997): 625-52; and Laura H. Korobkin, "'Can your Volatile Daughter ever Acquire your Wisdom?': Luxury and False Ideals in *The Coquette*," *Early American Literature* 41.1 (2006): 79-107.

78    Rosemarie Zagarri, *Revolutionary Backlash*, (Philadelphia: University of Pennsylvania Press, 2007): 171

79    Pauline Schloesser, *The Fair Sex: White women and Racial Patriarchy in the Early American Republic* (New York: New York University Press, 2002): 8, 53.

80    See also Washington, *Medical Apartheid*; Doyle, *Maternal Bodies*, esp. Chapter 1; and Owens, *Medical Bondage*.

81    Bard, *A Compendium* (1812), 25, emphasis added.

82    *Ibid.*, 26.

83    Bard, *A Compendium* (1819), 1, emphasis added.

84    *Ibid.*, 4.

85    *Ibid.*, 35

86    *Ibid.*, 134

87    Tyler, *The Conrast*, 94.

88    See for instance, Hoffert, *Private Matters*; Ulrich, *The Midwife's Tale*; Leavitt, *Brought to Bed*; and Wertz and Wertz, *Lying-in*.

89    Bard, *A Compendium* (1819), 70.

90    *Ibid.*, 41.

91    See Lacqueur, *Making Sex*, 161-63.

92    Mary Wollstonecraft, *A Vindication of the Rights of Women*. 2nd Ed. Ed. Carol H. Poston (New York: Norton, 1988), 138.

93    Sarah Knott, "Female Liberty? Sentimental Gallantry, Republican Womanhood, and Rights Feminism in the Age of Revolutions," *William and Mary Quarterly* 71.4 (2014): 426.

94    Nancy Cott, "Passionlessness: An Interpretation of Victorian Sexual Ideology, 1790-1850," *Signs* 4.2 (1978): 221. See also Barbara Welter, "The Cult of True Womanhood, 1820-1860," *American Quarterly* 18.2 (1966): 151-174.

95    Cott, "Passionlessness," 233.

96   *Ibid.*, 236.

97   Samuel Gregory, *Man-Midwifery Exposed and Corrected* (Boston: George Gregory, 1848): 5.

98   Peachey Harrison, "Observations on Impregnation. By Peachey Harrison, in a Letter to the Editor," *Philadelphia Medical Museum* (Philadelphia: Thomas Dobson, 1806): 422.

99   William Potts Dewees, "Reply to Dr. Peachey Harrison's Observations on Impregnation," *Philadelphia Medical Museum* (Philadelphia: Thomas Dobson, 1807): 36. 33.

100  Harrison, "Answer to Dr. Dewees's Reply to Dr. Peachey Harrison's Observations on Impregnation," *Philadelphia Medical Museum* (Philadelphia: Thomas Dobson, 1808): 102.

101  Dewees, "Remarks on Dr. Peachey Harrison's Reply," *Philadelphia Medical Museum* (Philadelphia: Thomas Dobson, 1808): 168. Emphasis in original.

102  Dewees, "Reply to Dr. Peachy Harrison's," 33.

103  Harrison, "Answer to Dr. Dewees's Reply," 101.

104  Bard, *A Compendium* (1819), 35.

# Coda: Heroes in Our Own Stories

Although this was not my original plan for ending this book, I am going to close with a personal medical story—one that is lengthy, overly intimate, and humiliating, but that, for me, encapsulates how gender and power still play out on the examination table.

Recently, I injured my labia minora. When I called my medical provider, my regular gynecologist did not have any openings for weeks, but the understanding receptionist was able to get me in to see a Certified Nurse Midwife (CNM) the next day. At my appointment, I first explained my situation to the intake nurse, who asked if I have considered labiaplasty. I answered, no, I was there about injured, not healthy, tissue. Then I had to repeat my story to the CNM, who was clearly empathetic and caring, but who also asked if I have considered labiaplasty. I again said no, that there is nothing wrong with my labia in general. There is a lot of variation in the size and shape of vulvas— had she ever seen Jamie McCartney's *The Great Wall of Vagina*—an art piece that displays the casts of over 400 vulvas to celebrate their diversity[1] —and proceeded to show her images of it on my phone.

After the examination, she was pretty sure she could treat me, but she wanted to first confer with the new urogenital specialist, whom she assured me, was "great." When he came in, he made small talk—asked what I do for a living, and I responded that I teach literature and gender studies. He then complained that his son's gender studies class at university made too much of physician abuse of patients, which, he assured me, he had never personally seen. I made some defensive comment about it still being a problem. Then he asked what my weekend plans were, to which I responded to clean my house and to attend a local Black Lives Matter demonstration being held in response to George Floyd's recent murder.[2]

For the third time, I repeated my story and for the third time I was asked to consider labiaplasty. At this point, the CNM asked the physician if he knew about *The Great Wall of Vagina*, so I told him about Jamie McCartney's art piece, to which he dismissively responded, wasn't she a VJ on MTV? After more awkward small talk and my attempts to humorously make light of my embarrassing situation, the urogenital specialist proceeded to the physical examination. Unfortunately the CNM had to leave before this to see other patients, so in the room was just he, his nurse, and I. I was lying half-naked, feet in stirrups, while he proceeded to poke and prod my genitals, when he asked me what I think about all the protests. "Black lives matter," I responded. Yes, he answered, what do I think about that? "That black lives matter." To which he responded, "But what about black-on-black crime?"

I ask you to picture my situation—I am an educated, self-confident, white woman, lying exposed, feet in stirrups, gripping the edges of the examination table in pain and anxiety, as minor surgery was being performed on my genitals. At that moment of incredible vulnerability, I found myself arguing that black lives matter and that criminality has nothing to do with scourge of police brutality with this seemingly dispassionate, white male physician, who could at any moment "slip" and do me untold, intimate, grievous injury, and who doesn't believe that physicians abuse their patients. After what seemed like an eternity, but was in actuality only a few minutes, I finally sharply suggested that arguing politics while he operated on my genitals was not a good idea. So he proceeded to turn the conversation to my gender studies course and asked what my opinion was on female circumcision!

Fortunately, my ordeal was over shortly thereafter, but I walked away, healing yes, but stunned—utterly dumbfounded—by this exchange. The power dynamic—and the physician's seeming obliviousness to it—in that room nearly left me speechless. Yet, we were both white and "doctors"—in many ways social equals. What might be the situation of women and girls with less social status? Less education and self-confidence? How does this "great" doctor act toward women of color?

At the same time, I am certain that in his version of this event, this physician would be the hero helping a hapless woman with an embarrassing injury. In fact, with my argumentativeness, he might even think of me as a modern-day equivalent of the "unmanageable" women William Smellie complained about. This is true not only because we are always the heroes in our own stories, but also because, the story of the physician-as-hero has become the cultural norm.

Often considered the first hero-doctor in fiction, George Elliot's Tertius Lydgate in *Middlemarch* (1871) dreams of being a medical hero. Filled with tales of the heroic discoveries and interventions of his predecessors—and no doubt with their self-presentations as heroes—he seeks professional glory, desiring to reform the practice of medicine and pursue scientific research. Lydgate "did not simply aim at a more genuine kind of practice than was common....He was fired with the possibility that he might work out the proof of an anatomical conception and make a link in the chain of discovery."[3] Unfortunately, the cares and responsibilities of a wife and family stymie his ambitions, and although he "gained an excellent practice" before his early death, "he always regarded himself as a failure"[4] because he had not joined the ranks of great medical researchers and writers. *Middlemarch* is the culmination of more than a century of medical self-fashioning and self-aggrandizement. Having spent gallons of ink convincing themselves and each other about their heroism—and the development of some effective therapeutics—the public at large became convinced of the medical man's heroic status. The hero-doctor was born and thereafter, with few exceptions, fictional doctors are heroes— men who stand between the masses of humanity and death.[5] This heroic narrative still captivates audiences in television series like *ER* and *House*, in which the physicians may be flawed, but they are always fighting to save the hapless from death.[6]

This cultural mythos of the heroic physician has enabled many to abuse patients, despite the doubts of my "great" urogenital specialist. For example, famous medical monster Larry Nassar got away with abusing hundreds of girls for nearly two decades, and when he was finally brought to justice, still maintained that he was a "wonderful doctor."[7] Sarah Yahr Tucker's harrowing 2018 exposé of the "epidemic" of ob-gyns and their nurses abusing patients in labor demonstrates just how widespread and mundane medical abuse can be.[8] Tucker's research into "obstetric violence" relies heavily on first-hand accounts from doulas who have witnessed and tried to protect their clients from such violence. The exposé leaves readers with the question of what happens to women who do not have such a "bodyguard" to defend them?

The conflict between traditional midwifery and the medical professions of obstetrics and gynecology are especially salient in the United States with its juggernaut of privatized medicine, labyrinthine networks of public and private medical insurance, and abysmal maternal and infant death rates.[9] In European nations, including the United Kingdom, midwifery has been incorporated into national healthcare systems. Although this has resulted in the loss of autonomy and some compromise with a techno-medical model of birth, traditional midwifery is respected and practiced without the heated controversies that exist in the U.S.[10] In the U.S., numerous legal and economic barriers exist to prevent women who want to be attended by a midwife or to give birth outside of the hospital setting. Moreover, within or without the hospital, the costs associated with birth, especially for the uninsured, can be ruinous.[11]

The current conflict between the doula or midwife and the ob-gyn invested in the techno-medical model of birth is, in many ways, a long continuation of the contest for authority recounted in the foregoing pages. This fact is powerfully demonstrated in Mary M. Lay's *The Rhetoric of Midwifery*, which recounts and analyzes the 1990s legal and medical drama around the failed attempts to establish licensing procedures and requirements for direct entry midwives in Minnesota. Lay examines the conflict, ongoing since the eighteenth century, between "medical authoritative knowledge" that views "a woman's body [as] imperfect and that medicine can 'improve on nature,' that every pregnant woman and her infant are at risk, and that 'you cannot assume that any birth is normal until it is over…'"[12] and the experiential knowledge of midwives that sees most pregnancies and births as normal, nonmedical events. This episode in medical history, as Lay points out, in many ways recapitulates the eighteenth-century debates between traditional midwives like Elizabeth Nihell and the men-midwives.

By styling themselves as medical heroes and traditional female midwives as ignorant, dangerous, and unreliable, eighteenth-century men-midwives eventually achieved the social and professional authority that obstetricians and gynecologists of whatever gender enjoy to this day. In their writings, eighteenth-century men-midwives deployed the tropes of hero-accoucheur and parturient damsel-in-distress. They envisioned the female body as a frightening and treacherous *terra incognita* that they were compelled to enter and explore, to map and "fix" in order to rescue the chaste damsel and her infant from her imperfect and dangerous female body.

On the one hand, men-midwives deployed these tropes, full of fear and desire, within the sentimental discourse of the day that accepted their truths without fully unpacking their contents. These tropes naturalized men-midwives' claims of authority over the female body, just as they naturalized the discovery of modesty, passivity, and weakness within that body. On the other, medical men attempted to coin a new, objective vocabulary with which to discuss the female body in order to distance their professional endeavors from the novels and bawdry with which they shared too much in common. Nevertheless, their coinages (vagina, labia, uterus, etc.) were not neutral. They were as little divested of ideology as their other rhetorical choices. Historical analyses of medicine such as this one should remind us to keep an eye on the cultural fears and desires that necessarily infect the medico-scientific objectivity of our own time. Language and rhetoric, even that of dry medico-scientific techno-speak, can never entirely divest themselves of their intrinsic quality of *dilatio*—of meanings that multiply, proliferate beyond intention or purpose. Language can never divest itself of its connotative tendencies, of its histories, nor of the cultural codes that imbue the signified.

I have mapped out the changing rhetorical valences of male-authored midwifery manuals through a comparative analysis among midwifery manuals and between versions and editions of the same titles. I have argued that these men borrowed the language of sentiment to construct a compelling professional identity that enabled them to centralize authority over the body, and in particular, over women's bodies. However, much work remains to be done. For instance, the nexus between natural history and midwifery is a fruitful one that has only begun to be explored, while the question of female reaction to and interaction with these texts is a looming question. Exploration of these avenues and others will continue to shed light on the vexed and vexing questions about the construction and maintenance of gender and gendered power in biomedical writings and in our culture at large. Maybe one day knowledge of the sexed body will not be the purview of the privileged few and the "secrets" of women will not be used to curtail the political and social freedom of women. It is my hope that my work, by tracing the history of biomedical power, will help unravel the ways in which the fact of female embodiment continues to be used against us in the examination room, the labor and delivery room, and in the world at large.

# Endnotes

1    Jamie McCartney, *The Great Wall of Vagina* (2015). https://jamiemccartney. com/portfolio/the-great-wall-of-vagina/. Accessed June 2, 2020.

2    The murder of George Floyd by police in Minneapolis on May 25, 2020, set off weeks of international protests against racism and police brutality. For an overview, see, for instance, the *Wikipedia* article on "The Killing of George Floyd" Last updated July 2, 2020. https://en.wikipedia.org/wiki/Killing_of_ George_Floyd Accessed July 2, 2020.

3    George Eliot. *Middlemarch*. Ed. David Carroll (Oxford: Clarendon, 1992), 143-44.

4    *Ibid*, 821.

5    See, for instance, Rosner, The *Most Beautiful Man*; Brown,. "'Like a Devoted Army'; M. Faith McLellan, "Images of Physicians in Literature: From Quacks to Heroes," *The Lancet* (1996): 458-60; Janine Marchessault, "Men in White, Women in Aprons: Utopian Iconographies of TV Doctors," In *Figuring it Out* Ann B Shteir and Bernard Lightman, eds (Hanover, NH: Dartmouth College Press, 2006), 315-336.

6    *ER*, created by Michael Crichton, ran on NBC from 1994-2009. *House,* created by David Shore and starring Hugh Laurie, ran on Fox from 2004-2012.

7    Quoted in Hadley Freeman, "How was Larry Nassar able to abuse so many gymnasts for so long?" *The Guardian*. (January 26, 2018). https://www. theguardian.com/sport/2018/jan/26/larry-nassar-abuse-gymnasts-scandal-culture

8    Sarah Yahr Tucker, "There is a Hidden Epidemic of Doctors Abusing Women in Labor, Doulas Say." *Broadly, Vice Media*. (May 8, 2018) https://broadly.vice. com/en_us/article/evqew7/obstetric-violence-doulas-abuse-giving-birth?utm_ source=vicefbus

9    In 2018, maternal mortality rate in the United States ranged from 12 out of 1,000 for white, non-Hispanic women to 40 out of 1,000 for African-American women. Similarly, infant mortality rate ranged 5 out of 1,000 among Asian or Pacific Islander Americans to nearly 15 out of 1,000 for African-American infants. See Amber Bellazaire and Erik Skinner, "Preventing Infant and Maternal Mortality: State Policy Options" National Conference of State Legislatures (2019). https://www.ncsl.org/Portals/1/Documents/Health/ Infant-Maternal-Mortality_v05_web.pdf

10    See, for instance, Hilary Marland and Anne Marie Rafferty, eds., *Midwives, Society and Childbirth* (London: Routledge, 1997); and Judith Pence Rooks, *Midwifery & Childbirth in America* (Philadelphia: Temple University Press, 1997), esp. chapter 15.

11    See Lauren K. Hall, "Rehumanizing Birth and Death in America," *Society* (2017): 226-37.

12    Mary M. Lay, *The Rhetoric of Midwifery* (New Brunswick, NJ: Rutgers University Press, 2000), 10.

# Bibliography

## Archives

| | |
|---|---|
| Bard College | BC |
| College of Physicians of Philadelphia | COP |
| Columbia University Butler Library | CUBL |
| Columbia University Health Sciences Library | CUHS |
| Franklin D Roosevelt Presidential Library | FDRPL |
| The Historical Society of Pennsylvania | HSP |
| New York Academy of Medicine | NYAM |
| New York Historical Society | NYHS |
| Wellcome Library | WL |

## Collections

Anderson Family Papers, 1797-1913. #1745. The Historical Society of Pennsylvania, Philadelphia, Pennsylvania.

Bard Collection, 1760-1820. Mss. arc. The New York Academy of Medicine, New York, New York.

Bard Family Papers. Stevenson Library, Bard College, Annandale-on-Hudson, New York.

Bard Family Papers. Rare Book and Manuscript Library, Columbia University Library. New York, New York.

Bard Family Papers, 1764-1941. New-York Historical Society. New York, New York.

Bard Family Papers, 1658-1898. Hudson River Valley & Dutchess County Manuscript Collection. Franklin Delano Roosevelt Presidential Library, Hyde Park, New York

Biography of Thomas Denman (1733-1815). MS 5620. Wellcome Library, London, United Kingdom.

Denman, Thomas (1773-1815) & Osborne, William (1736-1808). Wellcome Library, London, United Kingdom. MS 2099.

Letters of. Misc. Archives & Special Collections, Columbia University Health Sciences Library, New York, New York.

[Manuscript lectures; a collection of manuscript notes on various medical topics, in the same hand, [18--?].The College of Physicians of Philadelphia, Philadelphia, PA.

Michael Reynard papers. Rare Book and Manuscript Library, Columbia University Library, New York, New York.

Moses Champion Letters. Columbia University Health Sciences Library, New York, New York.

Notes from the lectures of Dr. T. C. James on midwifery by Isaac Hayes. Manuscript. [Philadelphia 18--]. The College of Physicians of Philadelphia, Philadelphia, Pennsylvania.

Notes from Dr. Osborn's and Dr. Clarke's Lectures on Midwifery by Thomas C. James, 1790-1791. Manuscript. The College of Physicians of Philadelphia. Philadelphia, Pennsylvania.

Thomas Denman (1733-1815), Physician and Obstetrician. MS 6014. Wellcome Library, London, United Kingdom.

William Martin's notes on lectures by Benjamin Rush, Joseph Black, and Adam Kuhn while studying at the University of Pennsylvania, Collection #920, The Historical Society of Pennsylvania. Philadelphia, PA.

## Primary

"Adollizing, or A Lively Picture of A Doll-Worship" (1748), *Eighteenth-Century British Erotica Set II*, Vol. 2. Ed. Deborah Needleman Armintor. London: Pickering and Chatto, 2004, 325-36.

Aitken, John. *Principles of Midwifery, or Puerperal Medicine* 3rd ed. London: J. Murray, 1786.

*The American Medical Recorder, or Original Papers and Intelligence in Medicine and Surgery.* "Article XVII." Philadelphia: James Webster, 1822. 528. *Hathi Trust.*

*Anatomical Lectures: or, The Anatomy of the Human Bones, Nerves, and Lacteal Sac and Duct.* By a Society of Gentleman. London, 1775. *Eighteenth Century Collections Online.*

*Aristotle's Complete Masterpiece* (London 1749). Ed. Randolph Turnbach. New York: Garland, 1986.

Austen, Jane. *Sense and Sensibility* (1811). Ed. Claudia L. Johnson. New York: Norton, 2001.

—. *Pride and Prejudice* (1813). Ed. Robert P. Irvine. Ontario: Broadview, 2002.

Bard, Samuel. *A Compendium on the Theory and Practice of Midwifery, Containing Instructions for the Management of Women during Pregnancy, in Labour, and in Child-Bed; Calculated to correct the Errors, and to improve the Practice, of Midwives; As well as to serve as an Introduction to the Study of this Art, for Students and Young Practitioners.* New York: Collins and Perkins, 1808. *Early American Imprints.*

—. *A Compendium on the Theory and Practice of Midwifery, Containing Instructions for the Management of Women during Pregnancy, in Labour, and in Child-Bed; Calculated to correct the Errors, and to improve the Practice, of Midwives; As well as to serve as an Introduction to the Study of this Art, for Students and Young Practitioners. Second Edition Enlarged.* New York: Collins and Perkins, 1812. *Early American Imprints.*

—. *A Compendium on the Theory and Practice of Midwifery, Containing Instructions for the Management of Women during Pregnancy, in Labour, and in Child-Bed; Calculated to correct the Errors, and to improve the Practice, of Midwives; As well as to serve as an Introduction to the Study of this Art. Third Edition Enlarged.* New York: Collins and Perkins, 1815. *Early American Imprints.*

—. *A Compendium on the Theory and Practice of Midwifery, Containing Practical Instructions for the Management of Women, During Pregnancy, in Labour, and in Child-Bed. Illustrated by Many Cases, and Particularly Adapted to the Use of Students. Fourth Edition Enlarged.* New York: Collins and Perkins, 1817. *Early American Imprints.*

—. *A Compendium on the Theory and Practice of Midwifery, Containing Practical Instructions for the Management of Women, During Pregnancy, in Labour, and in Child-Bed. Illustrated by Many Cases, and Particularly Adapted to the Use of Students. Fifth Edition Enlarged.* New York: Collins and Perkins, 1819. *Early American Imprints.*

Bard, Samuel and John W. Francis, "University of the State of New York— College of Physicians and Surgeons." *New York Medical and Philosophical Journal and Review* (January 1811). *American Periodical Series Online.*

—. "Domestic Intelligence." *The American Medical and Philosophical Register* (July 1813). *American Periodical Series Online.*

Beach, Wooster. *An Improved System of Midwifery, Adapted to the Reformed Practice of Medicine; Illustrated by Numerous Plates. To which is added, a Compendium of the Treatment of Female and Infantile Diseases, with Remarks on Physiological and Moral Elevation.* New York: Baker & Scribner, 1850.

Blundell, James. *The Principles and Practice of Obstetricy.* London: E. Cox, 1834.

—. *Observations on Some of the More Important Diseases of Women.* London: E. Cox, 1837.

—. "Lectures on the Diseases of Women and Children Delivered at Guy's Hospital." *The Lancet* (1828-9): 641-47. thelancet.com

Blunt, John [S. W. Fores]. *Man-Midwifery Dissected; or, The Obstetric Family Instructor.* London, 1793. *Eighteenth Century Collections Online.*

Borham, W. H. "A Case of Hour-Glass Contraction of the Uterus." *Lancet* 61 (1853): 19. thelancet.com

Bracken, Henry. *The Midwife's Companion, or a Treatise of Midwifery.* London, 1737. *Eighteenth Century Collections Online.*

Brontë, Charlotte. *Jane Eyre* (1847). Ed. Deborah Lutz. New York: Norton, 2016.

Buchan, William. *Domestic Medicine* 7ᵗʰ ed. London, 1781. *Eighteenth Century Collections Online.*

—. *Advice to Mothers* (Boston 1809). *The Physician and Childrearing: Two Guides 1809-1894.* Medicine & Society in America Series. Ed. Charles E. Rosenberg. New York: Arno, 1972.

Burney, Frances. *Evelina* (1778). Ed. Edward A. Bloom. Oxford: Oxford University Press, 2008.

Burns, Robert. *The Merry Muses of Caledonia.* Ed. G. Legman. New Hyde Park, NY: University Books, 1965.

Burton, John. *A Letter to William Smellie, M.D. Containing Critical and Practical Remarks upon his Treatise on the Theory and Practice of Midwifery.* London, 1753.

—. *An Essay towards a Complete New System of Midwifry, Theoretical and Practical.* London, 1751.

*A Catalogue of the Books Belonging to the Medical Library in the Pennsylvania Hospital.* Philadelphia, 1790. *Early American Imprints.*

de Cervantes, Miguel. *Don Quixote* (1615). Trans. Edith Grossman. New York: Harper Perennial, 2005.

Chapman, Edmund. *A Treatise on the Improvement in Midwifery,* 3ʳᵈ ed. London, 1759. *Eighteenth Century Collections Online.*

Cleland, John. *Fanny Hill, or Memoirs of a Woman of Pleasure* (1749). Ed. Gary Gautier. New York: Modern Library, 2001.

Cooper, James Fenimore. *The Pioneers* (1823). New York: Penguin, 1988.

—. *The Last of the Mohicans* (1827). Ed. Paul C. Gutahr. Ontario: Broadview, 2009.

Crichton, Michael, creator. *ER* (1994-2009). NBC.

Culpeper, Nicolas. *Directory for Midwives or a Guide to Women in their Conception, Bearing, and Suckling their Children* (London, 1651). *Early English Books Online.*

Defoe, Daniel. *Roxana, Or the Fortunate Mistress* (1724). Ed. John Mullan. Oxford: Oxford University Press, 1996.

Denman, Thomas. *A Collection of Engravings, Tending to Illustrate the Generation and Parturition of Animals and of the Human Species.* London, 1787.

—. *An Introduction to the Practice of Midwifery* (London 1788).

—. *An Introduction to the Practice of Midwifery* (New York 1792).

—. *An Introduction to the Practice of Midwifery Volume I.* (London: J. Johnson, 1794). *Eighteenth-Century Collections Online.*

—. *An Introduction to the Practice of Midwifery Volume II.* (London: J. Johnson, 1794). *Eighteenth-Century Collections Online.*

—. *An Introduction to the Practice of Midwifery* (New York 1802).

—. *Aphorisms on the Application and Use of the Forceps and Vectis.* Ed. Thomas James. Philadelphia: Benjamin Johnson, 1803.

Dewees, William. *An Abridgement of Mr. Heath's Translation of Baudelocque's Midwifery; with notes by William P. Dewees.* Philadelphia: Thomas Dobson, 1807.

—. "Reply to Dr. Peachy Harrison's Observations on Impregnation." *Philadelphia Medical Museum.* (Philadelphia: Thomas Dobson, 1807): 30-40.

—. "Remarks on Dr. Peachey Harrison's Reply." *Philadelphia Medical Museum.* (Thomas Dobson, 1808): 145-76.

"The Discovery," *The Cabinet of Love* (1739). *Eighteenth-Century British Erotica Set II*, Vol. 2. Ed. Deborah Needleman Armintor. London: Pickering and Chatto, 2004, 85-89.

Ducachet, Henry William. *A Biographical Memoir of Samuel Bard, M.D. LL.D. Late President of the College of Physicians and Surgeons of the University of the State of New-York, &c. With a Critique Upon His Writings. Read Before the New-York Historical Society, August 14ᵗʰ 1821.* Philadelphia, 1821.

Edgeworth, Maria. *Belinda* (1801). Ed. Katherine J. Kirkpatrick. Oxford: Oxford University Press, 2009.

Eliot, George. *Middlemarch.* (1871). Ed. David Carroll. Oxford: Clarendon, 1992.

Elliot, Charles. *C. Elliot, T. Kay, and Co's Catalogue of Books, in all the Different Branches of Medicine, Surgery, Anatomy, Natural History, &c. &c. For the Year 1788.* London, 1788. *Eighteenth Century Collections Online.*

*Encyclopaedia Britannica,* Vol. 7. Edinburgh 1781.

*Encyclopaedia; or, A Dictionary of arts, sciences and miscellaneous literature,* Vol. 11 Philadelphia: Thomas Dobson, 1798.

*The English Review; or, an Abstract of English and Foreign Literature for the Year M,DCC,LXXXIV.* "Article VIII." (London: J. Murray, 1789): 120. *Eighteenth Century Collection Online.*

Ewell, Thomas. *The Ladies Medical Companion: containing, in a series of letters, an account of the latest improvements and most successful means of preserving their beauty and health ; of relieving the diseases peculiar to the sex, and an explanation of the offices they should perform to each other at births ; with engraved figures explanatory ; also, the best means of nursing, preventing and curing the diseases of children.* Philadelphia: William Brown, 1818.

Franklin, Benjamin. "Old Mistress Apologue," *The Papers of Benjamin Franklin*, Vol. 3. Ed. Leonard W. Labaree. New Haven: Yale University Press, 1961, 30-33.

Gregory, John. *Observations on the Duties and Offices of a Physician; and on the Methods of Prosecuting Enqueries in Philosophy.* London: Strahan and Cadell. 1770. *Eighteenth Century Collections Online.*

Gregory, Samuel. *Man-Midwifery Exposed and Corrected.* Boston: George Gregory, 1848.

Goldsmith, Oliver. *The Vicar of Wakefield* (1766). Ed. Arthur Friedman. Oxford: Oxford University Press, 2008.

Hamilton, Alexander. *Elements of the Practice of Midwifery* London, 1775.

—.*Outlines on the Theory and Practice of Midwifery.* Edinburgh, 1784. College of Physicians, Philadelphia. Call number Ge 69. Annotations by Dr. Samuel P. Griffitts.

—. *Outlines on the Theory and Practice of Midwifery.* Philadelphia: Thomas Dobson, 1790.

—. *A Treatise of Midwifery, Comprehending the Management of Female Complaints and the Treatment of Children in Early Infancy* 1ˢᵗ ed. Edinburgh, 1781.

Harrison, Peachey. "Observations on Impregnation. By Peachey Harrison, in a Letter to the Editor." *Philadelphia Medical Museum.* (Philadelphia: Thomas Dobson, 1806): 421-26.

—. "Answer to Dr. Dewees's Reply to Dr. Peachey Harrison's Observations on Impregnation." *Philadelphia Medical Museum.* (Philadelphia: Thomas Dobson, 1808): 97-118.

Harvey, William. *On Generation. The Works of William Harvey.* Trans. Robert Willis. Philadelphia: University of Pennsylvania Press, 1989, 151-518.

Hopkinson, Francis. *An Oration which might have been Delivered to the Students in Anatomy on the Late Rupture Between the Two Schools in This City.* Philadelphia, 1789.

Hosack, David. "Original Communications: Sketch of the Origin and Progress of the Medical Schools of New York and Philadelphia." *The American Medical and Philosophical Register* (July 1811). *American Periodical Series Online.*

Hume, David. "Essay XXI: Of National Characters." *Essays Moral, Political, and Literary*. Ed. Eugene F. Miller. Indianapolis: Literary Fund, 1985. 197-215.

Hunter, John. *Essays and Observations of Natural History*. Vol. I. Ed. Richard Owen. London: Taylor and Francis, 1861.

Hunter, William. *The Anatomy of the Human Gravid Uterus Exhibited in Figures*. (London 1774). Birmingham: Classics of Medicine Library, 1980.

—. *Medical Commentaries Part I. Containing a Plain and Direct Answer to Professor Monro Jun. Interspersed with Marks on the Structure, Functions, and Diseases of Several Parts of the Human Body*. London: A Hamilton, 1762.

—. *Two Introductory Lectures, Delivered by William Hunter, to his last course of anatomical lectures at his theatre in Windmill-Street: As they were left corrected for the Press by Himself*. *London*: J. Johnson, 1784. *Eighteenth Century Collections Online*.

"Index Indicatorius." *The Gentleman's Magazine* Vol. II. (London: John Nichols, 1788): 1186. *Eighteenth Century Collections Online*.

Jennings, Samuel. *The Married Lady's Companion, or Poor Man's Friend* 2nd Ed. (New York 1808). Medicine & Society in America Series, Ed. Charles E. Rosenberg. New York: Arno, 1972.

von Krafft-Ebing, Richard. *Psychopathia Sexualis with Especial Reference to the Antipathetic Sexual Instinct. A Medico-Forensic Study*. Trans. F. J. Rebman. London: W. Heinemann, 1928. *Hathi Trust*.

Leake, John. *Dissertation upon the properties and efficacy of the Lisbon Diet Drink, and its Extract, in the Cure of Venereal Disease & Scurvy; Rheumatic Gout, the Scrophula, Consumption; and other Disorders proceeding from an impure State of the Blood; especially those of the Skin and Glands*. London: R. Baldwin, 1762.

—. *Dissertation upon the properties and efficacy of the Lisbon Diet Drink, and its Extract, in the Cure of Venereal Disease & Scurvy; Rheumatic Gout, the Scrophula, Consumption; and other Disorders proceeding from an impure State of the Blood; especially those of the Skin and Glands*. London: R. Baldwin, 1787.

Lennox, Charlotte. *The Female Quixote, or The Adventures of Arabella* (1752). Ed. Margaret Anne Doody. Oxford: Oxford University Press, 1989.

*Little Merlin's Cave* (1737). *Eighteenth Century British Erotica Set I*, Vol. 3, Ed. Patrick Spedding. London: Pickering & Chatto, 2002, 110-118.

MacKenzie, Henry. *The Man of Feeling* (1771). Ed. Brian Vickers. Oxford: Oxford University Press, 2009.

Maubray, John. *The Female Physician, Containing all the Diseases incident to that Sex, in Virgins, Wives, and Widows; Together with their Causes and Symptoms, their Degrees of Danger, and Respective Method of Prevention and Cure: To which is added, The Whole Art of New improv'd Midwifery; Comprehending the necessary Qualifications of a Midwife, and particular Directions for laying Women, in all Cases of Difficult and Preternatural Births; together with the Diet and Regimen of both the Mother and Child.* London: James Holland, 1724. *Eighteenth Century Collections Online.*

McCartney, Jamie. *The Great Wall of Vagina* (2015). https://jamiemccartney.com/portfolio/the-great-wall-of-vagina/. Accessed June 2, 2020.

McClintock, Alfred H. *Smellie's Treatise on the Theory and Practice of Midwifery. Edited, with Annotations.* Three Volumes. London: The New Sydenham Society, 1878.

M'Vickar, John. *A Domestic Narrative of the Life of Samuel Bard, M.D. LL.D.* New York, 1822.

Meigs, Charles. *Woman; Her Diseases. A Series of Lectures to his Class.* 2nd ed. Philadelphia: Lea and Blanchard, 1851.

—. *Obstetrics; the Science and the Art.* 5th Ed. Philadelphia: Henry C. Lea, 1867.

"Memoir of the Late Thomas Denman, M. D." *The Gentleman's Magazine* Vol. 2. London: Nichols, Son and Bentley, 1815. 566-67.

Munro, Jun., Alexander. *An Expostulatory Epistle to William Hunter, M.D.* Edinburgh: G. Hamilton and J. Balfour, 1762.

[Nicholls, Frank]. *Petition of the Unborn Babes to the Censors of the Royal College of Physicians of London.* London 1751.

Nihell, Elizabeth. *A Treatise on the Art of Midwifery* (1760). *Eighteenth-Century British Midwifery*, Vol. 6. Ed. Pam Lieske. London: Pickering & Chatto, 2008, 1-503.

—. *An Answer to the Author of the Critical Review, for March, 1760, Upon the Article of Mrs. Nihell's Treatise on the Art of Midwifery.* London, 1760. *Eighteenth-Century Collections Online.*

Ould, Fielding. *A Treatise of Midwifery, In Three Parts.* Dublin, 1742. *Eighteenth-Century Collections Online.*

Osborne, William. *Essays on the Practice of Midwifery, in Natural and Difficult Labours.* London: T. Cadell and J. Johnson, 1792. *Eighteenth-Century Collections Online.*

*Pennsylvania Packet and Daily Advertiser.* November 9, 1785. *America's Historical Newspapers Online Database*

"Proposed Union of the Medical Schools in New York." *The American Medical and Philosophical Register,* (July 1810). *American Periodical Series Online.*

Benjamin Pugh, *A Treatise of Midwifery, chiefly with Regards the Operation. With Several Improvements of the Art.* London: J. Buckland, 1754. *Eighteenth-*

*Century Collections Online.*

*Remarks on the Employment of Females as Practitioners in Midwifery by a Physician.* Boston 1820.

[Salmon, William]. *Aristotle's Compleat and Experienced Midwife.* London, 1731.

Seaman, Valentine. *The Midwife's Monitor and Mother's Mirror: Being Three Concluding Lectures of a Course of Instruction on Midwifery.* New York, 1800. *Early American Imprints.*

Sharp, Jane. *The Midwives Book* (London, 1671). Ed. Elaine Hobby. Oxford: Oxford University Press, 1999.

Shore, David, creator. *House* (2004-2012). Fox.

Smellie, William. *A Treatise on the Theory and Practice of Midwifery* Vol. I (London 1752). Birmingham: Classics of Medicine Library, 1990.

—. *A Collection of Cases and Observations in Midwifery to Illustrate His former Treatise, or First Volume, on that Subject.* Vol. II. London, 1754. *Eighteenth-Century Collections Online.*

—. *A Collection of Preternatural Cases and Observations in Midwifery, Completing the Design of Illustrating his First Volume, on that Subject.* Vol. III. London, 1764. *Eighteenth-Century Collections Online.*

—. *A Set of Anatomical Tables, with Explanations, and an Abridgement of the Practice of Midwifery With a View to Illustrate a Treatise on that Subject, and Collection of Cases* 2nd ed. London, 1761.

—. *A Treatise on the Theory and Practice of Midwifery Volume I. A New Edition. With A Set of Anatomical Tables, with Explanations.* London, 1779.

—. *A Set of Anatomical Tables, with Explanations, and an Abridgement of the Practice of Midwifery With a View to Illustrate a Treatise on that Subject, and Collection of Cases. A New Edition, Corrected; To which is added, Two Additional Tables with Explanations, By the late Dr. Thomas of Edinburgh, and Dr. John Evans of Oswestery Shropshire.* Edinburgh, 1785.

—. *An Abridgement of the practice of midwifery: and a set of anatomical tables with explanations: Collected from the works of the celebrated, W. Smellie, M. D.* Boston, 1796.

—. *An Abridgement of the practice of midwifery: and a set of anatomical tables with explanations: Collected from the works of the celebrated, W. Smellie, M. D.* Boston, 1796. College of Physicians, Philadelphia. Call number Ge 116. Annotations by Thomas Sewall, Sr. and others.

—. *Anatomical Tables, With Explanations and An Abridgment of the Practice of Midwifery, With a View to Illustrate A Treatise on that Subject, And Collection of Cases. By William Smellie, M.D. A New Edition, Carefully Corrected and Revised, With Notes and Illustrations, Adapted to the present Improved Method of*

*Practice. By A. Hamilton, M. D. F. R. S. Edin. And Professor of Midwifery in the University of Edinburgh.* Edinburgh: Elliott: 1787.

—. *A Set of Anatomical Tables, with Explanations, and an Abridgement of the Practice of Midwifery With a View to Illustrate a Treatise on that Subject, and Collection of Cases. By William Smellie, M.D. A New Edition, Carefully Corrected and Revised, With Notes and Illustrations, Adapted to the present Improved Method of Practice. By A. Hamilton, M. D. F. R. S. Edin. And Professor of Midwifery in the University of Edinburgh.* Edinburgh: Eliott, 1790.

—. *A Set of Anatomical Tables, with Explanations, and an Abridgement of the Practice of Midwifery With a View to Illustrate a Treatise on that Subject, and Collection of Cases. By William Smellie, M.D. To which are added, Notes and Illustrations, Adapted to the present Improved Method of Practice. By A. Hamilton, M. D. F. R. S. Edin. And Professor of Midwifery in the University of Edinburgh. First Worcester Edition. With a New Set of Plates, Carefully Corrected and Revised.* Worcester, MA: Isaiah Thomas, 1793.

Smollett, Tobias. *The Adventures of Roderick Random* (1748). Ed. Paul Gabriel Boucé. Oxford: Oxford University Press, 1999.

Steele, Richard. *Spectator* No. 155. *The Commerce of Everyday Life: Selections from 'The Tatler' and 'The Spectator.'* Ed. Erin Mackie. Boston: Bedford/St. Martin's, 1998, 213-16.

Stone, Sarah. *A Complete Practice of Midwifery.* London, T. Cooper: 1737. *Eighteenth Century Collections Online.*

[Stretzer, Thomas], *A New Description of Merryland* (London 1741) *When Flesh Becomes Word: An Anthology of Early Eighteenth-Century Libertine Literature.* Ed. Bradford K. Mudge. Oxford: Oxford University Press, 2004, 259-85.

Swift, Jonathan. "A Beautiful Young Nymph Going to Bed," *Jonathan Swift: The Complete Poems.* Ed. Pat Rogers. New Haven: Yale University Press, 1983. 453-55.

Tenney, Tabitha. *Female Quixotism: Exhibited in the Romantic Opinions and Extravagant Adventures of Dorcasina Sheldon* (1801). Eds. Jean Nienkamp and Andrea Collins. New York: Oxford University Press, 1992.

Thicknesse, Phillip. *Man Midwifery Analysed: And the Tendency of That Practice Detected and Exposed.* London, 1764. *Eighteenth Century Collections Online.*

Tyler, Royall. The Contrast: *Manners, Morals, and Authority in the Early American Republic.* Ed. Cynthia A. Kierner. New York: New York University Press, 2007.

US National Library of Medicine. *Historical Anatomies on the Web.* Last updated August 26, 2016. http://www.nlm.nih.gov/exhibition/

historicalanatomies/home.html.

Venette, Nicolas. *Conjugal Love; or the Pleasures of the Marriage Bed* (London 1720). Ed. Randolph Trumbach. New York: Garland, 1984.

Walker, Sayer. *Observations on the Constitutions of Women, and on Some of the Diseases to which they are more especially liable.* London, 1803.

White, Charles. *Treatise on the Management of Pregnant and Lying-in Women.* Worcester, MA: Isaiah Thomas, 1793.

Wollstonecraft, Mary. *A Vindication of the Rights of Women.* 2nd Ed. Ed. Carol H. Poston. New York: Norton, 1988.

## Secondary

Altick, Richard. *The Shows of London.* Cambridge: Harvard University Press, 1978.

Altshuler, Sari. *The Medical Imagination: Literature and Health in the Early United States.* Philadelphia: University of Pennsylvania Press, 2018.

Anderson, Benedict. *Imagined Communities: Reflections on the Origin and Spread of Nationalism.* London: Verso, 1983, 2006.

Andrikopoulou, M., L. Michala, S. M. Creighton, and L. M. Liao, "The Normal Vulva in Medical Textbooks," *Journal of Obstetrical Gynaecology* 33.7 (2013): 648-50.

Armintor, Deborah Needleman. Headnote to "Adollizing," *Eighteenth-Century British Erotica Set II,* Vol. 2. Ed. Deborah Needleman Armintor. London: Pickering and Chatto, 2004, 304.

Armstrong, Nancy. *Desire and Domestic Fiction: A Political History of the Novel.* New York: Oxford University Press, 1990.

Arner, Robert D. *Dobson's* Encyclopedia: *The Publisher, Text, and Publication of America's First* Britannica, *1789-1803.* Philadelphia: University of Pennsylvania Press, 1991.

Banks, Amanda Carson. *Birth Chairs, Midwives, and Medicine,* Jackson: University Press of Mississippi, 1999.

Baym, Nina. "Putting Women in their Place: *The Last of the Mohicans* and other Indian Stories." In *Feminism and American Literary History.* New Brunswick, NJ: Rutgers University Press, 1992. 19-35.

Bellazaire, Amber and Erik Skinner. "Preventing Infant and Maternal Mortality: State Policy Options" *National Conference of State Legislatures,* 2019. https://www.ncsl.org/Portals/1/Documents/Health/Infant-Maternal-Mortality_v05_web.pdf

Beneditto, Christopher. "A Most Daring and Sacrilegious Robbery." *New*

*England Ancestors* 6.2 (2005): 31-34.

Black, Shirley Burgoyne. *An Eighteenth-Century Mad Doctor: William Perfect of West-Malling*. Sevenoaks, Kent, UK: Darenth Valley, 1995.

Blackwell, Bonnie. "*Tristram Shandy* and the Theatre of the Mechanical Mother," *ELH* 68.1 (2001): 81-133.

Bloch, Sharon. *Rape and Sexual Power in Early America*. Chapel Hill, NC: University of North Carolina Press, 2006.

Bonner, Thomas Neville. *Becoming a Physician: Medical Education in Britain, France, Germany, and the United States, 1750-1945*. Baltimore: Johns Hopkins University Press, 1995.

Boucé, Paul-Gabriel. "Some Sexual Beliefs and Myths in Eighteenth-Century Britain." *Sexuality in Eighteenth-Century Britain* Ed. Paul-Gabriel Boucé. Manchester: Manchester University Press, 1982, 28-46.

—. "Chthonic and Pelagic Metaphorization in Eighteenth-Century English Erotica." *Tis Nature's Fault: Unauthorized Sexuality in the Enlightenment*. Ed. Robert Purks Maccubbin. Cambridge: Cambridge University Press, 1985, 202-16.

Brody, Stuart & Rui Miguel Costa. "Vaginal Orgasm is Associated with Less Use of Immature Psychological Defense Mechanisms." *Journal of Sexual Medicine* 5 (2008): 1167-1176.

Brown, Gillian. "Consent, Coquetry, and Consequences." *American Literary History* 9.1 (1997): 625-52.

Brown, Michael. "'Like a Devoted Army': Medicine, Heroic Masculinity, and the Military Paradigm in Victorian Britain." *Journal of British Studies* 49.3 (2010): 592-622.

de Ceglia, Francesco. "Rotten Corpses, a Disembowelled Woman, A Flayed Man. Images of the Body from the End of the 17th to the Beginning of the 19th Century. Florentine Wax Models in the First-hand Account of Visitors," *Perspectives on Science* 14.4 (2006): 417-56.

Chamberlain, Ava ."Bad Books and Bad Boys: The Transformation of Gender in Eighteenth-Century Northampton, Massachusetts," *New England Quarterly* 75.2 (2002): 179-203.

Chaplin, Simon. "RE: Anatomical specimen preservation techniques." Message to Marcia Nichols. December 14, 2009. Email.

Cody, Lisa Forman. "The Politics of Reproduction: From Midwives' Alternative Public Sphere to the Public Spectacle of Man Midwifery." *Eighteenth-Century Studies* 32.4 (1999): 477-95.

—. "Living and Dying in Georgian London's Lying-in Hospitals." *Bulletin of the History of Medicine* 78 (2004): 309-48.

—. *Birthing the Nation: Sex, Science, and the Conception of Eighteenth-Century Britons*. Oxford: Oxford University Press, 2005.

Connell, R. W. and James W. Meserschmidt. "Hegemonic Masculinity: Rethinking the Concept." *Gender & Society* (2005). 829-59.

Corner, Betsy Copping. *William Shippen, Jr.: Pioneer in American Medical Education*, Philadelphia: American Philosophical Society, 1951.

Cott, Nancy. "Passionlessness: An Interpretation of Victorian Sexual Ideology, 1790-1850." *Signs* 4.2 (1978): 219-36.

Datson, Lorraine and Peter Galison. *Objectivity*. New York: Zone Books, 2007.

Davidson, Cathy N. *Revolution and the Word: The Rise of the Novel in America*. Oxford: Oxford University Press, 2004.

D'Emillo, John and Estelle Freedman. *Intimate Matters: A History of Sexuality in America*. 2nd ed. Chicago: University of Chicago Press, 1997.

Dennis, Ian. "The Worthlessness of Duncan Heyward: A Waverly Hero in America." *Studies in the Novel* 29.1 (1997): 1-16.

Donegan, Jane B. *Women and Men Midwives: Medicine, Morality and Misogyny in Early America*. Westport, CT: Greenwood, 1978.

Donnison, Jean. *Midwives and Medical Men: A History of the Struggle for the Control of Childbirth*. 2nd Ed. London: Historical Publications, 1988.

Doyle, Nora. *Maternal Bodies: Redefining Motherhood in Early America*. Chapel Hill: University of North Carolina Press, 2018.

Dunn, P. M. "Dr. Thomas Denman of London (1733-1815): Rupture of the Membranes and Management of the Cord." *Archives of Diseases of Childhood* 67 (1992): 882-84.

"Episode 14: Labioplasty." *Hungry Beast*. ABC Australia. Originally aired 3/3/2010. Accessed 05/18/2010 on *Jezebel* http://jezebel.com/5535356/the-labiaplasty-you-never-knew-you-wanted-[nsfw]

Epstein. Abby, Director. *The Business of Being Born*. Perf. Ricky Lake. Barranca Productions, 2008.

Epstein, Julia. *The Iron Pen: Frances Burney and the Politics of Women's Writings*. Bristol: Bristol Classical, 1989.

—. *Altered Conditions: Disease, Medicine, and Storytelling*. New York: Routledge, 1995.

Erickson, Robert A. "'The books of generation': Some Observations on the style of the British Midwife Books, 1671-1764." *Sexuality in Eighteenth-Century Britain*. Ed. Paul-Gabriel Boucé. Manchester: Manchester University Press, 1982, 74-94.

Estes, J. Worth. "Patterns of Drug Use in Colonial America." *New York State*

*Journal of Medicine* 87 (1987): 37-45.

Etcoff, Nancy. *Survival of the Prettiest: The Science of Beauty.* New York: Anchor Books, 1999.

Evans, Gareth. "Rakes, Coquettes, and Republican Patriarchs: Class, Gender, and Nation in Early American Sentimental Fiction." *Canadian Review of American Studies* 25.3 (1995): 41-63.

Evans, Martin H. and Geoffrey Hooper. "Three Misleading Diaries: John Knyveton MD—from Navel Surgeon's Mate to Man-Midwife." *The International Journal of Maritime History* 26.4 (2014): 762-88.

Fabian, Ann. *The Skull Collectors: Race, Science, and America's Unburied Dead.* Chicago: University of Chicago Press, 2010.

Fausto-Sterling, Anne. *Sexing the Body: Gender Politics and the Construction of Sexuality.* New York: Basic, 2000.

Findley, Palmer. *Priests of Lucina: The Story of Obstetrics.* Boston: Little, Brown & Co. 1939.

Fissell, Mary E. "Making a Masterpiece: The Aristotle Texts in Vernacular Culture." *Right Living: An Anglo-American Tradition of Self-Help Medicine and Hygiene.* Ed. Charles E. Rosenberg. Baltimore: Johns Hopkins University Press, 2003, 59-87.

—. "Hairy Women and Naked Truths: Gender and the Politics of Knowledge in 'Aristotle's Masterpiece,'" *William and Mary Quarterly* 60.1 (2003): 43-74.

Foucault, Michel. *Discipline & Punish: The Birth of the Prison.* Trans. Alan Sheridan. New York: Vintage, 1977.

—. *The History of Sexuality: An Introduction.* Vol. 1. Trans. Robert Hurley. New York: Vintage, 1990.

—. *The Birth of the Clinic: An Archeology of Medical Perception.* Trans. A. M. Sheridan Smith. New York: Vintage, 1994.

Frappier-Mazur, Lucienne. "Truth and the Obscene Word in Eighteenth-Century French Pornography." *Invention of Pornography, 1500-1800: Obscenity and the Origins of Modernity.* Ed. Lynn Hunt. New York: Zone Books, 1993, 203-21.

Freeman, Hadley. "How was Larry Nassar able to abuse so many gymnasts for so long?" *The Guardian.* (January 26, 2018). https://www.theguardian. com/sport/2018/jan/26/larry-nassar-abuse-gymnasts-scandal-culture

Garvan Beatrice B. *Federal Philadelphia: The Athens of the Western World.* Philadelphia: Princeton Polychrome, 1987.

Gellner, Ernest. *Nations and Nationalism.* 2nd Ed. Ithaca, NY: Blackwell, 2008.

Gilman, Sander L. *Difference and Pathology: Stereotypes of Sexuality, Race and*

*Madness.* Ithaca, NY: Cornell University Press, 1985.

Glaister, John. *Dr. William Smellie and His Contemporaries.* Glasgow: James Maclehose & Sons, 1894.

Godbeer, Richard. *Sexual Revolution in Early America.* Baltimore: Johns Hopkins University Press, 2002.

Gray, Ernest. *The Diary of a Surgeon, 1751-1752.* New York, London: Appleton Century, 1937.

—. *Surgeon's Mate: The Diary of John Knyveton, Surgeon in the British Fleet during the Seven Years War, 1756-1762.* London: R. Hale Ltd., 1942.

—. *Man Midwife; the Further Experiences of John Knyveton, M.D., Late Surgeon in the British Fleet, during the Years 1763-1809.* London: Hale, 1946.

Gray, John. *Men Are from Mars, Women Are from Venus: A Practical Guide for Improving Communication and Getting What You Want in Your Relationships.* New York: Harpers Collins, 1993.

Green, James N. "'The Cowl knows best what will suit in Virginia': Parson Weems on Southern Readers." *Printing History* 17 (1995): 26-34.

—. "The Rise of Book Publishing." *History of the Book in America: Volume 2: An Extensive Republic: Print, Culture, and Society in the New Nation, 1790-1840.* Eds. Robert A. Gross and Mary Kelley. Chapel Hill, NC: University of North Carolina Press, 2010. 75-127.

Guerrini, Anita. "Anatomists and Entrepreneurs in Early Eighteenth-Century London." *Journal of the History of Medicine* 59.2 (2004): 219-34.

Hall, Lauren K. "Rehumanizing Birth and Death in America," *Society* 54 (2017): 226-37.

Halttunen, Karen. "Humanitarianism and the Pornography of Pain in Anglo-American Culture." *The American Historical Review* 100.2 (1995): 303-34.

Hartveit, Lars. *Workings of the Picaresque in the British Novel.* Oslo, Norway: Solum Forlag A/S, 1987.

Harvey, Karen. *Reading Sex in the Eighteenth Century: Bodies and Gender in English Erotic Culture.* Cambridge: Cambridge University Press, 2004.

Henderson, Andrea K. *Romantic Identities: Varieties of Subjectivity, 1774-1830.* Cambridge: Cambridge University Press, 1996.

Hill, Bridget. *Women, Work & Sexual Politics in Eighteenth-Century England.* Montreal: McGill-Queen's University Press, 1989.

Hoffert, Sylvia D. *Private Matters: American Attitudes toward Childbearing and Infant Nurture in the Urban North, 1800-1860.* Urbana, IL: University of Illinois Press, 1989.

Human Rights Watch. "US. Harmful Surgery on Intersex Children." July 25,

2017. https://www.hrw.org/news/2017/07/25/us-harmful-surgery-intersex-children

InterACT Advocates for Intersex Youth. Interactadvocates.org. Last updated 2018.

Intersex Society of North America. http://www.isna.org/ Last Updated 2008.

Jacob, Margaret C. "The Materialist World of Pornography." *The Invention of Pornography, 1500-1800: Obscenity and the Origins of Modernity.* Ed. Lynn Hunt. New York: Zone Books, 1993, 157-202.

Johnson, Thomas H. "Jonathan Edwards and the 'Young Folks' Bible.'" *New England Quarterly* 5.1 (1932): 37-54.

Johnstone, R. W. *William Smellie: The Master of British Midwifery.* Edinburgh: E & S Livingstone, 1952.

Jordanova, Ludmilla. *Sexual Visions: Images of Gender in Science and Medicine Between the Eighteenth and Twentieth Centuries.* Madison: University of Wisconsin Press, 1989.

—. "Gender, Generation, and Science: William Hunter's Obstetrical Atlas." *William Hunter and the Eighteenth-Century World.* Eds. W. F. Bynum and Roy Porter. Cambridge: Cambridge University Press, 2002, 385-412.

Kass, Amalie M. "The Obstetrical Casebook of Walter Channing, 1811-1822," *Bulletin of the History of Medicine* 67 (1993): 494-523.

—. *Midwifery and Medicine in Boston: Walter Channing, M. D. 1786-1876.* Boston: Northwestern University Press, 2002.

Keesling, Barbara. *Super Sexual Orgasm: Discover the Ultimate Pleasure Spot: The Cul-de-Sac.* New York: Harpers Collins, 1997.

Keller, Eve. *Generating Bodies and Gendered Selves: The Rhetoric of Reproduction in Early Modern England.* Seattle: University of Washington Press, 2007.

Kemp, Martin and Marina Wallace. *Spectacular Bodies: The Art and Science of the Human Body from Leonardo to Now.* Berkley: University of California Press, 2000.

"The Killing of George Floyd." *Wikipedia.* Last updated July 2, 2020. https://en.wikipedia.org/wiki/Killing_of_George_Floyd Accessed July 2, 2020.

King, Helen. *Midwifery, Obstetrics, and the Rise of Gynecology: The Uses of a Sixteenth-Century Compendium.* Burlington, VT: Ashgate, 2007.

—. *The Diseases of Virgins: Greensickness, Chlorosis and the Problems of Puberty.* London: Routledge, 2004.

Kinnick, Katherine N. "Pushing the Envelope: The Role of the Mass Media in the Mainstreaming of Pornography," *Pop/Porn: The Proliferation of*

*Pornography in American Pop Culture.* Eds. Ann C. Hall and Mardia J. Bishop. Westport, CT: Greenwood, 2007, 2-26.

Klepp, Susan E. *Revolutionary Conceptions: Women, Fertility, and Family Limitation in America, 1760-1820.* Chapel Hill, NC: University of North Carolina Press, 2009.

Knapp, Lewis Mansfield. "More Smollett Letters" *Modern Language Notes* 48.4 (1933): 246-49.

Knott, Sarah. *Sensibility and the American Revolution.* Chapel Hill: University of North Carolina Press, 2009.

—. "Female Liberty? Sentimental Gallantry, Republican Womanhood, and Rights Feminism in the Age of Revolutions." *The William and Mary Quarterly* 71.3 (2014): 425-56.

Kogan, Herman. *The Great EB: The Story of the Encyclopedia Britannica.* Chicago: Chicago University Press, 1958.

Komisaruk, Barry R., Carlos Beyer-Flores, & Beverly Whipple. *The Science of Orgasm.* Baltimore: Johns Hopkins University Press, 2006.

Korobkin, Laura H. "'Can Your Volatile Daughter ever Acquire your Wisdom?': Luxury and False Ideals in *The Coquette.*" *Early American Literature* 41.1 (2006): 79-107.

LaFleur, Greta. *The Natural History of Sexuality in Early America.* Baltimore: Johns Hopkins University Press, 2018.

Lamoine, George. "Lord Chesterfield's Letters as Conduct Books." In *The Crisis of Courtesy: Studies in the Conduct-Book in Britain, 1600-1900.* Ed. Jacques Carré. Leiden: E. J. Brill, 1994. 105-117.

Langstaff, John Brett. *Doctor Bard of Hyde Park.* Dutton & Co: New York, 1942.

Laqueur, Thomas. "Bodies, Details, and the Humanitarian Narrative." In *The New Cultural History.* Eds Aletta Biersack and Lynn Hunt (Berkley: University of California Press, 1989): 176-204.

—. *Making Sex: Body and Gender From the Greeks to Freud.* Cambridge, MA: Harvard University Press, 1990.

Lawrence, Susan C. *Charitable Knowledge: Hospital Pupils and Practitioners in Eighteenth-Century London.* Cambridge: Cambridge University Press, 1996.

Lay, Mary M. *The Rhetoric of Midwifery: Gender, Knowledge, and Power.* New Brunswick, NJ: Rutgers University Press, 2000.

Learned, M. D. and C. F. Brede. "An Old German Midwife's Record Kept Susanna Müller, of Providence Township, Lancaster County Pennsylvania, during the Years 1791-1815." *German American Annals* (1903): 73-96.

Leavitt, Judith Walzer. *Brought to Bed: Childbearing in America, 1750-1950.* Oxford: Oxford University Press, 1986.

Levin, Roy J. "The Clitoral Activation Paradox—Claimed Outcomes from Different Methods of its Stimulation." *Clinical Anatomy* (2018): 650-660.

Lewes, Darby. *Nudes from Nowhere: Utopian Sexual Landscapes.* Lanham: Roman & Littlefield, 2000.

Lieske, Pam. "Configuring Women: William Smellie's Obstetrical Machines and the Poor," *Studies in Eighteenth-Century Culture* 29 (2000): 65-86.

Lloyd, Josephine M. "The 'Languid Child' and the Eighteenth-Century Man-Midwife," *Bulletin of the History of Medicine* 75 (2001): 641-77.

Lord, Alexandra. "'The Great *Arcana* of the Diety': Menstruation and Menstrual Disorders in Eighteenth-Century British Medical Thought," *Bulletin of the History of Medicine* 73.1 (1999): 38-63.

Lyons, Clare A. *Sex Among the Rabble: An Intimate History of Gender and Power in the Age of Revolution, Philadelphia, 1730-1830.* Chapel Hill, NC: University of North Carolina Press, 2006.

Marchessault, Janine. "Men in White, Women in Aprons: Utopian Iconographies of TV Doctors," In *Figuring it Out: Science, Gender and Visual Culture.* Ann B Shteir and Bernard Lightman, eds (Hanover, NH: Dartmouth College Press, 2006): 315-336.

Marland, Hilary and Anne Marie Rafferty, eds. *Midwives, Society and Childbirth: Debates and Controversies in the Modern Period.* London: Routledge, 1997.

Martin, Emily. *The Woman in the Body: A Cultural Analysis of Reproduction.* Boston: Beacon, 1992.

Massey, Lyle. "Pregnancy and Pathology: Picturing Childbirth in Eighteenth-Century Obstetric Atlases," *Art Bulletin* 87.1 (2005): 73-91.

McCall, Colin. *Naval Warfare to Natal Care: A Brief Look at the Life and Works of Thomas Denman (1733-1815), a Founder and Contributor to Male Midwifery and Modern Medical Practice.* Matlock: SOLCOL, 2010.

McDougall, Warren. "Charles Elliot's Medical Publications and the International Book Trade," *Science and Medicine in the Scottish Enlightenment.* Eds. Charles W. J. Withers and Paul Wood. Glasgow: Tuckwell, 2002, 215-53.

McGrath, Roberta. *Seeing Her Sex: Medical Archives and the Female Body.* Manchester: Manchester University Press, 2002.

McGregor, Deborah Kuhn. *From Midwives to Medicine: The Birth of American Gynecology.* New Brunswick, NJ: Rutgers University Press, 1998.

McKeon, Michael. *The Secret History of Domesticity: Public, Private, and the Division of Knowledge.* Baltimore: Johns Hopkins University Press, 2005.

McLaren, Angus. *Reproductive Rituals: The Perception of Fertility in England from the Sixteenth to the Nineteenth Century.* London: Methuen & Co., 1984.

McLellan, M. Faith "Images of Physicians in Literature: From Quacks to Heroes," *The Lancet* (1996): 458-60.

Milder, Robert. "*The Last of Mohicans* and the New World Fall." *American Literature* 52.3 (1980): 407-49.

Moore, Wendy. *The Knife Man: The Extraordinary Life and Times of John Hunter, Father of Modern Surgery.* New York: Broadway, 2005.

Moscucci, Ornella. *The Science of Woman: Gynecology and Gender in England, 1800-1929.* Cambridge: Cambridge University Press, 1990.

Muir, Allison. "Imagining Reproduction: The Politics of Reproduction, Technology and the Woman Machine." *Journal of Medical History* (2009): 53-67.

Nead, Lynda. *The Female Nude: Art, Obscenity and Sexuality.* London: Routledge, 1992.

Nelson, Dana D. *Nationalist Manhood: Capitalist Citizenship and the Imagined Fraternity of White Men.* Durham, NC: Duke University Press, 1998.

Nichols, Marcia D. "A Colonial Man of Science: Imperial Fantasy in Merryland." In *Expanding Worlds: Travel Narratives, The New Science, and Literary Discourse.* Ed. Judy H. Hayden. Burlington, VT: Ashgate, 2013. 143.60.

—. "Venus Dissected: The Visual Blazon of Mid-Eighteenth Century Medical Atlases." In *Sex and Death in Eighteenth-Century Literature.* Ed. Jolene Zigarovich. New York: Routledge, 2013. 103-23.

O'Connell, Helen E., Kalavampa V. Sanjeevan, & John M. Hutson. "Anatomy of the Clitoris." *The Journal of Urology* 174 (2005): 1189-1195.

Ofek, Galia. *Representations of Hair in Victorian Literature and Culture.* Surrey: Ashgate, 2009.

Officer, Lawrence H, Samuel H. Williamson, et al. *MeasuringWorth.com.* Last updated 2020. http://www.measuringworth.com/index.php

Öllerer-Einböck, Birgit. *The English Picaresque Tradition: Beginnings to the Eighteenth Century.* Saarbrücken, Germany: VDM Verlag, 2008.

Owens, Dierdre Cooper. *Medical Bondage: Race, Gender, and the Origins of American Gynecology.* Athens, GA: University of Georgia Press, 2017.

Parker, Patricia. *Literary Fat Ladies: Rhetoric, Gender, Property.* London and New York: Methuen, 1987.

Peakman, Julie. *Mighty Lewd Books: The Development of Pornography in Eighteenth-Century England.* London: Palgrave, 2003.

Porter, Roy. "A Touch of Danger," *Sexual Underworlds of the Enlightenment.*

Eds. G. S. Rousseau and Roy Porter. Manchester: Manchester University Press, 1987, 206-33.

—. *Cambridge Illustrated History of Medicine*. Cambridge: Cambridge University Press, 1996.

—. "William Hunter: a surgeon and a gentleman." *William Hunter and the Eighteenth-Century Medical World*. Eds. W. F. Bynum and Roy Porter. Cambridge: Cambridge University Press, 2002, 7-34.

—. *Quacks: Fakers and Charlatans in Medicine*. Stroud: Tempus, 2003.

—. *Flesh in the Age of Reason: The Modern Foundations of Body and Soul*. Ed. Simon Schama. New York: Norton & Co., 2003.

Porter, Roy and Lesley Hall. *Facts of Life: The Creation of Sexual Knowledge in Britain, 1650-1950*. New Haven: Yale University Press, 1995.

Prause, Nicole, *et al*. "Clitorally Stimulated Orgasms Are Associated with Better Control of Sexual Desire, and Not Associated with Depression or Anxiety, Compared with Vaginally Stimulated Orgasms." *The Journal of Sexual Medicine* 13 (2016): 1676-1685.

Puppo, Vincenzo & Guilia Puppo. "Anatomy of Sex: Revision of the New Anatomical Terms Used for the Clitoris and the Female Orgasm by Sexologists." *Clinical Anatomy* (2014): 293-304.

Reifsnyder, Jennifer E. et al, "Nerve Sparing Clitoroplasty is an Option for Adolescent and Adult Female Patients with Congenital Adrenal Hyperplasia and Clitoral Pain following Prior Clitoral Recession or Incomplete Reduction, *The Journal of Urology* 195.4 (2016): 1270-1274

Reverby, Susan M. *Examining Tuskegee: The Infamous Syphilis Study and its Legacy*. Chapel Hill, NC: University of North Carolina Press, 2009.

Rhodes, Philip. *Doctor John Leake's Hospital: A History of the General Lying-In Hospital, York Road, Lambeth 1765-1971*. London: Davis-Poynter, 1977.

Richardson, Ruth. *Death, Dissection and the Destitute*. 2nd ed. Chicago: University of Chicago Press, 1987.

Riddle, John M. *Eve's Herbs: A History of Contraception and Abortion in the West*. Cambridge, MA: Harvard University Press, 1997.

Roberts, A. D. G., et al. "William Smellie and William Hunter: two great obstetricians and anatomists." *Journal of the Royal Society of Medicine* (2010): 205-06.

Romero, Lora. "Vanishing Americans: Gender, Empire, and New Historicism." *American Literature* 63.3 (1991): 385-404.

Rooks, Judith Pence. *Midwifery & Childbirth in America*. Philadelphia: Temple University Press, 1997.

Rosner, Lisa. *Medical Education in the Age of Improvement: Edinburgh Students and*

*Apprentices, 1760-1826.* Edinburgh: Edinburgh University Press, 1991.

—. "Thistle on the Delaware: Edinburgh Medical Education and Philadelphia Practice, 1800-1825," *The Society for the Social History of Medicine* (1992): 19-42.

—. "Student Culture at the Turn of the Nineteenth Century: Edinburgh and Philadelphia." *Caduceus* 10.2 (1994): 65-86.

—. *The Most Beautiful Man in Existence: The Scandalous Life of Alexander Lesassier.* Philadelphia: University of Pennsylvania Press, 1999.

Royal College of Physicians. "Thomas Denman." Lives of the Fellows. 2009. munksroll.rcplondon.ac.uk/Biography/Details/1235

Sappol, Michael. *A Traffic of Dead Bodies: Anatomy and Embodied Social Identity in Nineteenth-Century America.* Princeton: Princeton University Press, 2002.

Schiebinger, Londa. *Nature's Body: Gender in the Making of Modern Science.* New Brunswick, NJ: Rutgers University Press, 1993.

Schloesser, Pauline. *The Fair Sex: White women and Racial Patriarchy in the Early American Republic.* New York: New York University Press, 2002

Sedgewick, Eve Kosofsky. *Between Men: English Literature and Male Homosocial Desire.* New York: Columbia University Press, 1985.

Shelton, Don. "The Emperor's New Clothes." *Journal of the Royal Society of Medicine* (2010): 46-50.

Sher, Richard B. *The Enlightenment and the Book: Scottish Authors and Their Publishers in Eighteenth-Century Britain, Ireland, and America.* Chicago: University of Chicago Press, 2006.

Shipton, Clifford. K. *Isaiah Thomas: Printer, Patriot and Philanthropist.* Rochester, NY: Leo Hart, 1948.

Smith, Norah. "Sexual Mores and Attitudes in Enlightenment Scotland." *Sexuality in Eighteenth-Century Britain.* Ed. Paul-Gabriel Boucé. Manchester: Manchester University Press, 47-73.

Spacks, Patricia Meyer. "Oscillations of Sensibility." *New Literary History* 25.3 (1994): 505-20.

Thornton, John L. *Jan Van Rymsdyk: Medical Artist of the Eighteenth Century.* Cambridge, Oleander Press, 1982.

Tucker, Sarah Yahr. "There is a Hidden Epidemic of Doctors Abusing Women in Labor, Doulas Say." *Broadly, Vice Media.* (May 8, 2018). https://broadly.vice.com/en_us/article/evqew7/obstetric-violence-doulas-abuse-giving-birth?utm_source=vicefbus

Ulrich, Laurel Thatcher. *A Midwife's Tale: The Life of Martha Ballard, Based on her Diary 1785-1812.* New York: Vintage, 1991.

W., F. C. "John Norman." *Dictionary of American Biography*, Vol. XIII. Ed.

Dumas Malone. New York: Charles Scribner's Sons, 1934, 550-51.

Wagner, Peter. *Eros Revived: Erotica of the Enlightenment in England and America.* London: Paladin, 1988.

Wardrop, Stephanie. "Last of the Red Hot Mohicans: Miscegenation in the Popular American Romance," *MELUS* 22.2 (1997): 61-74.

Warner, Michael. *The Letters of the Republic: Publication and the Public Sphere in Eighteenth-Century America.* Cambridge, MA: Harvard University Press, 1990.

Washington, Harriet A. *Medical Apartheid: The Dark History of Medical Experimentation on Black Americans from Colonial times to the Present.* New York: Anchor Books, 2008.

Welter, Barbara. "The Cult of True Womanhood, 1820-1860." *American Quarterly* 18.2 (1966): 151-74.

Wertz, Richard W. and Dorothy C. Wertz. *Lying-In: A History of Childbirth in America.* Expanded Edition. New Haven, CT: Yale University Press, 1989.

Wheeler, Roxann. *The Complexion of Race: Categories of Difference in Eighteenth-Century British Culture.* Philadelphia: University of Pennsylvania Press, 2000.

Wicks, Ulrich. "The Nature of Picaresque Narrative: A Modal Approach," *PMLA* 89.2 (1974): 240-49.

Wilson, Adrian. *The Making of Man-Midwifery: Childbirth in England, 1660-1770.* Cambridge, MA: Harvard University Press, 1995.

—. "William Hunter and the varieties of man-midwifery," *William Hunter and the Eighteenth-Century World.* Eds. W. F. Bynum and Roy Porter. Cambridge: Cambridge University Press, 2002, 343-70.

Withycombe, Shannon. *Lost: Miscarriage in Nineteenth-Century America.* New Brunswick, NJ: Rutgers University Press, 2019.

Yang, Jennifer, Diane Felsen, and Dix P. Poppas. "Nerve Sparing Ventral Clitoroplasty: Analysis of Clitoral Sensitivity and Viability," *The Journal of Urology* 178.4 (2007); 1598-1601

Zagarri, Rosemaire. *Revolutionary Backlash: Women and Politics in the Early American Republic.* Philadelphia: University of Pennsylvania Press, 2007.

# Index

Onanism (Tissot), 72

one-sex theory of body, 7–8

orgasm, 1, 178–79

L'origine du Monde (Courbet), 104n11, 170

Osborne, William, 116, 136, 158–59, 161, 183n15

Ould, Fielding, 28

ovaries, 8–9, 24, 50, 128

ovulation, 29, 178, 180

pain: of examinations, 39, 53, 189; sensibility and, 119, 169; of sex, 169, 179

Paré, Ambrose, 32, 55n20, 134

parish laws, 20–21, 83

parturient damsel-in-distress: malformed pelvis and, 42, 49–50, 162, 169, 176–77; man-midwifery on, 14, 33, 49–53, 102, 191; midwives and pretender danger to, 53; pregnant women as, 4, 11, 14, 33, 163, 165, 173; Smellie on, 52–53, 83

passive and active voice, 33–37, 132, 141, 168

passivity: of women, 4–7, 9–11, 33, 51, 53, 65–66, 140, 191; of writing voice, 33–37, 132, 141, 168

patients: Accoucheur of Feeling on, 125–26, 143; American doctors on, 5, 150–51, 158; Bard, S., saving, 164, 167; Hunter and care of, 119; man-midwifery for paying, 138, 150, 158–60; medical bleeding of, 168, 177; Smellie and, 37–38, 52–53, 60n110, 188–89; as unmanageable, 52, 188–89. See also women

pediatric care, 32, 63n167, 119–20

pelvis, 8, 27; Bard, S., on, 174–77;

illustration of, 82; intervention and, 162; as malformed, 42, 49–50, 162, 169, 175–77; manual examination of, 169–70; parturient damsel-in-distress and, 42, 49–50, 162, 169, 176–77; Smellie on, 23–26, 42, 49–50, 65, 84, 99–100, 175–76; in Tables, 84, 99–100

Perfect, William, 161, 163–64

perineum, 41–43, 45, 80

Petition of the Unborn Babes to the Censors of the Royal College of Physicians in London (Nicholls), 19, 21

The Physician Struggling Against Death for Life (Saliger), 139–40

physicians, 2, 18

picaresque mode, 9, 14–17, 32–33, 51

picaro, 15–33

podalic version, 17, 32, 55n20

polygenesis, 142

poor women, 9; Cody on, 109n74; dissections of, 59nn75–76, 90, 110n82; female proprietors and, 110n78; man-midwifery on, 3, 6, 10, 16, 20–21, 43, 51; medical illustrations of, 82–83, 85, 87–88, 101–2; medical pornography and, 90; pay-for-view birth and, 88; propertied white women vs., 173–74; prostitutes and, 75, 88, 90, 109n72, 121; as public spectacles, 90; sexual voracity of, 87, 101–2; Sims on Irish, 85, 102; use of, 55n18

pornography: Edwards on, 98–99, 112n105; erotica and, 8, 21–22, 26–27, 73–75, 83–85, 89, 91, 121, 131, 169; medical images and, 26–27, 65–66, 69–73, 78, 86, 91, 98–101, 108n60, 170, 191; poor women and

25, 121–22, 192

white women: as educated, 85, 96, 98, 173, 189; experiments benefiting, 85, 102; as norm, 171, 173–74; over racial Others, 8–10, 173–74; poor vs., 173–74; pubic hair and, 75

Whitman, Walt, 11

Wick, Ulrich, 14–15

Wilson, Adrian, 6, 13–14, 44–45, 55*n22*

Wilson, David, 91

Wollstonecraft, 178

women: animals and, 8–9, 86, 115, 117, 123–25, 142; Bard, S., on, 173–74; biology of, 8; body metaphors on, 26–27, 58*n65*, 63*n171*, 123; body-as-machine metaphor on, 26, 57*n63*, 64–65, 118; in *A Collection of Engravings*, 126–30; conduct manuals on, 10–11, 114–15, 117, 122–23, 147*n70*; death struggle over, 139–40; as delicate and weak, 4–5, 9–11, 33, 115, 117, 125–26, 167–68, 173, 175–77, 191; Denman for privacy and, 133; ejaculation by, 142; fixing needed by, 50; humors of, 73, 118; malformed pelvis and fragile, 42, 49–50, 162, 169, 175–77; meddling midwifery by, 6, 33, 153, 162, 175, 191; medicine on inabilities and, 150–51; menstruation by human, 124, 177–78; as passionless, 1, 124, 178–80; as passive, 4–7, 9–11, 33, 51, 53, 65–66, 140, 191; on pregnancy, 124–25; Republican womanhood and, 165–66, 178; sensibility of animals and, 124; sexuality of, 86–87, 142, 178, 180; social respectability of, 87–88, 102, 131; *Tables* on unknowable, 10; as "the Sex," 8–9. *See also* poor women

women's bodies, 2; American doctors on, 5, 150–51, 158; Anglo-Atlantic society on, 91; containment and regulation of, 10, 68, 123, 173; *Encyclopedia* on normative, 99, 101; exhumation of, 107; as helpless and passive, 9–10; illustrations of, 10, 65–68; mechanisms of, 26–27; standards and deviations of, 66, 103*n10*, 140; *Tables* on normative, 96; as unruly, 10, 50–51, 53, 64, 68, 123, 191; as uteri, 6–7, 98; as victims, 11, 65, 139; as "waxen medical 'venuses,'" 72

X-ray, 25, 65, 137

Young, Thomas, 92–93

Zagarri, Rosemarie, 173

www.ingramcontent.com/pod-product-compliance
Lightning Source LLC
Chambersburg PA
CBHW070031100426
42740CB00013B/2654